Genocide

Genocide *Its Political Use in the*

Twentieth Century

LEO KUPER

New Haven and London: YALE UNIVERSITY PRESS

First published in 1981 in the United Kingdom by Penguin
Books Limited. First published in 1982 in the United States
of America by Yale University Press.

Set in Linotype Times Roman.
Printed in the United States of America.

Library of Congress Cataloging in Publication Data

Kuper, Leo.
  Genocide: its political use in the twentieth century.

  Bibliography: p.
  Includes index.
  1. Genocide. I. Title.
JX5418.K86   1981   341.7'7   81–16151
ISBN 0–300–02795–8   AACR2

10 9 8 7 6 5 4 3 2

To Herbert Machleder
with my deep gratitude

Contents

Preface

How is one to write on the theme of genocide? And how to convey in a comparative study, or indeed in any study, the suffering and the cruelty? The very act of comparison is an affront. Should not 'each human evil be understood in its own terms'? Yet even in the particular case, the enormity of the genocide seems to defy understanding. It is individual suffering which speaks to us most directly and meaningfully – the account of a survivor; the anguish of a mutilated baby; an Italian Consul's despair as witness to an episode in the Turkish genocide against Armenians; a young boy's first view of Auschwitz at the time of the German annihilation of Hungarian Jews; the narrative of a husband and wife moving from a Polish ghetto through the death camps to a heartbreaking reunion with their son. But I have been driven to this study by the realization that genocide is all too common in our own day, and that the organization charged with its prevention and punishment, the United Nations, responds with indifference, if not with condonation. It would seem that it can only be recalled to its duty by the mounting pressure of international opinion.

This study deals mainly with domestic genocides in the twentieth century. By domestic genocides, I mean those internal to a society, not a direct consequence of war. The selection of cases is by no means exhaustive, but it covers a wide range of genocide in its many forms: religious, racial, ethnic; on colonization and decolonization; in struggles for power or against defenceless groups, as scapegoats; against hunters and gatherers, and against assimilated urban populations; bureaucratic mechanized genocide, or more spontaneous and pre-industrial.

There is a preliminary problem in the choice of cases for inclusion. It involves a judgment that the case is in fact one of genocide. Inevitably this is a somewhat personal, and sometimes controversial, judgment, since there is no international criminal court to investigate charges of genocide, and the United Nations evades the issue. To meet this problem, I have selected, for the most part, cases where there has been

9

Genocide

massive slaughter under conditions suggesting genocide as defined by
the United Nations Convention on the Prevention and Punishment of
the Crime of Genocide. I have, however, broadened the scope of the
study in two respects. I have included cases where the victims of massacre were political groups (or economic classes). These are discussed
separately under the heading 'Related Atrocities', for the reason that the
'protection' of the Genocide Convention does not extend to these
groups. I have also included conflicts marked by genocidal massacres,
expressed characteristically in the annihilation of a section of a group
– men, women and children, as for example in the wiping out of whole
villages. This is in part because the genocidal massacre has some of the
elements of genocide. But I hope too that the inclusion of genocidal
massacre will reduce controversy over the selection of cases, so that
the human concern for the prevention of genocide may prevail over the
almost insuperable problem of precision in classification.

The study was made possible by help received from the University of
California, Los Angeles, and from colleagues and representatives of
human rights organizations. At the University of California, Los
Angeles, I would like to acknowledge with my thanks support from the
Senate Research Committee, and from the Committee on International
and Comparative Studies through its Ford Foundation grant. I wish to
thank the Public Affairs and Reference Sections of the Research Library
for their continuous help, and Lilian Choddar and Teresa Joseph for
their work in the preparation of the manuscript. Colleagues have commented on the whole or sections of this study, or have made suggestions
for approaches to the problems or directed attention to relevant sources.
I would especially like to thank Professors Richard Hovannisian, Hilda
Kuper, Peter Loewenberg, Hans Rogger, Sakkie Schapera, Pierre van
den Berghe, Stanley Wolpert, and my research assistant Mike Paolliso.
I also want to thank William Shawcross, Lek Hor Tan, United Nations
personnel, and many others who gave time to respond to issues I raised
in connection with the problem of international protection against genocide. Finally, I would like to express my deep appreciation for the help
I received through the award of a Spivak Fellowship by the American
Sociological Association.

Chapter 1

'An Odious Scourge'

The word is new, the crime ancient. The preamble to the Convention on Genocide, approved by the General Assembly of the United Nations in December 1948, describes genocide as an odious scourge which has inflicted great losses on humanity in all periods of history.

One recalls the more horrifying genocidal massacres, such as the terror of Assyrian warfare in the eighth and seventh centuries B.C., when many cities were razed to the ground and whole populations carried off or brutally exterminated, until the Assyrian empire itself became the victim of its own wars of annihilation; or the destruction of Troy and its defenders, and the carrying off into slavery of the women (as described in the legendary accounts and the Greek tragedies which have come down to us); or the Roman obliteration of Carthage, men, women and children, the site of the devastated city sown with salt, symbolic of desolation.

But the razing of cities and the slaughter of peoples were not isolated episodes in ancient times. One has only to refer to accounts of the many genocidal conflicts in the Bible and in the chronicles of Greek and Roman historians. However, when Hannah Arendt[1] writes that massacres of whole peoples were the order of the day in antiquity, she cannot have meant that this was the rule or the norm in warfare or conquest. Many circumstances affected the final outcome. Though it was common enough practice to destroy besieged cities and to slaughter their inhabitants, or their male defenders while taking the women and children into slavery, a city which surrendered might be spared this genocidal fate, and in exceptional cases, mercy might even be extended to a city taken by assault.[2]

The names of Genghis Khan and of Timur Lenk have become

1. Arendt 1969: 288.
2. See the discussion by T. A. Walker (1899) of the evolution of international law among the Israelites, the Greeks and the Romans.

Genocide

synonyms for the genocides of a later period. Of Genghis Khan, the Scourge of God, Lamb writes that

> when he marched with his horde, it was over degrees of latitude and longitude instead of miles; cities in his path were often obliterated, and rivers diverted from their courses; deserts were peopled with the fleeing and dying, and when he had passed, wolves and ravens often were the sole living things in once populous lands.[3]

As to Timur Lenk (Tamerlane), for the vast majority of those to whom the name means anything at all,

> it commemorates a militarist who perpetrated as many horrors in the span of twenty-four years as the last five Assyrian kings perpetrated in a hundred and twenty. We think of the monster who razed Isfarā'in to the ground in A.D. 1381; built 2,000 prisoners into a living mound and then bricked them over at Sabzawār in 1383; piled 5,000 heads into minarets at Zirih in the same year; cast his Lūrī prisoners alive over precipices in 1386; massacred 70,000 people and piled the heads of the slain into minarets at Isfahan in 1387; massacred 100,000 prisoners at Delhi in 1398; buried alive 4,000 Christian soldiers of the garrison of Sivas after their capitulation in 1400; and built twenty towers of skulls in Syria in 1400 and 1401.[4]

Again, these were not isolated actors and events in the history of genocide; the war practices of 'civilized' peoples in the Middle Ages were often marked by genocidal massacres.[5]

Meanwhile, the wars of religion had already started. They were of course a feature of ancient history, and they continue into our own times. They are merely one form in which the tyranny of an idea becomes charged with genocidal potential. Probably religious ideas do not often act in purity, being generally compounded with other motivations – struggles for power and for possessions, or destructive fury unleashed by threatening events. The religious differences however may indeed be the driving force in genocidal conflict, or they may define the lines along which other conflicts erupt. There may be religious authority for genocide, and even when genocide runs counter to the theology, the warrant for genocide may be found in religious praxis, with religious zeal supplying the fuel for genocide.

The Crusades against the Muslim 'infidel' and for the recovery of the holy places almost all started with pogroms against Jews. The first

3. Lamb, 1927:1.
4. Toynbee, 1947:347.
5. See Walker, op. cit., 123–37.

12

armies of Crusaders did no special harm to the Jews, they plundered Christians and Jews alike; but the hordes that followed 'began the holy work of plundering and murdering with the Jews'.[6] And the course of the Crusades was marked by the slaughter of Jewish communities. Thus, when the crusading army had finally taken Jerusalem by storm in the year 1099 and had massacred the Muslims, they drove the Jews into a synagogue, set fire to it and burnt all within its walls.[7] At times, Jews were able to offer effective resistance, or they were protected by rulers and by churchmen, or became converts to Christianity; at other times, rather than fall into the hands of the crusaders, whose piety sanctified murder and pillage, they took refuge in mass suicide.

It was not only the Crusades which unleashed these attacks. The Inquisition engaged massively in holy murder. Indeed, whatever the religious conflict, it served as licence for the slaughter of Jews. In the suppression of the Christian Albigensian sect in southern France, Jews in that region inevitably suffered with the members of the sect. When the city of Béziers was stormed in A.D. 1209, the crusading army, organized at the instigation of the Pope and the monk Arnold of Cîteaux, spared 'neither dignity, nor sex nor age, nearly 20,000 human beings have perished by the sword ... After the massacre the town was plundered and burnt, and the revenge of God seemed to rage upon it in a wonderful manner'.[8] Since even orthodox Catholics were not spared ('Strike down; God will recognize His own'), there was little reason for indulgence to Jews. In the fifteenth century, Jews were massacred in the suppression of the Hussite sect; and the Crusaders (the German imperial army) threatened, on their return from victory over the Hussites, to wipe the Jewish people from the face of the earth.[9]

Quite apart from religious conflicts, or religious occasions such as Easter, almost any catastrophe might set off massacres of Jews. Thus they were charged with responsibility for the Black Death which ravaged Europe in the fourteenth century, and large numbers of Jewish communities were annihilated, notwithstanding opposition from the Pope, some European rulers and city councils.[10] It is startling to find

6. Graetz, 1894: Vol. III, 298–9.

7. ibid., 308.

8. Account given by the monk Arnold to the Pope, Graetz, op. cit., Vol. III, 502.

9. Graetz, op. cit., Vol. IV, 225.

10. See ibid., 100ff., and Sachar, 1967: Ch. 15: 'similar accusations were made, with similar results, at innumerable local plagues down to the mid-sixteenth century' (Cohn, 1967:261).

within Christian practice in the period of the Crusades, the Inquisition and the religious wars, all the elements in the major genocide of our day, that of the Nazis against the Jews. There were the laws corresponding to the Nuremberg laws, there were the distinguishing badges, the theory of a Jewish conspiracy, appointed centres of annihilation corresponding to Auschwitz, and some systematic organization, with the Dominican friars for example providing the professional expertise and the bureaucratic cadres in the Inquisition.

The massacre of Jews, however, was quite peripheral to the main religious conflicts between Christians and Muslims, and between Catholics and Protestants. Many genocidal massacres marked the course of these conflicts, which culminated in the persecution of the Huguenots in France and in the Thirty Years War in Germany. The Massacre of Saint Bartholomew in 1572 and the great exodus from France following the revocation of the Edict of Nantes, stand out in the tragic history of the Huguenots. The Thirty Years War in the seventeenth century has always seemed the symbol of the extreme devastation wrought by the unbridled passions of religious conflict. It is generally regarded as dividing 'the period of religious wars from that of national wars, the ideological wars from the wars of mere aggression. But the demarcation is as artificial as such arbitrary divisions commonly are. Aggression, dynastic ambition and fanaticism are all alike present in the hazy background behind the reality of the war, and the last of the wars of religion merged insensibly into the pseudo-national wars of the future.'[11] In any event, the ideological wars, including religious wars, are very characteristic of the contemporary world.

In our own era, there are the genocidal conflicts linked to the march of colonization and to the process of decolonization. The tyranny of faith persists as a source of genocidal conflict, but more often in the form of political ideology rather than religious belief. Advanced technology facilitates the obliteration of whole communities in the course of international warfare. But the major arena for contemporary genocidal conflict and massacre is to be found within the sovereign state: it is particularly a phenomenon of the plural society.

In much contemporary writing on colonization, especially radical writing, there is a tendency to equate colonization with genocide. This is a conception expressed by Sartre[12] in his indictment of the U.S.A. on a charge of genocide in Vietnam. He writes that since the blatant aggres-

11. Wedgwood, 1939:525.
12. Sartre, 1968:37–42.

sion of colonial conquests kindles the hatred of the civilian population, and since the civilians are potentially rebels and soldiers, the colonial troops maintain their authority by perpetual massacres. These are aimed at the destruction 'of part of an ethnic, national, or religious group', so as to terrorize the remainder and wrench apart the indigenous society; they are thus genocidal in character. Sartre introduces the qualification that in situations where there is an infra-structural contradiction arising from the dependence of the colonizers on the labour of the colonized, there are restraints on the extent of the physical destruction of local populations. He introduces no such qualification in his description of colonization as by its very nature an act of cultural genocide: colonization, he argues, cannot take place without systematically liquidating all the characteristics of the native society.

This is a quite unbalanced perspective. If Dakar, the capital of Senegal, suggests a French provincial town, the visitor is under no illusion as he moves round Dakar and into the interior that he is moving among French provincials. If he visits Uganda, he cannot really believe that he is in the English countryside and meeting with the rather curious English locals: nor does Calcutta remind him of Liverpool or Manchester or indeed of any English city whatsoever. He finds himself, in previously colonized countries, in the presence of vigorous indigenous cultures. Culture change, borrowing of items of culture, transformation of institutions – these do not constitute cultural genocide. If one is thinking of the intention to commit cultural genocide, then the term should be reserved for a deliberate policy to eliminate a culture: there are indeed many examples of this intent in the history of colonization, but it is certainly not a universal feature of colonization. If however one is thinking of the actual extinction of a culture, then this is a less common phenomenon, and I would suppose that it is only effected by the physical extinction of the bearers of the culture or their absorption into another group.

So, too, it is overstated to equate colonization with physical genocide. The issue of decolonization could not arise in countries where there had been extensive genocide, and much of colonization has proceeded without genocidal conflict. But certainly the course of colonization has been marked all too often by genocide. In the colonization of North and South America, the West Indies, Australia and Tasmania, many native peoples were wiped out, sometimes as a result of wars and massacres, or of disease and ecological change, at other times by deliberate policies of extermination.

15

Genocide

Moreover, where a somewhat enduring relationship between colonizer and colonized is established, the situation may still be conducive to genocidal massacre. The relationship may be deeply charged with conflict from its inception in an extremely brutal conquest, as in the French conquest of Algeria, with its massacres and other atrocities, and its deliberate destruction of homes and orchards – the ravaging of a land and its people. The struggle to impose and maintain political control is generally accompanied by appropriation of land and other productive resources, giving rise to systematic political and economic exploitation, supported by justifying ideologies. This may have the effect of separating colonizer and colonized into almost distinct species, thereby encouraging extremes of violence. Revolts, or even riots, were often suppressed with great destruction of life and property, or by admonitory massacres. The slaughter of the Herero by the German rulers of South West Africa in 1904 was among the most exterminatory and horrifying of the reprisals for rebellion.

If the religious war is not a major contemporary phenomenon, religious differences have nevertheless been the basis of division in a number of twentieth-century genocides and genocidal conflicts. There were religious differences in the Turkish genocide against Armenians during the First World War and in the genocidal pogroms in the Ukraine at the end of the war. These genocides were followed in the Second World War by the German genocide against Jews. At the end of the Second World War, the partition of India resulted in a genocidal conflict, as an estimated ten million Hindus, Sikhs and Muslims changed lands, approximately one million never reaching their promised land alive. While a boundary force, largely infected with communal fever, stayed for the most part in barracks, cleaning weapons and boots, 'trainloads of Sikh refugees moving east were slaughtered by Muslims in Pakistan and Muslims headed west were butchered by Sikhs and Hindus in India'.[13] In 1975 and 1976, there was the genocidal conflict in Lebanon, a conflict powered by many different social forces, but appreciably mobilizing Christians and Muslims in enemy camps.[14] And can one doubt the possibility in the Middle East of a genocidal conflict, coloured by religious difference, with an international component chillingly reminiscent of the Nazi era.

13. Wolpert, 1977:348.
14. See Desjardins (1976: 55–6), who discusses the complexity of group alignments in the civil war, not reducible to a simple conflict between Muslims and Christians.

16

However, the role of religious ideas as warrant for, or stimulus to, genocide, has now been taken over by totalitarian political ideologies, of absolute commitment to the remaking of society in conformity with radical specifications, and a rooting out of dissent, as extreme as in the Inquisition. The major examples of the genocidal potentialities of these ideologies in our day are provided by the Nazi regime with its conception of a brave new world of racially tolerated and ordered societies under German hegemony; the Soviet regime, under Stalin, with the Gulag Archipelago receiving, as a sort of 'rubbish bin of history', the successive blood sacrifices of the communist utopia; and the recent Pol Pot regime in Cambodia, freely and righteously exterminating in total dedication to a starkly elemental blueprint for living.

In international warfare, technological change facilitates genocidal massacre, as in the bombing of Hiroshima and Nagasaki. An American marine serving in the Vietnam war comments that battlefield 'ethics seemed to be a matter of distance and technology. You could never go wrong if you killed people at long range with sophisticated weapons.'[15] And the long-range, sophisticated weapons encourage a sort of egalitarian approach to slaughter, drawing no distinction between combatants and non-combatants, the able-bodied and the infirm, the old and the young. While the sheer destructiveness of nuclear warfare imposes restraint on the great powers in the use of this ultimate weapon, no such restraint seems to operate against the use of the more conventional weapons of their advanced technological armoury. If the great powers do not themselves directly engage in the internal conflicts of smaller nations, as the Americans did in Vietnam, they do not hesitate to supply the contending parties with the sophisticated arms for mutual annihilation.

Many of the genocidal conflicts referred to in these pages are internal to the sovereign state. They are particularly a phenomenon of the plural or divided society, in which division persists between peoples of different race or ethnic group or religion, who have been brought together in the same political unit. Colonization, in its arbitrary delineation of metropolitan domains, has been a great creator of plural societies, and there have been many genocides in the process of decolonization or as an early aftermath of decolonization. The struggles for power between Hutu and Tutsi in Rwanda and in Burundi, and between mainland Africans and Arabs in Zanzibar, became genocidal. Partition, as in

15. Caputo, 1977:229–30.

Genocide

India, and repression of secessionary movements, as in Bangladesh, and some would say as in Nigeria, have taken a genocidal form.

It is a massive toll of genocidal conflict, if one adds to the civil wars of decolonization, the destruction of scapegoat groups, and the ideological, ethnic and religious massacres. And it is a particularly threatening scourge of our day and age, facilitated by international concern for the protection of the sovereign rights of the state, by international intervention in the arming of contending sections, and by United Nations *de facto* condonation, which serves as a screen for genocide.

Chapter 2

The Genocide Convention

'It was a complete delusion to suppose that the adoption of a convention of the type proposed, even if generally adhered to, would give people a greater sense of security or would diminish existing dangers of persecution on racial, religious or national grounds.'
[Sir Hartley Shawcross, representative of the United Kingdom, in the debate on the Genocide Convention (United Nations General Assembly, Legal Committee, *Summary Records and Annexes*, Session 3, Part 1, Sept.– Dec. 1948, 17)]

The Convention on Genocide, approved by the General Assembly of the United Nations on 9 December 1948, defines the crime of genocide as follows:

In the present Convention, genocide means any of the following acts committed with intent to destroy, in whole or in part, a national, ethnical, racial or religious group, as such:

(a) Killing members of the group;

(b) Causing serious bodily or mental harm to members of the group;

(c) Deliberately inflicting on the group conditions of life calculated to bring about its physical destruction in whole or in part;

(d) Imposing measures intended to prevent births within the group;

(e) Forcibly transferring children of the group to another group.

Prior to the Convention, the right of humanitarian intervention on behalf of populations persecuted in a manner shocking to mankind had long been considered part of the law of nations. Giving judgment in one of the Nuremberg trials of Nazi war criminals, the court referred to many precedents for such international intervention.[1] In 1827, England, France and Russia had intervened to end the atrocities in the Greco-Turkish war. In 1840, the President of the United States, through his Secretary of State, intervened with the Sultan of Turkey on behalf of the persecuted Jews of Damascus and Rhodes. The French intervened to check religious atrocities in Lebanon in 1861. There were protests by various nations to the governments of Russia and Romania

1. Trial of Joseph Altstötter and Others, *Law Reports of Trials of War Criminals*, 1948: Vol. VI, 46–7.

with respect to pogroms and atrocities against Jews, and to the government of Turkey on behalf of the persecuted Christian minorities. In 1902, the American Secretary of State addressed to Romania a remonstrance 'in the name of humanity' against Jewish persecutions, stating that his government could not be a tacit party to such international wrongs, and in his message to Congress in 1904, the President of the United States declared, with reference to the Kishniev pogrom in Russia and the 'systematic and long-extended cruel oppression of the Armenians', that 'there are occasional crimes committed on a vast scale and of such peculiar horror as to make us doubt whether it is not our manifest duty to endeavour at least to show our disapproval of the deed and our sympathy with those who have suffered by it'.

To these, we should add the declaration of 24 May 1915 by the governments of France, Great Britain and Russia, denouncing the massacres of the Armenian population 'as crimes against humanity and civilization for which all members of the Turkish government will be held responsible together with its agents implicated in the massacres'. And on similar lines, the Commission of Fifteen Members of the Preliminary Peace Conference in its report of 29 March 1919 referred to the liability to criminal prosecution of all those 'guilty of offenses against the laws and customs of war or the laws of humanity'.[2]

It was the devastation of peoples by the Nazis which provided the impetus for the formal recognition of genocide as a crime in international law, thus laying the basis for intervention by judicial process. Many declarations bear testimony to the sense of outrage as nations experienced or witnessed the atrocities of genocidal warfare. There was the declaration of St James's Palace in January 1942 by representatives in London of nine European countries overrun by the Nazis. This was made following the German occupation of large areas of Russia and expressed determination to secure the punishment not only of war criminals, but of all those guilty of a violence against civilian populations, having nothing in common with acts of war or political crimes, as understood in civilized countries. The horror was still nameless. In

2. Goldenberg, 1971:4–5. American members of the Commission issued a dissenting report on the grounds that a judicial tribunal deals only with existing law, leaving to another forum infractions of moral law and actions contrary to the laws and principles of humanity, and that standards of humanity were relative to time, place and circumstance. The ratified treaties make no reference to the laws of humanity, and the Treaty of Lausanne was accompanied by a 'Declaration of Amnesty'. See discussion by Schwelb, 1946:181–3.

December 1942, a declaration by allied governments expressed the resolve to punish those responsible for the 'bestial policy of cold-blooded extermination' against the Jews. Then there were the declarations by Churchill following the slaughter of hostages (the martyrs of Châteaubriant); by Molotov in response to the declaration of St James's Palace; by Roosevelt after the annihilation of the villages of Lidice and Ležáky in a collective reprisal for the assassination of the protector of Bohemia-Moravia; and finally, the Declaration of Moscow in October 1943, in which England, Russia and the U.S.A. issued a warning that those responsible for, or participants in, the atrocities, massacres or executions would be sent back for judgment and punishment to the countries in which they had committed their abominations.[3]

The Moscow Declaration was the basis for the Four-Power Agreement of 8 August 1945 between the governments of England, France, Russia and the U.S.A. It established the Charter for the International Military Tribunal which tried the major war criminals at Nuremberg. Article 6 of the Charter specifies three types of crime falling under the jurisdiction of the tribunal:

(a) Crimes against peace: namely, planning, preparation, initiation or waging of a war of aggression, or a war in violation of international treaties, agreements or assurances, or participation in a common plan or conspiracy for the accomplishment of any of the foregoing.

(b) War Crimes: namely, violations of the laws or customs of war. Such violations shall include, but not be limited to, murder, ill-treatment or deportation to slave labour or for any other purpose of civilian population of or in occupied territory, murder or ill-treatment of prisoners of war or persons on the seas, killing of hostages, plunder of public or private property, wanton destruction of cities, towns or villages, or devastation not justified by military necessity.

(c) Crimes against humanity: namely, murder, extermination, enslavement, deportation and other inhumane acts committed against any civilian population, before or during the war, or persecutions on political, racial or religious grounds of execution of or in connection with any crime within the jurisdiction of the Tribunal, whether or not in violation of the domestic law of the country where perpetrated.

The crimes against peace and the crimes against humanity were then embryonic categories of international law:[4] war crimes were already established as offences under international law. Genocide would con-

3. Donnedieu de Vabres, 1947 : 81–9, and Schwelb, 1946 : 183–8.
4. See Goldenberg, op. cit., 2.

stitute a crime against humanity, though it could also take the form of a war crime, there being much overlapping between the two categories.

The term genocide was now coming into use. It was coined by the jurist, Raphael Lemkin, whose remarkable achievement it was to initiate a one-man crusade for a genocide convention.[5] As early as 1933, he had submitted to the International Conference for Unification of Criminal Law a proposal to declare the destruction of racial, religious or social collectivities a crime (of barbarity) under the law of nations.[6] In his very detailed study of Axis Rule in Occupied Europe, published in 1944, he repeated this proposal in somewhat different form. In Chapter IX, devoted to genocide, he wrote that 'by "genocide" we mean the destruction of a nation or of an ethnic group. This new word, coined by the author to denote an old practice in its modern development, is made from the ancient Greek word *genos* (race, tribe) and the Latin *cide* (killing), thus corresponding in its formation to such words as tyrannicide, homicide, infanticide, etc.' He explained that generally speaking, genocide does not necessarily mean the immediate destruction of a nation, except when accomplished by mass killings of all members of a nation, but is intended rather to signify a coordinated plan of different actions aiming at the destruction of essential foundations of the life of national groups, with the aim of annihilating the groups themselves.

The term appears in the indictment of the major German war criminals at Nuremberg in 1945, and I think that this must be the first formal recognition of the crime of *genocide*. The defendants were charged with having 'conducted deliberate and systematic genocide, viz., the extermination of racial and national groups, against the civilian populations of certain occupied territories in order to destroy particular races and classes of people and national, racial or religious groups, particularly Jews, Poles and Gypsies, and others'. But though the Nuremberg Tribunal dealt at great length in its judgment with the substance of the charge of genocide, it did not use this term, nor make any reference to the conception of genocide.[7] In a later trial of one of the Nazi war criminals by the Supreme National Tribunal of Poland, held in August and September 1946, the Prosecutor charged the accused with the crime of genocide (claiming it to be a *crimen laesae humanitatis*) and the Court found that the wholesale extermination of Jews and also of Poles

5. See Hohenberg, 1968:86–7.
6. Lemkin, 1947: 146.
7. *Law Reports of Trials of War Criminals*, op. cit., Vol. VII, 8.

had all the characteristics of genocide in the biological meaning of the term, and embraced in addition the destruction of the cultural life of those nations.[8]

About this time, however, the problem of the prevention and punishment of genocide was already becoming an issue for the United Nations as a result of the lobbying of Raphael Lemkin, and on 11 December 1946 the General Assembly passed the following resolution (96–I):

Genocide is a denial of the right of existence of entire human groups, as homicide is the denial of the right to live of individual human beings; such denial of the right of existence shocks the conscience of mankind, results in great losses to humanity in the form of cultural and other contributions represented by these groups, and is contrary to moral law and to the spirit and aims of the United Nations. Many instances of such crimes of genocide have occurred, when racial, religious, political and other groups have been destroyed, entirely or in part. The punishment of the crime of genocide is a matter of international concern.

The General Assembly Therefore, Affirms that genocide is a crime under international law which the civilized world condemns, and for the commission of which principals and accomplices – whether private individuals, public officials or statesmen, and whether the crime is committed on religious, racial, political or any other grounds – are punishable.

The resolution continues with an invitation to member states to enact the necessary legislation for the prevention and punishment of genocide, a recommendation for international cooperation in attaining these ends, and a request to the Economic and Social Council of the United Nations to undertake the necessary studies with a view to drawing up a draft convention.

It is important to note that the crime of genocide in this resolution is wholly independent of crimes against peace or of war crimes. A severe limitation in the Nuremberg Charter, as interpreted by the International Military Tribunal, was the linking of crimes against humanity with aggressive war or conventional war crimes. Seemingly a great advance had been made by the resolution of the United Nations General Assembly. The way was now cleared for the protection of racial, religious, political and other groups against genocidal assaults, not only

---

8. ibid., 1–10. For a discussion of early trials for genocide, see United Nations, *Study of the Question of the Prevention and Punishment of the Crime of Genocide*, E/CN. 4/Sub. 2/416, dated 4 July 1978, 6–7. This includes a comprehensive study of the Convention, and the controversies in the debates.

by foreign governments but also by their own governments, and not only in times of war but also in times of peace.

It is very depressing to read the reports of the debates in the Economic and Social Council, in its Ad Hoc Committee, and in the Sixth (Legal) Committee, as the proposals moved from the first draft of the Secretariat, through the second draft prepared by the Ad Hoc Committee, to the final version adopted by the General Assembly on 9 December 1948. One can see, in the controversies about the wording of the Convention, many of the forces which have rendered it so ineffective. Yet this may be too pessimistic a view. As compared with the failure of the United Nations for very many years even to agree on a definition of aggression for the purpose of defining the crime of aggressive war, it was an appreciable achievement to arrive quite speedily at a definition of genocide and at an agreement on some measures for its prevention and punishment.

In the deliberations of the Committees, there were major controversies regarding the groups to be protected, the question of intent, the inclusion of cultural genocide, the problem of enforcement and punishment, the extent of destruction which would constitute genocide, and the essential nature of the crime. Almost every conceivable argument was advanced, and critically tested. The representatives of many nations had considerable experience of genocide on which to draw, and even where there had been no direct exposure in the Second World War, as in the case of Peru, there were historic memories of genocide to inform comment and perspective.

The Nazis had freely exterminated their political opponents within Germany, notably the communists and social democrats. Quite naturally then, in response to the immediate experience of the Second World War, the United Nations resolution of December 1946 referred to the many instances of genocide in which racial, religious, political and other groups were destroyed, and declared genocide to be a crime under international law whether committed on religious, racial, political or any other grounds. The resolution was passed unanimously. However, in the deliberations on the framing of the Convention to give effect to this resolution, the Russian representatives launched a vigorous attack in the different committees, starting with the Ad Hoc Committee in spring 1948, against the inclusion of political groups among the groups to be protected. They were supported strongly by the Polish representatives, and also by representatives of other nations.

The Russian representatives argued that the inclusion of political groups was not in conformity 'with the scientific definition of genocide and would, in practice, distort the perspective in which the crime should be viewed and impair the efficacy of the Convention', giving 'the notion an extension of meaning contrary to the fundamental conception of genocide as recognized by science'. 'It was during the Nürnberg trials that the term "genocide" was used for the first time, in particular in the bill of indictment and the reasons adduced for the sentence, where it was defined as follows: extermination of racial and religious groups in the occupied territories.'[9] They contended that while the Nazis had exterminated members of political groups, this was because they formed the intellectual elements of populations to be subjugated: the principal objective, however, was the wholesale destruction of the civilian populations which were to be conquered and colonized in pursuance of the Nazi plan for German domination over the world. This was the historical point of departure in the conception of genocide as a crime against racial and national groups, though to be sure this did not make the crimes committed against other groups any the less odious.[10] Some representatives had mentioned historic crimes which might be classed as genocide. In the Russian view, these examples were interesting but had no modern application. Genocide was essentially bound up with fascist and Nazi ideologies, and other similar racial theories spreading national and racial hatred, and aiming at the domination of the so-called 'superior' races and the extermination of the so-called 'inferior' races.[11]

The etymology of the term, the Russian representative, argued, favoured this thesis, as did the juridical aspect. The criterion for defining the groups subject to genocide must have an objective character, which excludes the subjective qualities of individuals. 'On the basis of that fundamental concept, the groups could easily be distinguished: they were the racial and national groups which constituted distinct, clearly determinable communities.' As to the willingness of the delegation of the Soviet Union to include religious groups in parentheses after racial and national groups, this was for the reason that in all known

9. U.N. *Economic and Social Council, Official Records*, Session 7, 26 August 1948, 721; U.N. *Report of the Ad Hoc Committee on Genocide*, 5 April–10 May 1948; and U.N. *Legal Committee, Summary Records, and Annexes*, Session 3, Part 1, 14 October 1948, 104.
10. U.N. *Legal Committee*, cited above, 104–5.
11. U.N. *ECOSOC*, Session 7, 26 August 1948, 721–2.

Genocide

cases of genocide perpetrated on grounds of religion, it had always been evident that nationality or race were concomitant reasons. Placing religious groups in parentheses after racial or national groups would stress the fact that the persecution was always directed against national groups, even when it took the form of religious strife.[12]

Supporting arguments advanced by representatives of different nations sought to establish the distinctive character of membership in a political organization. The Iranian representative argued that if a distinction were recognized 'between those groups, membership of which was inevitable, such as racial, religious or national groups, whose distinctive features were permanent, and those, membership of which was voluntary, such as political groups, whose distinctive features were not permanent, it must be admitted that the destruction of the first type appeared most heinous in the light of the conscience of humanity, since it was directed against human beings whom chance alone had grouped together. Although it was true that people could change their nationality as their religion, such changes did not in fact happen very often; national and religious groups therefore belonged to the category of groups, membership of which was inevitable.'[13] The Polish representative argued that 'the inclusion of provisions relating to political groups, which because of their mutability and lack of distinguishing characteristics did not lend themselves to definition, would weaken and blur the whole Convention'.[14]

These arguments as to the transient and unstable nature of political groups constituting an obstacle to their inclusion in the Genocide Convention, were advanced repeatedly. In so doing, representatives disclaimed any intention of denying protection to political groups, but contended that this protection was, or should be, given by national legislation, and that at the international level, the appropriate instruments were those being prepared by the Human Rights Commission.[15] Fears were expressed that inclusion of political groups in the Convention would expose nations to external intervention in their domestic concerns, and 'might endanger the future of the Convention because many states would be unwilling to ratify it, fearing the possibility of

12. U.N. *Legal Committee*, Session 3, Part 1, 14 October 1948, 105.
13. ibid., 99
14. U.N. *ECOSOC*, Session 7, 26 August 1948, 712.
15. U.N. *Legal Committee*, Session 3, Part 1, 15 October 1948. See also the comment by the Yugoslav representative, U.N. *Legal Committee*, Session 3, Part I, 30 September 1948, 10.

being called before an international tribunal to answer charges made against them, even if those charges were without foundation. Subversive elements might make use of the Convention to weaken the attempts of their own Government to suppress them.'[16] The appeal to expediency, that 'the fear of impairing their power to take defensive action against domestic disorders might prevent many states from signing the Convention',[17] was however explicitly rejected by the Soviet representative as a supporting argument, in favour of a decision based on principle.

The counter-arguments attacked the conception of genocide as linked only to fascism-nazism, and hence to the destruction of racial and national groups, but not of political groups. The French representative argued that the relationship between the crimes of nazism-fascism and genocide was not an established historical fact[18] (implying presumably that genocide was not a necessary part of Nazi-fascist doctrine). The report of the Ad Hoc Committee pointed out that there was genocide before nazism-fascism, and that 'as regards the future, it was possible that crimes of genocide would be based on other motives. It would be dangerous to create the idea that genocide should only be punished if it were a product of fascism-nazism, and that the Convention was concerned only with that historical accident.'[19]

In a much later session, the French representative commented that '... whereas in the past crimes of genocide had been committed on racial or religious grounds, it was clear that in the future they would be committed mainly on political grounds',[20] and this view received strong support from other representatives.[21] As for the proposed Russian amendment to indicate that religious persecution was always associated with racial and national persecution, the Yugoslav representative objected on the ground of his country's recent experience of genocide for religious motives, as a result of which it had passed laws for the prevention and suppression of religious genocide as such.[22]

Two objections were advanced to the etymological argument, the first on the ground that 'there was no absolute concept of genocide ... Member States themselves must decide whether they intended to exclude

16. ibid., 7 October 1948, 58.
17. U.N. *ECOSOC*, Session 7, 26 August 1948, 705.
18. ibid., 26 August 1948, 723.
19. U.N. *Report of the Ad Hoc Committee on Genocide*, op. cit., 3.
20. U.N. *ECOSOC*, Session 7, 26 August 1948, 723.
21. See U.N. *Legal Committee*, Session 3, Part 1, 14 October 1948: Bolivia, 99; Haiti, 103; Cuba, 108.
22. ibid., 15 October 1948, 117.

them or not', and furthermore, 'the etymology of the word "genocide" could not determine its definitive meaning, for words evolved and changed in meaning even in legislative texts. Thus, there were no decisive reasons against including the political group in the Convention.'[23] A second line of argument sought to define genocide as 'the physical destruction of a group which was held together by a common origin or a common ideology ... The definition might even be broadened still further to include economic groups. There was nothing to prevent that; the word "genocide" meant the destruction of a group without implying any distinction between the various groups.'[24] The United States delegation did in fact introduce an amendment to extend protection to economic groups, but did not press the issue.

A plethora of attacks was directed against the argument that political groups were too unstable and lacking in identifiability for protection under the Convention. The Nazis had of course found no difficulty in identifying the German communists and social democrats whom they destroyed. If they were identifiable and stable enough to be exterminated, they were identifiable and stable enough to be included among the groups accorded protection against genocide. The United States representative added, among further examples of the identifiability of political groups, the decision of the Allied Control Council to proclaim the abolition of the Nazi Party, and the U.S.S.R. constitution which recognized the organization of the Communist Party as authorized to nominate candidates for the elections, thus proving that the Communist Party was a coherent and perfectly identifiable group.[25]

An important argument against the exclusion of political groups was that 'those who committed the crime of genocide might use the pretext of the political opinions of a racial or religious group to persecute and destroy it, without becoming liable to international sanctions'.[26] The representative from Haiti developed the argument further: '... since it was established that genocide always implied the participation or complicity of Governments, that crime would never be suppressed: the Government which was responsible would always be able to allege that the extermination of any group had been dictated by political considera-

---

23. ibid., 14 October 1948, 107; 15 October 1948, 114.
24. ibid., 14 October 1948, 98–9.
25. ibid., 102. See also the comments of the representative of the United Kingdom on 7 October 1948, 60.
26. ibid., 14 October 1948, 100.

tions, such as the necessity for quelling an insurrection or maintaining public order.'[27] (These were indeed the grounds on which the government of Burundi defended its recent genocidal massacres of Hutu.)

Granted that political groups should be protected, the Convention on Genocide was the proper instrument for their protection. 'The point at issue was not to protect freedom of opinion (that question came within the scope of the protection of human rights) nor was it to prevent States from maintaining internal order in the political field. The issue was to protect political groups against violence, followed by destruction.' The proposed protection 'applied only to the most horrible form of the crime against a group, that of its physical destruction. It seemed that all States could guarantee that limited measure of protection to political groups.'[28]

Political groups survived for many sessions and seemed securely ensconced in the Convention, but on 29 November 1948, the issue was reopened in the Legal Committee on a motion by the delegations of Iran, Egypt and Uruguay. A compromise seems to have been reached behind the scenes. The United States delegation, though still committed to the principle of extending protection to political groups, was conciliatory. It feared non-ratification of the Convention, and rejection of the proposal for an international tribunal, if political groups were included.[29] On a vote, political groups were expunged. The Convention, as adopted by the United Nations on 9 December 1948, limits genocide to the destruction of national, ethnical, racial or religious groups.[30]

It would be cynical to suggest that many nations were unwilling to renounce the right to commit political genocide against their own nationals. One must acknowledge that there was cause for anxiety that the inclusion of political groups in the Convention would expose nations to external interference in their internal affairs: this, after all, was the purpose of the Convention, to prevent and punish genocide. The United States was not among the eighty-four nations which ratified the Convention by 31 December 1978. In recent hearings before the Senate Foreign Relations Committee, reference was made to earlier objections, *inter alia*, that the American constitution prevented ratification because

27. ibid., 15 October 1948, 113.
28. ibid., 14 October 1948, 99, and 15 October 1948, 114.
29. ibid., 29 November 1948, 662.
30. See below, Appendix 1, Article II (p. 210).

Genocide

genocide was a domestic matter, and though the Committee dismissed
the arguments, the United States has still not ratified the Convention.[31]
If a relatively stable country such as the U.S.A., which took a leading
role in the Nuremberg trials and the Genocide Convention, has reservations about ratification of the Convention, one can understand the reaction against extending protection to political groups in other countries,
particularly those in which the political process is very violent (as
argued by the Venezuelan delegate).[32] I think though that one may
fairly say that the delegates, after all, represented governments in power,
and that many of these governments wished to retain an unrestricted
freedom to suppress political opposition.

The scope of genocide under the Convention is defined not only by the
number of 'protected groups', but also by the range of actions qualified
as genocide. Raphael Lemkin, in his detailed study of *Axis Rule in
Occupied Europe*,[33] listed the fields in which genocide was being carried
out as the political, social, cultural, economic, biological, physical,
religious and moral. Three of these categories appear in the first draft
of the Convention by the Secretariat – 'physical' genocide (acts causing
the death of members of protected groups or injuring their health or
physical integrity), 'biological' genocide (restriction of births) and
'cultural' genocide (destruction of the specific character of the persecuted 'group' by forced transfer of children, forced exile, prohibition
of the use of the national language, destruction of books, documents,
monuments, and objects of historical, artistic or religious value).[34]
The draft of the Ad Hoc Committee retained these categories with
many changes, the 'biological' in a much weakened form, and the
'cultural' defined as:

any deliberate act committed with the intent to destroy the language, religion,
or culture of a national, racial or religious group on grounds of the national
or racial origin or religious belief of its members such as:
1. Prohibiting the use of the language of the group in daily intercourse
or in schools, or the printing and circulation of publications in the language
of the group;

31. On this issue, see *United States Department of State Bulletin*, 62 (16 March
1970; Goldberg and Gardner, 1972; *The Fact Finder*, Vol. 31, no. 15 (16 June
1973); and *Hearings before the Committee on Foreign Relations, United States
Senate, Ninety-fifth Congress*, First Session, 24 and 26 May 1977.
32. U.N. *Legal Committee*, Session 3, 7 October 1948, 58.
33. Lemkin, 1944:82–9.
34. See Robinson, 1960:19, and annexed drafts of the Convention.

30

2. Destroying or preventing the use of libraries, museums, schools, historical monuments, places of worship or other cultural institutions and objects of the group.

The inclusion of cultural genocide became an issue of controversy. In this controversy,[35] the roles of the national delegations were somewhat reversed. The Soviet Bloc pressed for inclusion of cultural genocide in the Convention, the Western European democracies opposed. The issue was not whether groups should be protected against attempts to destroy their culture. There were many expressions of horror at cultural genocide, with the Nazi experience still vivid in the perspectives of the delegates. The issue was rather whether the protection of culture should be extended through the Convention on Genocide or in conventions on human rights and rights of minorities. This conflict of views was not sharply ideological, but presumably the representatives of the colonial powers would have been somewhat on the defensive, sensitive to criticism of their policies in non-self-governing territories.

In the result, cultural genocide was excluded from the Convention, though vestiges remain. The Convention makes special reference to the forcible transfer of children from one group to another, and the word ethnical has been added to the list of groups covered by the Convention. This would have the effect of extending protection to groups with distinctive culture or language.[36]

Though cultural genocide has disappeared as a crime under the Convention, it is commonly treated as such in much contemporary writing where it is described as ethnocide. This might be defined as the commission of specified acts 'with intent to extinguish, utterly or in substantial part, a culture. Among such ethnocidal acts are the deprivations of opportunity to use a language, practice a religion, create art in customary ways, maintain basic social institutions, preserve memories and traditions, work in cooperation toward social goals.'[37]

The initial draft of the Convention by the Secretariat described genocide as constituted by deliberate acts directed against specified groups, with the purpose of destroying the group *in whole or in part*. The phrase *in whole or in part* is omitted from the draft by the Ad Hoc Committee, but reappears in the final text adopted by the General Assembly of the United Nations. Its interpretation is a matter of some difficulty, and

35. See the arguments, *pro* and *con*, in U.N. *Legal Committee*, Session 3, Part 1, 193–7, 201, 205; U.N. *ECOSOC*, Session 7, 707, 718, 719, 723, 725.
36. See the explanation offered by the Swedish representative who proposed the amendment (U.N. *Legal Committee*, 13 October 1948, 97–8).
37. Beardsley, 1976:86.

there were conflicting views in the discussions of the Legal Committee. What numbers or proportion or sections would constitute a *part* within the definition? From a humanist point of view, it is quite repugnant to weigh the number of deaths which would accord significance in terms of the Convention: death and suffering and ignominy are hardly matters for mathematical calculation. From a legal point of view, which interested the members of the Legal Committee, could one argue that the murder of an individual should be considered genocide if it took place 'with a connecting aim', that is to say, if it were directed against persons of the same race, or nationality, or ethnic, or religious group?[38]

I will assume that the charge of genocide would not be preferred unless there were a 'substantial' or an 'appreciable' number of victims. I would have no difficulty in applying the term to the slaughter of a stratum of the educated of a racial or ethnic group, a common enough occurrence, provided there are 'appreciable' numbers. In other cases, as for example the obliteration of a village or villages by the French in Algeria after the riots in Sétif in 1945, or the slaughter of fifty French hostages, the martyrs of Châteaubriant, or the destruction of Lidice and Ležáky as reprisals for the assassination of German officials in the Second World War, I will use the term 'genocidal massacre'. I need hardly emphasize the arbitrary nature of this procedure in dealing with a wide range of actions, from the total obliteration of a small village (the 'genocidal massacre') to the systematic extermination of millions of Jews by the Nazis.

The crime of genocide under the Convention is not committed simply by the destruction, in whole or in part, of a racial, national, ethnic or religious group. There must be the intention to destroy. The Convention defines genocide as constituted by specified acts 'committed with intent to destroy, in whole or in part, a national, ethnical, racial or religious group, as such'. The 'inadvertent' wiping out of a group is not genocide.

The draft of the Ad Hoc Committee had offered a more complex formulation of intent in its definition of genocide as 'any of the following *deliberate* acts committed with the *intent* to destroy a national, racial, religious or political group, *on grounds of the national or racial origin, religious belief, or political opinion of its members*'. This stimulated a complex debate, which was to be expected, given the varied conceptions of law and of the nature of crime among these representatives of different national legal systems. Often the discussions seemed to be

38. See U.N. *Legal Committee*, 7 October 1948, 62, and 13 October 1948, 90–93. See also Robinson, op. cit., 63, and Drost, 1959:84–5.

governed by purist preoccupations with legal niceties, or the logic of rigorous analysis, rather than by concern with the substantive issues. The inclusion of intent in the definition of genocide introduces a subjective element, which would often prove difficult to establish. An attempt to substitute an objective measure proved unsuccessful, and in the result 'intent' was retained, the word 'deliberate' being deleted as redundant. There still remained the question of further intent, or of motive, represented by the phrase 'on grounds of national or racial origin' etc. This limited the grounds which would be necessary to constitute genocide, so that the destruction of a group for profit or because of personal rivalry between tribes could not be charged as genocide. To these examples given in the debate, one might add that presumably the destruction of a group in order to create a brave new world would also not fall within the concept of genocide. The Soviet delegation, consistent with its earlier stand for the exclusion of political groups from the list of protected groups, wished to delete from the enumerated grounds the words 'or political opinion of its members'. The effect of this would have been equally bizarre – the United Nations declaring that the destruction of an ethnic group because of its political beliefs (say Hutu in Burundi) would not be considered genocide. Understandably, the United Kingdom representative argued that the phrase under discussion was completely useless (the concept of intent having already been expressed at the beginning of the article), and that its inclusion was indeed dangerous, 'for its limitative nature would enable those who committed a crime of genocide to claim that they had not committed that crime "on grounds of" one of the motives listed in the article'. The United Kingdom delegation proposed its deletion.[39] In this impasse, the committee adopted a compromise solution proposed by the Venezuelan representative, namely, the substitution of the word 'as such' for the enumeration of grounds. This introduces an ambiguity,[40] the resolution of which would presumably rest with the court called upon to try a charge of genocide.

In contemporary extra-judicial discussions of allegations of genocide, the question of intent has become a controversial issue, providing a ready basis for denial of guilt. Thus in March 1974, the International League for the Rights of Man, joined by the Inter-American Association for Democracy and Freedom, charged the government of Paraguay with complicity in genocide against the Guayaki Indians. In a protest

39. U.N. *Legal Committee*, 15 October 1948, 118–21.
40. ibid., 16 October 1948, 123, 131–6.

Genocide

to the United Nations Secretary General, the organizations alleged the following violations, leading to the wholesale disappearance of the Guayaki (Aché) ethnic group, namely:

(1) enslavement, torture, and killing of the Guayaki Indians in reservations in eastern Paraguay;
(2) withholding of food and medicine from them resulting in their death by starvation and disease;
(3) massacre of their members outside the reservations by hunters and slave traders with the toleration and even encouragement of members of the government and with the aid of the armed forces;
(4) splitting up of families and selling into slavery of children, in particular girls for prostitution; and
(5) denial and destruction of Guayaki cultural traditions, including use of their language, traditional music, and religious practices.

This was followed by an attack in the United States Senate, supported by intellectuals and churchmen in Paraguay. To these protestations, the Defence Minister replied quite simply that there was no intention to destroy the Guayaki. 'Although there are victims and victimizer, there is not the third element necessary to establish the crime of genocide – that is "intent." Therefore, as there is no "intent," one cannot speak of "genocide." '[41]

A similar issue arose in relation to charges of genocide against the Indians in the Amazon river region of Brazil, to which the Permanent Representative of Brazil replied that

... the crimes committed against the Brazilian indigenous population cannot be characterized as genocide, since the criminal parties involved never eliminated the Indians as an ethnic or cultural group. Hence there was lacking the special malice or motivation necessary to characterize the occurrence of genocide. The crimes in question were committed for exclusively economic reasons, the perpetrators having acted solely to take possession of the lands of their victims.[42]

'Intent' was also an issue in the debate on the nature of the involvement of the U.S.A. in Vietnam. In the latter stages of the war, there was 'an increasing disposition by critics of American involvement to consider the indiscriminateness and magnitude of destruction on the peoples of Vietnam, Laos and Cambodia as "genocidal" '.[43] If one draws

41. Lewis, 1976:62–3.
42. United Nations, H. R. Communication No 478, 29 September 1969.
43. Falk, 1974:123–4.

34

a legal distinction between the act and the intention, and if one ignores
or discounts the circumstances of the American involvement in Vietnam,
then it is possible to make the argument that the level and nature of the
destruction rained on Vietnam by the U.S.A. was suggestive of genocide.
Sartre, in his address to the non-governmental International War Crimes
Tribunal, spoke of the alternatives offered the people of South
Vietnam – 'villages burned, the populace subjected to massive bombing,
livestock shot, vegetation destroyed by defoliants, crops ruined by toxic
aerosols, and everywhere indiscriminate shooting, murder, rape and
looting. This is genocide in the strictest sense : massive extermination.
The other option : what is *it*? What are the Vietnamese people supposed
to do to escape this horrible death? Join the armed forces of Saigon or
be enclosed in strategic or today's "New Life" hamlets, two names for
the same concentration camps.' We might add to this list the establishment of free-fire zones, the search and destroy missions, the obliteration
bombing, the use of high-technology weapons in counter-insurgency,
and the devastation model of pacification.

The problem of establishing intent is more complex. On this issue
Sartre was hesitant. He did not assert that there was proof that the
United States did in fact envision genocide, but simply that nothing
prevented the United States from envisaging it, that the genocidal intent
was implicit in the facts, and that those who fight the war of the greatest
power on earth against a poor peasant people 'are *living out* the only
possible relationship between an overindustrialized country and an
underdeveloped country, that is to say, a genocidal relationship imple-
mented through racism – the only relationship, short of picking up and
pulling out'.[44] Sartre's argument was weakened by extravagant general-
ization, but the case is made persuasively by others in more measured
legal terms. One can see in these and other controversies how difficult
it may be to establish intent in a court of law: governments hardly
declare and document genocidal plans in the manner of the Nazis. At a
different level, too, that of the forum of public opinion, the requirement
of 'intent' provides an easy means for evading responsibility. Its omission from a definition of genocide as quite simply the destruction of a

44. See Sartre, 1968 : 39–42. See also the careful analysis of Sartre's argument
from a legal point of view, with an examination of possible approaches to the
proof of intent, in Bedau, 1974. Note too that United States action in Vietnam
has given currency to the concept of *ecocide*, as the intentional destruction of the
physical environment needed to sustain human health and life in a given geographical region (see Bedau, op, cit., 44).

human group might have been some contribution to the suppression and punishment of this crime.

The declared purpose of the Convention, in terms of the original resolution of the General Assembly of the United Nations, was to prevent and punish the crime of genocide. Its effectiveness depends in some measure on the procedures devised, and the institutions established, for these purposes. The nature of the provision to be made for enforcement became one of the most controversial issues in the debates, which saw a steady whittling away of the initial proposals.

The first draft, that of the Secretariat, incorporated the principle of universal enforcement, and made provision for both national and international jurisdiction. The principle of universal enforcement had been applied in the suppression of the international crime of piracy on the high seas; the state, whose authorities had arrested the pirates, was competent to exercise jurisdiction, whatever the nationality of the pirates, and wherever on the high seas the crime had been committed. On similar lines, the Secretariat's draft included in the preamble a pledge by the contracting parties to prevent and repress acts of genocide *wherever they may occur*, and in Article VII a further pledge to punish any offender under the Convention within any territory under their jurisdiction, irrespective of the nationality of the offender or of the place where the offence was committed. The principle of universal validity was also incorporated in the provision that the contracting parties might call on the competent organs of the United Nations to take measures for the suppression or prevention of genocide in any part of the world, in which case the parties would do everything in their power to give full effect to the intervention of the United Nations. In the final text, however, the principle of universal repression was eliminated, save to the extent that the United Nations may take action within the scope of its general competence. This was to be expected, for otherwise the representative of one of the great powers, on a visit say to Uganda under Amin, might find himself arraigned on a charge of genocide before the courts of that country. I do not doubt that if pirates had been properly represented at the international convention on piracy, they too would have voted against the principle of universal repression.

In addition to the pledge to punish offenders in areas under their jurisdiction, the Secretariat's draft also imposed on the parties the obligation to provide in their municipal (national) laws for acts of genocide and their punishment, and to commit all persons 'guilty' of genocide for trial by an international court, when (1) they are themselves unwilling to try such offenders or to grant extradition to another country, (2) if the acts of genocide were committed by individuals acting as organs of the State or with the support or toleration of the State. It was particularly the provision in regard to an international penal court which aroused a storm of protest.

The establishment of international criminal jurisdiction was attacked as an infringement of national sovereignty, which might stand in the way of the acceptance of the Convention. It implied the existence of an international criminal tribunal, which the Convention however did not establish. States were therefore being asked to accept the creation, at a future date, of an international tribunal, the period of existence and competence of which were left entirely vague. Moreover, since the Convention envisaged that members of governments might be authors of the crime, there was the danger that the attempt to punish offenders through an international tribunal might jeopardize peace.[45]

The arguments in support of an international tribunal emphasized especially the role of governments in genocide. The French delegation had proposed an amendment in the definition of the crime to include the phrase 'it is committed, encouraged or tolerated by the rulers of a State'. The French representative argued that genocide was bound up with the action, or the culpable abstention from action, of the State.

The theoreticians of nazism and fascism, who had taught the doctrine of the superiority of certain races, could not have committed their crimes if they had not had the support of their rulers; similarly, pogroms had occurred frequently only in countries where no severe legal measures were taken against the perpetrators. Thus the experience of history showed the way; it was inconceivable that human groups should be exterminated while the government remained indifferent; it was inadmissible that the central authority should be powerless to put a stop to mass assassination when homicide was the first of punishable crimes. When the crime of genocide was committed, it was committed either directly by the Governments themselves or at their behest; alternatively, they remained indifferent and failed to use the power which every Government should have in order to ensure public order. Thus, whether as perpetrator, or as accomplice, the Government's responsibility was in all cases implicated.

Hence the task of suppression of the crime could not be left to the governments themselves. It was necessary for international society to intervene; otherwise one would arrive at the absurd position of the

45. U.N. *ECOSOC*, 26 August 1948, 704–5, 713–14.

future criminal being entrusted with ensuring his own punishment.[46] There was criticism of the conception of genocide as exclusively a crime of governments. The representative of Pakistan argued that such organizations as fascist or terrorist organizations might commit genocide, not connected in any way with the government in power, as had been the case in Germany under the Weimar Republic, where the government had been unable to take effective action. So too in India, terrorist organizations had been able to massacre hundreds of thousands of people with impunity, for the simple reason that the government was powerless to prevent and suppress these acts of terrorism. The Yugoslav representative thought that, in theory, the French amendment was justified, since in most cases genocide was committed, encouraged or tolerated by governments, but that in practice it was generally very difficult to establish government responsibility, as for example in Czechoslovakia in 1945, Poland in 1946, and Yugoslavia in 1948, when genocidal bands were introduced into these countries.[47]

In the result, the Legal Committee decided by a narrowly divided vote to eliminate the provision for an international penal tribunal. Later, however, the issue was reopened, after acceptance of a draft resolution that the International Law Commission be requested to study the desirability and possibility of establishing an independent international criminal court for the punishment of persons guilty of genocide, or a criminal chamber of the International Court of Justice. The deletion of political groups from the list of groups protected by the Convention had removed some of the objections to the establishment of an international tribunal, and it became feasible to reintroduce provision for international jurisdiction, though in an optional and conditional form.[48] The final clause in the Genocide Convention (Article VI) now provides for trial by a competent tribunal of the State in the territory of which the act was committed, 'or by such international penal tribunal as may have jurisdiction with respect to those Contracting Parties which shall have accepted its jurisdiction'.

Further developments have not been encouraging. On the same day as the adoption of the Genocide Convention, the General Assembly

46. U.N. *Legal Committee*, 19 October 1948, 146–7.
47. U.N. *Legal Committee*, 20 and 21 October 1948, 153–4, 167. See also the argument by the British representative, 1 October 1948, 17–18.
48. See the analysis by Robinson, op. cit., 80–82, and the United Nations' *Study of the Question of the Prevention and Punishment of the Crime of Genocide*, 47–86.

invited the International Law Commission to 'study the desirability and possibility of establishing an international judicial organ for the trial of persons charged with genocide or other crimes over which jurisdiction will be conferred upon that organ by international conventions'. This resulted in a Revised Draft Statute. Meanwhile, by an earlier resolution, the International Law Commission had been instructed to prepare a Draft Code of Offences against the Peace and Security of Mankind. This draft code, published in 1954, includes among the offences the crime of genocide. It reads, sadly, like a manual for contemporary international practice. In the General Assembly, discussion of the Revised Draft Statute for an international tribunal 'was made contingent upon satisfactory drafting of the Code of Offences against the Peace and Security of Mankind, which in turn was made contingent upon a satisfactory definition of "aggression", which problem was assigned to a Special Committee in 1954 and to a further Committee of 35 States in 1967, which has met repeatedly since that time . . .'[49] A definition of aggression was finally arrived at in 1974, but the project for an international penal tribunal to try charges of genocide still remains in disheartening abeyance.

There were many other controversies in the debate on the Genocide Convention, not central to my argument, and I have omitted them from this discussion. I shall follow the definition of genocide given in the Convention. This is not to say that I agree with this definition. On the contrary, I believe a major omission to be in the exclusion of political groups from the list of groups protected. In the contemporary world, political differences are at the very least as significant a basis for massacre and annihilation as racial, national, ethnic or religious differences. Then too, the genocides against racial, national, ethnic or religious groups are generally a consequence of, or intimately related to, political conflict. However, I do not think it helpful to create new definitions of genocide, when there is an internationally recognized definition and a Genocide Convention which might become the basis for some effective action, however limited the underlying conception. But since it would vitiate the analysis to exclude political groups, I shall refer freely, in the following discussion, to liquidating or exterminatory actions against them, while reserving some more specific comments for the chapter on 'Related Atrocities'.

49. Goldenberg, op. cit., 23 and 18–26.

Chapter 3

Theories of Genocide

'Genocide was such a vile act that even savages and wild beasts were incapable of committing it.'

[Australian Representative, United Nations General Assembly, 9 December 1948, 822]

Given the great variety of historical and social contexts of acts of genocide, it would hardly seem possible to develop a general theory of genocide. There has in fact been very little theorizing on the subject, but we do have a number of specific theories, *ad hoc* theories or theories directed to a special set of circumstances, from which we can abstract more general comment.

Hunting and gathering peoples have often been the victims of genocidal attacks, as for example the San (Bushmen) in Southern Africa, or many Indian groups in the U.S.A. and Latin America, or the systematic annihilation of Aborigines in Tasmania. I cannot do better than quote Eric Wolf on this genocidal process.

One thing is certain: the Aché are not alone in their dying. Hunters and gatherers like them have been dying and continue to die all along the internal margins of Latin America. Hundreds and thousands like them – in Peru, Brazil, Venezuela, Colombia – are driven daily from their former hunting territories to make room for incoming settlers and plantations, roads, airstrips, pipelines, oil wells. And this is hardly a new process, only the latest episode in the onward march of civilization. Wherever civilization advances, it spells the doom of the non-civilized. Out of the total range of human possibilities, civilization can tolerate only a few. In Latin America, this battle of the civilized against the non-civilized is fought by men who classify themselves as 'men of reason' (*gente de razón*) against those who, bereft of that particular reason, can be classified with the animals. The Guarani-speaking Paraguayans who hunt the Aché, and the Aché, both speak varieties of the same language stock, Tupi-Guarani. But the Guarani-speaking settlers are men of reason, while the hunting and gathering Aché are in their terminology merely Guayaki, 'rabid rats'; and rabid rats must be exterminated. As the Aché die, others inherit their land. The progress of civilization across the face of the earth is also a process of primary accumulation, of robbery in the name of reason. Nor is this process confined to Latin America. What goes

40

on there now is but what went on in North America when the land was 'discovered' and taken from its first occupants. It is only that in North America the process has been dignified by the passage of centuries: 'dead men tell no tales.'[1]

Wolf adds a further dimension to the contrast between 'real people' and 'animals', namely the distinction between political Indians with states, and savage, stateless societies. For the encroaching Spaniards and Portuguese, political Indians were domesticable Indians, in contrast to the savages, for whom the alternatives of action were genocide, or survival, along with other endangered species, in a national park, or ethnocide, the taming of Indians in reservations.

Somewhat related is the genocide against the so-called 'pariah' groups. This is a term I find objectionable in the present context. It derives from the perspective of dominant strata. It carries the implication that the group has characteristics which place it outside the bounds of human society, and that this failure in human quality contributes to, or indeed even justifies, genocide. Thus, for example, one continually hears in academic discourse the charge that Indians in East Africa, as members of an exploitative trading class, isolating themselves from intimate contact with Africans, brought their fate upon themselves. The fate, to be sure, falls far short of genocide, but it involves nevertheless the systematic expulsion, and robbery, of Indian communities from Uganda, and a process of attrition in Kenya and Tanzania. In taking this view of Indians in East Africa as in some measure their own executioners, no comparison is made with the practices of other trading groups, nor for that matter with the practices of African traders themselves. By attributing to the entire community the presumed failings of the traders amongst them, collective guilt is assumed, and collective responsibility imposed. There is, in all this, a genocidal calculus.

The term 'stranger' peoples is often used to describe these rejected groups. This is a broader category than 'pariah' peoples and again derives from the perspective of the host society. I would prefer the phrase 'hostage' peoples, as directing analysis away from the qualities of the victims to those of the victimizers, and as emphasizing the arbitrary nature of their fate. It does not imply, however, that genocide against these groups is never an end in itself, but always related to some further objective, and I think this implication invalid. In any event, whatever term is used, Jewish communities have been major victims of

1. Wolf, 1976:52–3.

Genocide

this type of genocide and massacre in many different European countries and over long periods of European history. For a theory of this form of genocide, I will draw on the study by Norman Cohn of exterminatory anti-semitism in his book *Warrant for Genocide*.

Cohn distinguishes exterminatory anti-semitism from other forms. He writes[2] that there is a kind of anti-semitism which is fairly closely related to the role played by Jews, or at least by some Jews, in the society in question. 'For instance, it has happened again and again that Jews, because of their peculiar history, have been pioneers in trade and money-lending in predominantly agricultural societies, while at the same time living more or less segregated from the population around them. In such cases they have attracted the same kind of hostility as, say, Indian traders in south-eastern Africa or Chinese traders in Java.'

This, Cohn contrasts with the anti-semitism that leads to attempts at genocide, which he argues can exist almost regardless of the real situation of Jews in society. 'It can prosper where Jews form a large, cohesive and clearly recognizable minority, but also where the only Jews are a few scattered individuals who hardly regard themselves as Jews at all. And if it thrives on the spectacle of rich and influential Jews, it does not necessarily wilt where all Jews are poor. Most striking of all, it can be found among people who have never set eyes on a Jew and in countries where there have been no Jews for centuries.'[3] This deadliest kind of anti-semitism, he argues, has little to do with real conflicts of interest between living people. At its heart lies the belief in a Jewish world conspiratorial body, employed in medieval times by Satan for the spiritual and physical ruination of Christendom, and in modern times, banded together for the ruin and domination of the rest of mankind.[4] Over a period of some eight centuries, and over a wide range of countries, the myth of a Jewish world conspiracy has enabled organized groups to kill Jews, by providing them with an ideology and by bewildering the rest of the population. The indications are that the presence of these organized killers is a necessary condition. 'Pogroms as spontaneous outbreaks of popular fury seem to be a myth, and there is in fact no established case where the inhabitants of a town or village have simply fallen upon their Jewish neighbours and slaughtered them.'[5]

2. Cohn, 1967:251–2.
3. ibid., 252.
4. ibid., 16.
5. ibid., 266.

42

Centuries of propaganda had produced a general atmosphere of super-stitious dread of Jews. 'Particularly in periods of exceptional strain, anxiety, and disorientation, multitudes of people yielded to the tempta-tion to blame all their troubles on the machinations of those uncanny beings – reacting to social and economic crises, for instance, very much as their ancestors had reacted to the plague.'[6]

Probably some such theory of 'demonization' is required to explain the prevalence and virulence of the genocidal massacres of Jews in Christian societies over so many centuries, and the rapid spread of Nazi doctrines, as envisaged by Hitler. The prosecution in the Nuremberg trials quoted the following prediction by Hitler.

> Anti-Semitism is a useful revolutionary expedient. Anti-Semitic propaganda in all countries is an almost indispensable medium in the extension of our political campaign. You will see how little time we shall need in order to upset the ideas and criteria of the whole world simply and solely by attacking Judaism. It is beyond question the most important weapon in our propaganda arsenal.[7]

But this is the extreme case. The main elements in the scapegoat type of genocide are, first, an identifiable and differentiated group within a society. Where there are problems in recognizing members of this group, a solution may be found by the use of devices to ensure identifiability. Usually, perhaps invariably, hostile stereotypes are projected onto the victims, and vilifying propaganda directed against them. These often take the form of 'dehumanizing' the target group. Vulnerability seems to be an essential element: the group is an easy prey. The ability of a group to defend itself, and to exact reprisals, is of course some guarantee against genocide. Commonly, there are material advantages to be gained – funds for war or other projects, elimination of competition in trade, distribution of spoils to one's followers, loot for the mob. But the group serves also as scapegoat, as diversion, as surrogate. This was a marked feature of the massacres of Jews, charged with responsibility for the Black Death in the fourteenth century, or massacred as liberals and as the cause of Russian misfortunes in the early twentieth century, or

---

6. ibid., 267. I have not taken up Cohn's view that the wide currency of the myth, and its imperviousness to rational argument, suggest that the myth answers to deep and enduring unconscious needs, which project a conception of Jews collectively as the 'bad' son and the 'bad' father (Conclusion, 251–74). I do not know what to make of the argument.

7. Vol. XIX of the *Proceedings of Nuremberg*, 437–8 (*Law Reports of Trials of War Criminals*, 1948).

Genocide

slaughtered as Jews and as Bolsheviks in the Ukrainian genocide after the First World War.[8]

I have referred, in Chapter 1, to Sartre's version of the theory of an affinity between colonialism and genocide.[9] Sartre bases his argument on his conception of the nature of capitalism. In the competition for markets between antagonistic bourgeois nationalisms, war becomes total, by reason of the involvement of civilians in war production, the siting of factories near towns, and the participation of the masses in politics; it is increasingly difficult to distinguish between civilians and military. However, since the belligerent nations are the industrial powers, a certain initial balance acts as a deterrent against the possibility of real extermination.

Sartre contrasts this situation with colonization, asserting that there have been countless acts of genocide by the capitalist powers in the colonial empires they established from the year 1830. Since victory, easily achieved by overwhelming fire-power, provokes the hatred of the civilian population, and since civilians are potentially rebels and soldiers, the colonial troops maintain their authority by the terror of perpetual massacre, genocidal in character. This is accompanied by cultural genocide, made necessary by colonialism as an economic system of unequal exchange in which the colony sells its raw materials and agricultural products at a reduced price to the colonizing power, and the latter in return sells its manufactured goods to the colony at world market prices. However, the dependence of the settlers on the sub-proletariat of the colonized protects the latter, to a certain extent, against physical genocide.

In the struggles for national independence after the Second World War, Sartre argues that the superiority of the colonialists in weapons, and of the colonized in numbers, determines the strategies employed. The insurgents rely on terrorism, ambushes, harassment, and extreme mobility, made possible by the support of the entire population, which feeds, hides and replenishes the liberation forces. Against partisans supported by the whole population, the only effective strategy is to

8. See Torrès, 1928, and Comité des Délégations Juives, 1927, This genocide was centrally organized with calls to Ukrainian regiments – Save the Ukraine: Kill the Jews. The same procedures were followed in the different towns and villages – the exacting of ransom, charges of Bolshevism, the humiliation of the representatives of the community, followed by massacres of men, women and children carried out with the most extreme cruelty and atrocity.
9. Sartre, 1968.

'empty the sea of its water', that is, to destroy the people, men, women and children. But since this is not possible without destroying also the colonial economy and the whole colonial system, the settlers panic, the colonial powers grow weary of the cost, and the mass of the people in the mother country oppose the continuation of an inhuman war: the colonies become sovereign states. In this process, infra-structural contradictions have stood in the way of genocide. Where, however, the genocidal response is not checked by infra-structural contradictions, as Sartre argues was the case in the imperialist aggression by the U.S.A. in Vietnam, then total genocide emerges, in his view, as the absolute basis of an anti-guerrilla strategy.

The date selected by Sartre for the beginning of his survey of capitalist colonialism, the year 1830, is revealing. It is the year in which the French invaded Algeria. The context of his speech is the Sartre-Russell International War Crimes Tribunal to consider U.S. actions in Vietnam, and it is clear that the generalizations he offers as to the genocidal nature of colonialism are derived primarily from his observations on Algeria and Vietnam. He gives no consideration to the wide range of variation in the process of colonization and decolonization. It would be necessary to study colonialism in its complex diversity in order to establish the conditions under which it sometimes took a genocidal form.

Nevertheless, given the many genocidal massacres in colonial history, I think the argument of an affinity between colonialism and genocide can be accepted, though with much qualification, and we can extract from Sartre's argument some of the significant elements in this relationship. There is the nature of the initial conquest, particularly brutal in the case of Algeria, accompanied by genocidal massacres and the devastation of settled areas, and extending over a long period of 'pacification'. Then there is the type of exploitation, taking the form in Algeria of unequal conditions of exchange, destruction of the economic infrastructure with dispossession of land, and the development of a subproletariat. To this one might add systematic discrimination resulting in the division of the society into two categories of being, the colonizers and the colonized, giving point to Sartre's comments that the colonized 'live in their underworld of misery like dark phantoms ceaselessly reminded of their subhumanity'. It is this creation of generalized categories which may be conducive to genocide under certain conditions. It is the basis 'for the symbiosis between the liberation forces and the masses of the people', encouraging a genocidal response by the colonizers in the attempt to deny the insurgents their popular support.

The restraints on genocide to which Sartre refers, dependence on the labour of the subject peoples and the preservation of the colonial economy, are of a functional nature. The corollary would be that the impulse to genocide will be given freer rein where there are no material advantages to be derived from restraint, as in the genocides against hunting and gathering peoples. This conception of functional restraints on genocide seems to have some general applicability.

There is no reference in Sartre's analysis to a frequent source of genocide in decolonization, that is, the struggle between different racial, or ethnic, or religious sections for power. This is one of the consequences flowing from the arbitrary grouping together of different peoples in colonial possessions, and the disruptive impact of the rewards of power with independence.

Sartre's theory is not only a theory of genocide in colonization: it is also a theory of genocide in the international relations of the great powers. The changing nature of warfare, with a movement to total warfare, and the technological means for the instantaneous annihilation of large populations, creates a situation conducive to genocidal conflict. This potential was realized in the Second World War, when Germany employed genocide in its war for domination; but I think the term must also be applied to the atomic bombing of the Japanese cities of Hiroshima and Nagasaki by the U.S.A. and to the pattern bombing by the Allies of such cities as Hamburg and Dresden. At the present time, the ability to retaliate, the horror of a nuclear war, presumably some respect for international obligation, and the pressures of international relations, keep genocide in check at the international level. However, the transposition of the arena of conflict between the great powers to intervention in domestic struggles for national domination between different sections, particularly in Third World countries, heightens the potentiality for domestic genocide.

Of course, we need to bear in mind that genocide in warfare preceded the discovery of the highly destructive atomic bomb and other armaments. Military hordes, armed with relatively primitive weapons, were quite capable of wiping out whole populations, and there were periods in history when conquering armies annihilated their enemies.

I have referred to the theory advanced by the Russian delegation in the debates on genocide, namely, that there is an organic link between genocide and nazism-fascism-racism. Genocide, so the argument ran, was essentially bound up with fascist and Nazi ideologies and other similar racial theories, spreading national and racial hatred, and aiming at the domination of the so-called 'superior' races and the extermination of the so-called 'inferior' races: as to religious groups, in all known cases of genocide on grounds of religion, nationality or race were concomitant reasons. The objections advanced against this theory in the debate seem valid enough – the founding of a general theory of genocide on the basis of one particular manifestation. Moreover, exterminatory racism it not a necessary part of fascist doctrine. Still, the theory draws attention to the potential role of ideologies of racial or national or ethnic superiority in genocide, and presumably also to the relevance of certain forms of totalitarian centralized and terroristic governments.

A surprising feature of the arguments presented by the Russian representatives and their supporters was the absence of any Marxist analysis or theory of genocide. Speculating on the form such an analysis might have taken, one would perhaps have anticipated the theory of nazism-fascism as a last ditch stand of capitalism. But this would not explain the genocidal content of Nazi ideology: and in any event, it was hardly feasible to launch an attack of this nature on capitalism in gatherings designed to arrive at a convention on genocide. Another possibility would have been to develop the Marxist theory of class struggle as a driving force in history into a theory of genocide. Given the conception of an increasing polarization of class relations leading to revolutionary change, the class struggle would seem to be charged with the potentiality for genocide, at any rate against the ruling class. But argument along these lines would hardly have been acceptable to Marxists, and in any event it was excluded in the genocide debates by the insistence of the Russian representatives that genocide was a crime committed against racial or national (or religious) groups.

Sartre's discussion of colonialism and its affinity for genocide is well within the tradition of Marxist-Leninist analysis of capitalism in its imperialist phase. This model of overseas conquest and colonization is now being applied to the internal domestic relations between dominant (or privileged) and subordinate (or underprivileged) racial or ethnic groups in the concept of internal colonialism.

In the early years of the United Nations the Belgians had attempted to broaden the concept of colonialism to include all ethnically distinct minorities discriminated against in their home countries; and Leo Marquard used the term 'internal colonialism' many years ago to describe internal race relations in South Africa. More recently it has been adopted in Marxist interpretations of black–white relations in the U.S.A.

and of Catholic–Protestant relations in Northern Ireland, and it has come into wide currency. Presumably the genocidal conflicts in Burundi and Lebanon would also be analysed in these terms. In this use of internal colonialism, there is an identification of ethnic (or racial) group with class. But the concept has also been applied directly to class conflicts. Thus, Gouldner[10] combines theories of class conflict, and of internal colonialism, between an urban-centred Bolshevik power élite and a largely rural society ('to which they related as an alien colonial power'), to explain the liquidation of many millions of *kulaks* and other peasants, following Stalin's decree in December 1929 for the liquidation of the *kulaks* as a class.

The German genocide in the Second World War was particularly shocking to Western sensibility, and stimulated inquiry into the causes of the regression of 'civilized' man to 'barbarism'. Psychological and psychoanalytic theories were applied to the interpretation of German society. There were studies of national character structure, of child-rearing and other cultural patterns, of deviations in the maturing of the Nazi leaders, and of the interaction between these leaders and the psychic demands of their followers.[11] Many of these studies emphasize the significance of psychopathological personality development in their interpretation of the German genocide.

At the different level of socio-historical perspectives, Rubenstein offers an analysis of the German genocide against Jews, the Holocaust, which has broad relevance for theories of contemporary genocide. He comments first on such obvious features as the defeat of Germany in the First World War after four years of unprecedented violence, and the conjunction of the charismatic leadership of Hitler, the bureaucratic competence of the German police and civil service, and the mood of the German people at a particular moment in history. But he argues that more was involved, that 'the Holocaust was an expression of some of the most significant political, moral, religious and demographic tendencies of Western civilization in the twentieth century'.[12]

In regard to the demographic tendency, Rubenstein places the Holocaust within the context of twentieth-century mass death, commenting

10. Gouldner, 1977–8.

11. For references to the literature, see Loewenberg, 1975 and 1971, as well as the brief comments in the United Nations' *Study of the Question of the Prevention and Punishment of the Crime of Genocide*, E/CN. 4/Sub. 2/416, dated 4 July 1978, 173–7.

12. Rubenstein, 1975:6.

that never before had human beings been so expendable. This he documents in support of the argument that the foundations of twentieth-century *military* slaughter on a mass scale were laid during the First World War, and the foundations of mass *civilian* slaughter immediately thereafter in the Russian sphere (as a result of revolution, civil war, demographic violence and large-scale famine), and, generally, in Central and Eastern Europe. And he asks whether there might not be some regulating mechanism at work to reduce population surplus – a blind mechanism in the First World War, but deliberate and explicit under the Nazi leaders.

As for the political changes, Rubenstein refers to Hannah Arendt's observation that with the signing of the minorities' treaties after the First World War, the transformation of the state from an institution of law into an instrument of the dominant national community had been completed; surplus population might be readily deprived of meaningful human rights by denationalization, and disposed of by expulsion. Moreover, bureaucratic political and social organization in the Christian West had come to full development. This was the result of the growth of an ethos of secularization, of disenchantment of the world and of rationalization, derived from fundamental tendencies in occidental religion. With this development in bureaucracy, it became possible to overcome the moral barrier that had prevented the systematic riddance of surplus populations in the past, and to contemplate the extermination of millions. Thus, far from being a regression to a barbaric paganism, bureaucratic dehumanization and mass murder were within the mainstream of Western culture.[13]

To these theories focused on specific contexts or strata, one might add any of the more general theories of violence such as frustration and aggression theory.[14] Then too, given the fact that genocide is almost invariably a crime of governments, or of organized groups, it is to be expected that élite theory should be invoked. The following proposition seems plausible enough: 'When the ruling élites decide that their continuation in power transcends all other economic and social values, at that point does the possibility, if not the necessity, for genocide increase qualitatively. For this reason, genocide is a unique strategy for totalitarian regimes.'[15]

13. ibid., 27–31.
14. For an application of frustration-aggression theory, see the discussion of the Turkish genocide against Armenians by Dadrian, 1947.
15. Horowitz, 1976:38–9.

In a somewhat different form, élite theory has been applied in the interpretation of genocidal conflict between racial and ethnic groups. Thus in Burundi, after the massive genocide by Tutsi against Hutu in 1972, the Catholic bishops wrote in their pastoral letter of January 1973 that although the main problem appeared to lie in the divisive processes and policies of nepotism, racism or tribalism, and regionalism for personal gain, they themselves were persuaded that the root cause was the egoism of Hutu and Tutsi élites. So too in interpretations of the massacres of Ibos in Northern Nigeria, and in analyses of the highly destructive civil war between the forces of the federal government of Nigeria and the Ibo, many commentators place the responsibility on élites, mobilizing ethnic support in a struggle for power. I would add my own view that whatever the responsibility of élites, they are working with social forces present within the society, and not creating a genocidal situation out of a vacuum or transforming a harmonious equilibrium into a genocidal conflict.

It seems hardly conceivable that functional theories should be applied to genocide, but they have already appeared in different forms in the theories discussed above. They appear in the conception of hunting and gathering groups as standing in the way of economic development, and their elimination as serving the interests of economic progress. They appear in discussions of Nazi anti-semitism. Thus we read that 'the Jew has of course served as the master symbol of the adversary of the German people and their mission. One of his most important functions is to unify the different evils which beset them in a single tangible symbol – above all to bring capitalism and bolshevism together.'[16] And anti-semitism served Nazi interests, as envisaged by Hitler, in gaining political support, not only in Germany, but in many other countries where it spawned Nazi movements. Sartre makes use of functional theory in his analysis of the role of genocidal massacres in the colonial conquest of markets for an expanding capitalism: and he relies on functionalism to explain the restraints on genocide arising from infrastructural contradictions, and to interpret U.S. strategy in Vietnam in terms of its potential function as an admonitory genocide for the Third World.

In a specifically structural functional analysis, Dadrian advances the proposition that 'even though in conception, design and execution, genocide may be regarded as a phenomenon *sui generis*, in terms of underlying structural contingencies and projective goals, it is functional;

16. Parsons, 1949:337.

Theories of Genocide

it subserves the ultimate end of equilibrium of a system beset by disarray through acute group conflict'.[17] Using the Turks and Armenians as a case study, he interprets the genocide as a response to the imbalances set in motion by the economic success of a merchant class of the subordinate Armenians, by critical events in the First World War, and by the tension between Turkish nationalism and Armenian ethnocentrism. Since genocide must result in radical change in a social system where the target group is as numerous as the Armenians in Turkey, I think the argument should not be phrased in terms of functions for the social system, but of functions (and dysfunctions) *for the dominant group* that commits the genocide.

In addition to these sociological theories, there are theories of human destructiveness which would derive genocide from the biological nature of man or his personality structure as moulded by the advance of civilization. For Lorenz, the human destructiveness expressed in the killing of members of one's own species flows from instinctual aggression in man. In the course of evolution, this aggression has taken an exaggerated form: and unexpected explosions of devastatingly destructive violence may result from its frustration. This is all the more likely, Lorenz argues, since the invention of weapons has the effect of destroying the functional equilibrium between the aggressive instinct and mechanisms which inhibit the killing of members of one's own species; particularly in modern warfare, impersonal methods of killing at everincreasing distances remove these inhibitions. Moreover, the danger of intra-species killing is intensified by militant enthusiasm, an autonomous instinct which evolved out of a communal defence response of our prehuman ancestors, and which can be applied equally to ethical or destructive goals. 'That indeed is the Janus head of man: The only being capable of dedicating himself to the very highest moral and ethical values requires for this purpose a phylogenetically adapted mechanism of behaviour whose animal properties bring with them the danger that he will kill his brother, convinced that he is doing so in the interests of these very same high values.'[18]

Koestler, in a discussion of man's persistent pursuit of intra-specific warfare,[19] describes him as alone (apart from some controversial phenomena among rats and cats) in killing members of his own species on an

17. Dadrian, 1974–5:123.
18. Lorenz, 1977:265, 228–90; and 1970:3–5, 51–6. See also the critical discussion of Lorenz's theory by Fromm, 1975:22–5, 37–54, 94–5, 98.
19. Koestler, 1978:Prologue.

Genocide

individual and collective scale, for motives ranging from sexual jealousy
to quibbles about metaphysical doctrines. Homo sapiens, he argues, may
be an aberrant biological species, an evolutionary misfit, afflicted by an
endemic disorder, the source of which lies in the conflict between the
new and the old structures of the brain. The neo-cortex, seat of our
intellect, has failed to establish proper control over our ancient brain,
seat of archaic emotion-based beliefs, the horse and the crocodile which
we carry inside our skulls.[20]

By contrast, Fromm places the emphasis, in his analysis of human
destructiveness, on the interaction of various social conditions with
man's existential needs. He distinguishes two different types of aggression, defensive aggression and malignant aggression, defensive aggression being part of human nature and a benign form of aggression.
'However, man differs from the animal by the fact that he is a killer;
he is the only primate that kills and tortures members of his own
species without any reason, either biological or economic, and who feels
satisfaction in doing so. It is this biologically nonadaptive and non-
phylogenetically programmed "malignant" aggression, that constitutes
the real problem and the danger to man's existence as a species.'[21] The
malignant forms of aggression arise out of man's reactions to conditions
which are unfavourable to the development of his genuine needs and
capacities, his human self-activity and creative power as ends in themselves.[22]

The paucity of theoretical speculation about genocide may be due
to the fact that it is seen as an extreme manifestation of a broader
phenomenon – of violence, of destructiveness, of aggression. This would
also explain why the more focused theories tend to deal with specific
cases or types of genocide. However, there are some general theoretical
observations which we can derive from the preceding discussion.

Though animals do engage in intra-species killing, genocide is essentially a human crime. But this does not mean that it is rooted in human
nature. There are convincing arguments to the contrary. Conflict of a
potentially genocidal character is not the normal pattern of interaction
between social groups. Even in our contemporary world, ravaged as it
is by genocidal conflicts, most societies develop and relate to each other
without interruption by group annihilating destruction. Some analysts

20. For critical reviews of this theory, see Gould, 1978, and Jonas, 1978.
21. Fromm, op. cit., 26.
22. ibid., 482–3.

would add the further argument that in the so-called 'simple' hunting-gathering societies, warfare was 'characteristically unbloody',[23] but this may be controversial. In any event, the source of genocide is to be found in the social conditions of man's existence. This is central to Fromm's thesis. But the social factors also have some significance in Lorenz's approach,[24] as in his discussion of the discovery of weapons as disturbing the equilibrium between the ability and the inhibition to kill; or the effect on human aggression of the deviation of the ecological and sociological conditions created by culture from those to which human instinctive behaviour is phylogenetically adapted; or the genesis of militant enthusiasm in the interaction between an instinctive behavioural pattern and culturally ritualized social norms and rites; or in such suggestions for avoiding aggression as the promotion of personal acquaintance and, if possible, friendship between individual members of different nations, thereby activating the inhibition against killing.

Turning then to these social conditions, since genocide is a crime against a collectivity, it implies an identifiable group as victim. The more specifically focused theories we have been discussing deal with hunting and gathering peoples; hostage groups; the colonized; other nations; the racial and ethnic sections of a society. Maximum identifiability is present where there are marked racial differences: but cultural differences may be equally divisive. In cases where the groups appear to an outside observer to share the same culture, the members of the society may themselves be highly sensitive to minutiae of cultural differences, which in the course of the genocidal conflict cry out for murder. Where there is a high level of segregation, there is no need to rely on personal identifying features. The I.R.A. terrorist who throws a bomb into a public house in Belfast, Northern Ireland, will know from its location that his victims will be Protestant: he can fire indiscriminately on pedestrians in particular localities with reasonable certainty as to their Protestant identity. In situations where there are no obviously identifying physical differences, identifiability can be assured by systems of registration or such other devices as the compulsory wearing of badges. Even political groups recruited from the same population may be readily differentiated from each other as victimizers and victims, and are so differentiated in many societies. The fact that identification on racial, ethnic, religious or political grounds may not be precise is, of course, no obstacle to genocidal assault.

23. See the references cited in ibid., 159, 170–76.
24. Lorenz, op. cit., Chs. 13 and 14.

The plural society, which I discuss in the next chapter, is by definition characterized by the presence of identifiable groups. I use the term, in a tradition which derives from Furnivall, to describe societies with persistent cleavages between racial, ethnic or religious groups. They are a major arena for genocidal conflict. Partly as a result of colonization, which has left numerous states in the Third World with a diversity of peoples between whom a stable accommodation has not yet been achieved, there are many contemporary plural societies with a relatively high potential for genocidal conflict. At the same time, ease of contact and communication between different nations most effectively translates the internal pluralism into international relations and international conflicts. With nuclear armament acting as a deterrent to war between the great powers, they transfer their warring to struggles for domination over smaller nations, whose conflicts with each other and whose domestic conflicts between different sections provide a point of entry and a field of deployment of conventional, but increasingly sophisticated and devastating, weapons. The destructive potentialities of the plural society are thereby greatly magnified.

There must have been periods in the history of human societies when groups committed genocide without benefit of ideologies to incite or justify commission of the crime. In the genocides of our own era, they seem to be invariably present. They are an aspect of many of the theories we have been discussing. Thus in the comments on genocide against hunters and gatherers, we quoted a reference to the Aché people as 'rabid rats' in the eyes of their persecutors. This is a common phenomenon, the equating of hunting and gathering peoples with animals, and the hunting them down in the same way as animals. There are similar processes of dehumanization in the ideologies against 'hostage' or 'stranger' groups, taking the extreme form of demonization in the theory of the Jewish world conspiracy, and rendering the groups readily available as scapegoats and as sacrifices. The elaboration of denigrating and justifying ideologies was an intrinsic part of the colonizing process, and these ideologies are often described as significant factors in the genocidal attacks against colonial peoples.[25] They are present also in the struggles for power between different groups in the process or aftermath of decolonization. And nazism was quite specific in its ideological ordering of peoples on a genocidal scale.

In the debate on the Genocide Convention, one of the delegates

25. See my discussion of the role of ideologies in *Race, Class and Power*, 1974: Part One.

argued for the inclusion of political groups among the protected groups, on the ground that 'strife between nations had now been superseded by strife between ideologies. Men no longer destroyed for reasons of national, racial or religious hatred, but in the name of ideas and the faith to which they gave birth.' There can be no doubt that political ideologies, not revolving round race, ethnicity or religion, may be a significant element in many highly destructive conflicts, dehumanizing the opposition, and promoting self-righteous conceptions of expendable human groups.

Since genocide is a crime against a collectivity, policies which have the effect of collectivizing the members of the society into polarized sections increase the potentiality for genocide. Thus, in the attempt to deny guerrillas a popular base, there may be a vast relocation of the indigenous people into ill-equipped settlements, with punitive action in the form of collective punishment against whole communities, and a progressive identification of ordinary civilians with the enemy. The use of highly destructive weapons, deployed at long range, against guerrilla forces which disappear into the local population, as in Vietnam, also fails to discriminate between combatants and non-combatants. These processes, and reciprocity in violence, resulting in increasing polarization, may escalate the conflict to a genocidal level. There may however be no struggle, no reciprocity in violence, but a deliberate decision to annihilate a group, and the overwhelming power to carry out the annihilation, as in the German genocide against Jews.

The argument advanced in the debates on the Genocide Convention, that genocide is essentially a crime of governments, has validity, though I would emphasize that it is not exclusively a crime of governments. This involvement of governments directs attention to the role of ruling strata, of élites, in organizing or unleashing genocide or acting in complicity with other groups in the commission of genocide. The strategies and goals of élites may thus be a crucial factor in genocide, whether the genocide takes the form of a direct attack on contending élites and the groups from which they draw support, as in the Tutsi genocide against Hutu in Burundi, or whether it consolidates power indirectly, as in the scapegoat genocidal massacres.

Governments engage in large-scale genocidal massacres not only against racial, ethnic and religious groups. The liquidation of political groups is a speciality of governments, though not their exclusive prerogative. The line between these forms of annihilation is quite arbitrary, more particularly since political motives usually enter into the genocides against racial, ethnic or religious groups. It is only in order to follow the definition in the Genocide Convention that I treat the crimes against political groups as a related atrocity. However, there are significant differences which do warrant some separate treatment. The liquidation of political groups may, but does not generally, take the form of root and branch extermination, expressed in the slaughter of men, women and children.

The involvement of governments and élites in many genocides is a reminder that human actors make choices and decisions, and carry out actions which constitute, or lead to, genocide. Genocide is not an inevitable consequence of certain social conditions within a society. There may be extreme pluralism in a society, with highly antagonistic, polarizing ideologies, division expressed in religion, segregation, employment, social networks, and political party affiliation, a long history of reciprocal violence, and periods of highly escalated conflict. Yet the struggle may stop short of genocide. Northern Ireland is an example of such a society. Notwithstanding the periodic conflagrations in the nineteenth and twentieth centuries, there have been no large-scale genocidal massacres during this period, which also takes in a civil war. I will describe societies of this type as non-genocidal societies, in the sense that there are effective restraints against genocide, even though many social factors are conducive to the commission of the crime. The study of these societies should offer insight into inhibitions against genocide even under conditions of the sharpest conflict and the most acute stress.

These themes of structure, ideology, process, the involvement of governments and the non-genocidal society are discussed in the following chapters.

Chapter 4

Social Structure and Genocide
Colonization, Decolonization and Succession

1. The subjection of peoples to alien subjugation, domination and exploitation constitutes a denial of fundamental human rights, is contrary to the Charter of the United Nations and is an impediment to the promotion of world peace and co-operation.

2. All peoples have the right to self-determination; by virtue of that right they freely determine their political status and freely pursue their economic, social and cultural development.

6. Any attempt aimed at the partial or total disruption of the national unity and the territorial integrity of a country is incompatible with the purposes and principles of the Charter of the United Nations.

[Declaration on the Granting of Independence to Colonial Countries and Peoples: General Assembly Resolution 1514 (XV) of 14 December 1960]

The plural society provides the structural base for genocide, the presence of a diversity of racial, ethnic and/or religious groups being the structural characteristic of the plural society, and genocide a crime.committed against these groups. This is not to say that genocide is inevitable in the history of plural societies, but only that plural societies offer the necessary conditions for domestic genocide. The many genocidal conflicts in plural societies (as for example in India on partition, or in Bangladesh, or in Rwanda and Burundi) suggest an intimate relationship between the plural society and genocide.

I do not use the term plural society to mean simply the presence of a diversity of racial, ethnic and/or religious groups. The effect of this would be to classify the overwhelming majority of societies as plural societies. I use the term rather, in a tradition deriving from J. S. Furnivall, to describe societies with persistent and pervasive cleavages between these sections. It is a distinctive type of society, recognized as such in the literature under a variety of names – divided societies, communally fragmented societies, multi-ethnic or multiple societies, composite societies, segmented societies and internally colonized societies.

In the plural society, racial or ethnic or religious differentiation is elaborated in many different spheres. There is generally inequality in the mode of political incorporation, as in the constitutional provisions which exclude Africans from the vote for members of the South African parliament. Even where there is formal recognition of political equality, there may be practical inequality, as in Northern Ireland, where Protestants succeeded in maintaining an entrenched political domination over Catholics, notwithstanding a democratic constitution. The political inequality is usually associated with economic discrimination – in opportunities for employment, in wages, in access to the means of production. There is almost certain to be discrimination also in provision for education, sometimes with quite startling differences in expenditure for dominant groups as compared with subordinate. Segregation may be imposed in many spheres, including prohibition against intermarriage, or an increasing segregation may develop in the course of conflicts protracted over many years. Differences in culture and social organization may add further to division between the different sections.

The plural society, in its *extreme* form, is characterized by a super-imposition of inequalities. The same sections are dominant or subordinate, favoured or discriminated against, in the political structure, in the economy, in opportunities for education, in human rights, in access to amenity. And issues of conflict tend also to be superimposed along the same lines of cleavage and inequality. These structural conditions are likely to be conducive to genocidal conflict. They aggregate the population into distinctive sections, thereby facilitating crimes against collectivities. The divisions being so pervasive, and relatively consistent in so many spheres, issues of conflict may move rapidly from one sector to another, until almost the entire society is polarized. A quite local racial disturbance, for example, of seemingly minor significance, may set off a chain of reactions – rioting at distant geographical points, demonstrations, strike action, police reprisals, reciprocal terrorism and violent political confrontation at a national level. So too, by reason of the superimposition of issues of conflict, particular issues, however specific in their origin, become generalized to a wide range of grievance. And if there is a long history of struggle, with its models, for the dominant group, of effective violent repression, and its memories, for the subordinate group, of past injustice and atrocity, it will give an emotional charge to the conflict, which may escalate to high levels of destructive violence. But this is by no means an inevitable development. A society which one might characterize as an extreme plural society on the basis of objective measures may remain quiescent for long periods, perhaps indefinitely, lacking the subjective reactions and opportunity to sustain a destructive conflict.

In the examples which follow, I have drawn on case studies of highly destructive violence to establish the argument of a genocidal potential in the conflicts between racial, ethnic or religious sections of a plural society. I would not personally describe each of the case studies as genocide. But they are all conflicts in which the charge of genocide has been made – though this charge is often made in a loose and exaggerated way. And they are all conflicts in which there has been massive slaughter, with episodes of genocidal massacre, whole communities of the target group being annihilated.

Colonization has been a major creator of plural societies, and many colonial and settler societies conformed to the extreme type of plural society. But colonies varied greatly in the manner of the initial colonization, in the structure of the relationships established, in the mode of decolonization, and in the violence attending these historical phases.

Many variables are relevant to these differences in colonial societies, and in the incidence of violent confrontation. There is the familiar distinction between limited settlement, as in the early Iberian pre-capitalist colonization of Central and South America, substantial settlement, as in Algeria and South Africa, and massive settlement, engulfing the indigenous peoples, as for example Indians in the U.S.A. and Canada, Maoris in New Zealand, Aborigines in Australia. Then there is the extent of intermarriage, with milder forms of racism prevailing where intermarriage was a predominant mode, as in Mexico, and maximal racism, with exclusion of intermarriage. The period of colonization, related to the forms of economic exploitation, is specially significant, as in the search for raw materials at the lowest possible cost in an earlier period, and for market outlets for finished goods at a later period. The time factor is also relevant to the ideological justifications and the policies of the different colonial powers. So too, of particular significance for the introduction of new groups, with increasing pluralism of the society, is the failure of attempts by the colonizers to enslave, or to harness to production, indigenous groups, and the consequent resort to slaves or contract labourers from the outside; and the need in certain situations to encourage the immigration of middlemen accustomed to a

Genocide

technological culture and a money economy.[1] This has been a source of
small hostage groups in former colonies, and also of substantial populations, strong enough to challenge the indigenous peoples in the struggles
for power on decolonization.

I have already discussed, in theories of genocide, the vulnerability of
hunting and gathering groups in the process of colonization, and, more
generally, the incidence of genocidal massacres in the establishment and
maintenance of colonial domination. The colonization of Algeria in the
nineteenth century, and its decolonization by revolution in 1954–61, are
among the most bloody conflicts in the history of modern colonialism.
The brutality of the initial conquest and 'pacification', with whole communities annihilated and areas of fair settlement and cultivation deliberately laid waste, was recalled in revolutionary writings, and became part
of the political consciousness in the struggle for liberation, achieved by
the Algerians at enormous cost in human life and in the uprooting of
millions of Algerians from their traditional homes.

Fanon wrote in 1959, during the revolution, of 'the genocide that is
rife in Algeria'. Sartre, as we have seen, was more cautious in the charge
he made at the Russell Tribunal, introducing the qualification that the
settlers could not carry massacre to the point of physical genocide,
because of their need to exploit the native peoples; by exterminating
the sub-proletariat in Algeria, they would have exterminated themselves
as settlers.[2] I do not see how the Algerian struggle can really be described
as genocide within the terms of the United Nations definition, but it was
certainly marked by genocidal massacres. In 1945, at Sétif, and under
police provocation, Muslims participating in the celebration of victory
in the Second World War, spread through the city, savagely attacking
and murdering the Europeans they encountered. This was followed by
attacks in the countryside with armed bands of Muslims killing, raping,
mutilating, pillaging, burning. The French and settler reprisals were
vastly more savage. There were summary executions and reprisal massacres of Arabs; Senegalese troops and legionnaires pillaged, burnt, raped
and slaughtered in full freedom; a cruiser bombarded coastal areas;
planes destroyed forty-four villages. In the final count, the French dead

1. In this discussion of relevant variables, I have been drawing on the work of
Schermerhorn, 1970: Ch. 4. See also, M. G. Smith's analysis of different patterns in
the Caribbean, 1974, and my paper on *The Theory of the Plural Society, Race and
Conquest* (see Bibliography).
2. In *The Pity of It All*, 1977:247–75, I analyse the processes of polarization in
Algeria.

numbered 103, and there were some hundred wounded and mutilated. The French authorities estimated the Muslim dead as 1,500; the liberation movement placed the Muslim death toll at 50,000.[3]

In the Constantine area, during the course of the revolution, massacre and counter-massacre re-enacted the tragedy of Sétif. In Philippeville, in August 1955, Arabs mounted a devastating attack. At Constantine, bombs exploded throughout the city; and at El Halia, a mining centre in which fifty European families lived among 2,000 Arabs, under conditions of complete equality in employment, and seemingly in perfect harmony, the Europeans were relentlessly slaughtered. When the military finally arrived, wading through pools of blood, they found the bodies of men and women sexually mutilated, women and children with their throats cut and disembowelled by billhook. The reprisals in Constantine took the form of the indiscriminate slaughter of Arabs; in Philippeville, young Muslims were rounded up and shot down in the stadium, while the villages from which some of the assailants originated were destroyed by mortar. The toll of reprisals, according to the count of the revolutionary forces, was 12,000 Muslims dead or missing.[4]

To these pogrom-type massacres must be added the indiscriminate killing of Muslims or of settlers in the escalation of the struggle, with its increasing polarization and reciprocal cycles of terrorism, as in the discharging of a bomb in the densely populated Muslim Casbah, or the bombing of a European milk bar and other public places, or the Muslim terrorist attack followed by the settler *ratonnade* (pogrom), or Muslim massacre and massive French settler vigilante massacre, or the random gunning down of non-combatants.[5] In all this, one can see the genocidal potential of violent conflict in plural societies.

Where there were two tiers of domination in the colonial structure, decolonization was particularly charged with genocidal potential. Plural societies preceded colonial imperialism,[6] and in some cases, capitalist colonization of a plural society resulted in the superimposition of an additional layer of domination on an earlier domination. In a number of these societies, decolonization detonated explosive genocidal conflicts,

3. ibid., 66–70.
4. ibid., 70–73. In the account of these conflicts, I relied on the work of Courrière, 1969:179ff.
5. *The Pity of It All*, 74–83, 128–45.
6. See M. G. Smith's discussion of pluralism in pre-colonial African societies, 1969. See also Lemarchand's analysis of revolutionary phenomena in stratified societies, 1968.

as the earlier rulers and their one-time subjects engaged in violent struggle under the impetus of electoral contests in a democratic idiom, introduced by the colonial powers in the movement to independence.

A major genocide of this type was carried out by a minority of Tutsi against a Hutu majority in Burundi in 1972. In both Rwanda and Burundi, domination had been established centuries earlier by invading Tutsi pastoralists over Hutu agriculturalists and small numbers of Twa hunters and gatherers. Under Belgian mandate, the traditional lines of domination remained clearly defined in Rwanda in a relationship often described by commentators as caste. The sharpness of division was, however, somewhat softened by a great network of patron-client relationships, by a seeming acquiescence in inequality, and by loyalty to the Mwami, the king. The restraints on divisive ethnic confrontation broke down, however, under the impact of reforms introduced by the Belgian government, including a progressive system of electoral representation. Political parties consolidated on mainly ethnic lines, and terrorism, initiated by the Tutsi, and the violent reactions of Hutu, rapidly polarized the society, and escalated electoral contest to violent confrontation.

In March 1962, in one of the regions of Rwanda, the murder by Tutsi bands of two policemen in one raid, and of four Hutu (including one policeman and two civil servants) in another raid, led to massive indiscriminate reprisal in which between 1,000 and 2,000 Tutsi men, women and children were massacred and buried on the spot, their huts pillaged and burned and their property divided among the Hutu population. In December 1963, with Rwanda independent under Hutu domination, a minor, but threatening, invasion by Tutsi set off genocidal massacres. In the prefecture of Gikongoro, at the instigation of the local prefects, Hutu armed with clubs, pangas and spears methodically began to murder all Tutsi in sight – men, women and children. An estimated 5,000 were massacred in Gikongoro, and perhaps another 5,000–9,000 in other areas. The constitutional procedures established by the Belgian government with continuous United Nations intervention had served as catalyst for this escalating conflict in the plural society of Rwanda, terror and ultimately genocidal massacre becoming the instruments of political change.[7]

In Burundi, the colonial situation seemed promising for ethnic accommodation. Relations were more fluid. As in Rwanda, the Tutsi were a

7. I have analysed this genocide in *The Pity of It All*, op. cit., 170–97. The major analysis of this conflict is provided by Lemarchand, 1970.

minority (some 14 per cent in a population of perhaps three-and-a-half million in the period of decolonization). There were divisions within the dominant stratum of dynastic families, and the Tutsi and Hutu were themselves internally divided. Regional differences, and differences in wealth, power and status among Tutsi and among Hutu, added to the structural complexity of the society, which offered many social bases, and the stimulus of varied interests, for the transcending of ethnic exclusiveness. And initially, in the movement to decolonization, political division did not flow along ethnic lines. But very rapidly the society became ethnically polarized, as Tutsi élite sought to eliminate their Hutu opponents by terrorism and assassination, and Hutu responded by counter-terrorism.

Within three years of independence, ethnic conflict had escalated to genocidal massacre. In 1965, on the failure of a Hutu attempted coup, and in reaction also to massacres of Tutsi in the countryside, the army, assisted by civilian defence groups, and the government acting through a Council of War, killed some 2,500 to 5,000 Hutu, virtually liquidating Hutu leadership. This was a precursor, as it were, to the genocide of 1972, which re-enacted, on a vastly destructive scale, the events of 1965. In the southern provinces of Burundi, Hutu rebels, with some assistance by rebels from Zaire, slaughtered and mutilated every Tutsi they could find and of whatever age or sex, as well as the few Hutu who refused to join them. In the reprisals in which some 100,000 Hutu were slaughtered, the employed and the educated and the semi-educated were the special targets for revenge, which was also directed indiscriminately against Hutu.[8] Nor did 1972 see the end of these massacres, which continued into 1973, with intermittent killings thereafter.

In India, the conflicts in the process of decolonization were aggravated by religious cleavages. At the time of partition, the relationship between the British, Hindus and Muslims was hardly comparable to the two-tier structure of Rwanda under Belgian mandate. Hindus were in a great majority, some 300 million Hindus as against 100 million Muslims. They were separated from Muslims not only by their religion, but also by caste prohibitions on intermingling. They had been more ready than Muslims to seize the opportunities for British education, and they were largely the administrators of India for the British. It was mainly from their ranks too that India's businessmen, financiers and professionals

8. For accounts of this genocide and the background to it, see Lemarchand, 1970: Part III; Lemarchand and Martin, 1974: 5–25; Martin, 1974:29–34; Greenland, 1975: Vol. IV, 97–133; and Kuper, 1977:87–107, 197–208.

were recruited.[9] To be sure, the great majority of Hindus and Muslims must have been living in equal poverty. Still, in an independent India, politically unified but communally divided, Hindus would have dominated the society.

Partition transformed this situation, giving dominance to the majority, Muslim or non-Muslim, in the partitioned sections. But the distribution of populations, with substantial religious minorities in areas dominated numerically by members of other religions, or with much intermingling of people of different religion, or with segregated enclaves, did not permit of an easy severance into a Hindu India and a Muslim Pakistan. The structure thus gave opportunity for the persecution of minorities, and for retaliation in massacre, as reprisal provoked counter-reprisal in areas of mixed living, and as atrocity against Hindus or Sikhs in Muslim areas, or against Muslims in areas of Hindu or Sikh dominance, set off counter-massacres in a continuous spiral of escalating violence.

Already massacres had started in some areas prior to partition, when communal sentiment became inflamed in the troubled course of constitutional negotiation. In Calcutta, following the proclamation by the Muslim League of 16 August 1946 as Direct Action Day, Muslim

mobs howling in a quasi-religious fervor came bursting from their slums, waving clubs, iron bars, shovels, any instrument capable of smashing in a human skull ... They savagely beat to a pulp any Hindu in their path and left the bodies in the city's open gutters ... Later, the Hindu mobs came storming out of their neighbourhoods, looking for defenseless Muslims to slaughter. Never, in all its violent history, had Calcutta known twenty-four hours as savage, as packed with human viciousness. Like water-soaked logs, scores of bloated cadavers bobbed down the Hooghly river toward the sea. Other corpses, savagely mutilated, littered the city's streets. Everywhere, the weak and helpless suffered most ... By the time the slaughter was over, Calcutta belonged to the vultures. In filthy grey packs they scudded across the sky, tumbling down to gorge themselves on the bodies of the city's six thousand dead.[10]

And the Calcutta massacres triggered off other massacres not only in neighbouring areas, but across the continent in Bombay.

Relationships were particularly explosive in the Punjab. This was a Muslim majority province, but Muslims constituted only about 57 per cent of the population of over 34,000,000 enumerated in the 1941 census. In the west they were markedly predominant: in the east both their

9. Collins and Lapierre, 1975:38–9.
10. ibid., 41–2.

numbers and dominance fell away. Here lay the homelands of the Sikhs who had ruled over most of the province only some hundred years earlier, and of the Hindu Jats, a peasantry also with martial traditions.[11] In the city of Lahore, almost equally balanced populations pressed their rival claims. The city of Amritsar, built around the Golden Temple, was the main religious and political centre of the Sikhs, who numbered some six million, concentrated mostly in the Punjab. And beyond these cities was the province's 'mosaic of communal pockets set haphazardly amongst one another'.[12]

Inevitably, partition into a Muslim west and a Hindu east was highly disruptive. Lahore went to Pakistan, Amritsar to India. The Sikhs, split in two by partition, became the principal actors in the tragedy of the Punjab. Five million Sikhs and Hindus were left in Pakistan's half of the Punjab, over five million Muslims in India's half.[13] It was an invitation to massacre.

Massacre in the Punjab had preceded partition. In the village of Kahuta, where 2,000 Hindus and Sikhs and 1,500 Muslims lived in peace, a Muslim horde had set fire to the houses in its Sikh and Hindu quarters with buckets of gasoline. Entire families were consumed by the flames. Those who escaped were caught, tied together, soaked with gasoline and burnt alive like torches. 'A few Hindu women, yanked from their beds to be raped and converted to Islam, had survived; others had broken away from their captors and hurled themselves back into the fire to perish with their families.'[14] In Lahore, a tolerant city of some 500,000 Hindus, 100,000 Sikhs and 600,000 Muslims, a Sikh leader had precipitated violence by hacking down a Muslim League banner with a cry of death to Pakistan. In the riots which followed, more than 3,000 were killed, most of them Sikh. On the eve of independence, 15 August 1947, the city was a scene of desolation. 'Almost a hundred thousand Hindus and Sikhs were trapped inside Old Lahore's walled city, their water cut, fires raging around them, mobs of Muslims stalking the alleys outside their *mahallas*, waiting to pounce on anyone venturing out.' In Amritsar, 'murder was as routine an occurrence in its bazaars and alleyways as public defecation. The city's Hindus devised the cruel tactic of walking up to an unsuspecting Muslim and splashing his face

11. Moon, 1962:29. The Jats were the predominant agricultural tribe in the Punjab prior to partition; there were Muslim, Hindu and Sikh Jats (ibid., 30).
12. Collins and Lapierre, op. cit., 248–50; Moon, op. cit., 31.
13. Collins and Lapierre, op. cit., 319–20, 340–41.
14. ibid., 131–2.

with a vial of nitric or sulphuric acid. Arsonists were in action everywhere.' While the city authorities were performing the independence day rituals, 'an enraged horde of Sikhs was ravaging a Muslim neighbourhood less than a mile away. They slaughtered its male inhabitants without mercy or exception. The women were stripped, repeatedly raped, then paraded shaking and terrified through the city to the Golden Temple, where most had their throats cut.' In the countryside, Sikh bands attacked Muslim villages and neighbourhoods. 'A particular savagery characterized their killings. The circumcised penises of their Muslim male victims were hacked off and stuffed into their mouths or into the mouths of murdered Muslim women.'[15]

Campbell-Johnson, Press Attaché to the last British Viceroy of India, wrote[16] that perhaps the most horrifying feature of the communal insanity was the lust of the strong to seek out the weak for massacre: hospitals and refugee trains were the special targets of these crazed assassins. There were periods of four and five days at a stretch during which not a single train reached Lahore or Amritsar without its complement of dead and wounded.[17] In some of the trains, almost all the passengers had been most horribly slaughtered. So too, the refugee columns on the roads became an easy target for loot and massacre.

Many of these genocidal massacres were carried out by mobs in murderous frenzy. They were not a centrally organized government-directed type of genocide. Hindu and Muslim leaders gave assurances of protection to minority communities, and on 22 July 1947, shortly before partition, spokesmen for the prospective governments of India and Pakistan in a joint statement solemnly guaranteed protection to all citizens. This guarantee, it was stated, 'implies that in no circumstances will violence be tolerated in any form in either territory. The two Governments wish to emphasize that they are united in this determination.'[18] There was seemingly a remarkable faith in the effectiveness of the projected boundary force. But the leaders had greatly underestimated the extent and destructiveness of the communal passions unleashed by partition, and they were powerless to control the conflagration in the Punjab.

15. ibid., 225–6, 295, 252, 309, 251. I have been following closely the account of Collins and Lapierre.

16. Campbell-Johnson, 1951 : 184.

17. Collins and Lapierre, op. cit., 356. See also ibid., 309–10 and 354–8, and the novel by Khushwant Singh, *Mano Majna* (1956), set in a Muslim and Sikh village in the remote reaches of the northern frontier.

18. Moon, op. cit., 93–4.

Part of the difficulty was that the forces of law and order proved unreliable, having become infected by communal fears and hatreds. The police, the military, railway clerks and other officials, were often themselves involved in the massacres or did not intervene. In a trading town north of Lahore, the entire Hindu and Sikh community were herded into a huge warehouse and machine-gunned by Muslim police and army deserters.[19] There are many accounts of the police and the army standing by, or taking part, in the looting and killing. In the neighbouring princely state of Bahawalpur, where the authorities actively sought to protect the Hindu and Sikh minorities, a major problem was the unreliability of the army: and one of the most terrible massacres was perpetrated by the military against a band of some 2,000 Sikh refugees they were escorting across the border.[20] There may have been a difference between the governments of East (Hindu) Punjab and West (Muslim) Punjab. Campbell-Johnson[21] mentions collective fines being imposed by the government of East Punjab on villages known to be involved in the disorders. Moon, the British Revenue and Public Works Minister in Bahawalpur during partition, complains of the West Punjab government that 'despite noble professions there was no real desire to punish those who robbed, raped and murdered the minority communities; rather there was a disposition to punish those who tried to protect them.'[22] However, we need also to add his judgment that the excesses against Muslims in East Punjab 'exceeded in scale and atrocity the outrages perpetrated by Muslims in West Pakistan'.[23]

It would be misleading to think of all the peoples of the Punjab as given over to destructive communalism. There were many acts of protection of minorities by public servants, and of human sympathy extended, and refuge offered, across communal divisions.

In Calcutta, in the province of Bengal, the structure of the city, with its communal divisions and its history of violence, threatened a spilling of blood that 'would have made anything that happened in the Punjab look like a bed of roses'[24] Collins and Lapierre write of the awful miles of

human sewer packed with the densest concentration of human beings on the face of the earth. It included 400,000 beggars and unemployables, 40,000

19. Collins and Lapierre, op. cit., 343.
20. Moon, op. cit., 231–6.
21. Campbell-Johnson, op. cit., 202.
22. Moon, op. cit., 237.
23. ibid., 9.
24. Comment of the former Viceroy in Collins and Lapierre, op. cit., 254.

lepers. The slums they inhabited were a fetid, stinking horror. Their streets were cluttered lanes lined with open sewers overflowing with their burden of garbage, urine and excrement, each nourishing its hordes of rats, cockroaches, its buzzing clouds of flies and mosquitoes ... Once a week, down those lanes, the pitiless *zamindars* stalked in search of the rent for each corner in hell. At the moment when India was about to attain her freedom, three million human beings in Calcutta lived in a state of chronic undernourishment, existing on a caloric intake inferior to that given the inmates of Hitler's death camps.[25]

In this most violent city, men murdered 'for a mouthful of rice'. Already in August 1946, there had been 'The Great Calcutta Killings' and organized gangs continued to take their toll in communal murder. The scene was set for a vast conflagration on partition.

It was here on 13 August 1947, thirty-six hours before independence, that Gandhi moved in, as a sort of one-man boundary force. He was received initially with hostility, and indeed violence, by Hindu crowds. But almost immediately his message of non-violence and peace began to prevail. On independence day, there were half a million Hindus and Muslims at his prayer meeting, and thousands paraded through the streets chanting slogans of unity and friendship. At the end of August and the beginning of September, when there was a recurrence of communal violence, he restored the peace by fasting. The 'miracle of Calcutta' continued to endure.[26]

The main genocidal conflict had been in the Punjab. The estimated numbers of those slaughtered ranges from 200,000 (or less) to half a million (or more). Figures for the refugees in a gigantic exchange of population are more reliable – some ten and a half million, most of the movement in a period of three months from August to November. Another million were exchanged under more peaceful circumstances in Bengal.[27]

In the successor states on decolonization, persistent cleavages between racial, ethnic and religious groups provided the structural basis for highly destructive conflicts. These arose in the course of movements for liberation, or for greater regional autonomy or for secession, or in the

25. ibid., 269.
26. ibid., 353, 361–7.
27. See Moon, op. cit., 261, 268–9, 293; Collins and Lapierre, op. cit., 399. Campbell-Johnson, op. cit., Ch. 17, discusses the mass migrations in some detail.

course of struggles for power between élites, mobilizing the communal bases for their support.

One may distinguish a range from an earlier two-tier structure of domination, with the persistence of the traditional internal domination on decolonization, to situations of relative equality, at any rate initially, between the different sections. The settler societies, such as Burundi, South Africa and Northern Ireland, would be examples of the continuity of an internal domination – by Tutsi over Hutu in Burundi, whites over all other sections in South Africa, and Protestants over Catholics in Northern Ireland. But only in Burundi was there massive genocidal slaughter. Large-scale genocidal massacres are by no means inevitable in the racial, ethnic or religious conflicts of even the most extreme type of settler, plural society. This is a problem to which I shall return in Chapter 10. I should add that the term 'settler society' is not very satisfactory. Societies in which the indigenous peoples were substantially annihilated, as in Australia and the U.S.A., are not generally described as settler societies. But is it a more appropriate description, if the initial settlement is centuries old, and the indigenous peoples retain their identities and continue to multiply?

The division into successor societies with a previous two-tier structure of domination and assumption of power by the traditionally dominant section, and societies with equality between the subordinate sections, is by no means clear-cut. There is a wide range of variation, and sometimes it is not easy or profitable to classify societies in these terms. Colonization may have interrupted an earlier movement of conquest, which is now resumed. Or relative numbers, or greater access to education under colonial rule, or differences in regional development under colonization, may have laid the basis for domination by one section, however egalitarian the constitution on independence.

The Sudan, Nigeria and Bangladesh are among the successor societies in the decolonized world which had highly destructive conflicts. The number of deaths in the south of the Sudan in the war against the guerrilla movement, and in reprisals against, and massacres of, civilians, and by famine and disease, during the period 1955–72, is often estimated at 500,000 or more. Estimates of refugees seem more reliable, over 1,000,000 from a southern population of some 3,000,000.[28]

28. In the 1956 census, the population of the three southern provinces is given as 2,793,000 (about one-fourth of the total population of 10,263,000). However, there would already have been some flight of southerners from these troubled

In the conflict between the northern and southern sections of the highly plural society of the Sudan, the pluralism derives from ethnic and religious differences, from historical relationships, from differential development and discrimination, and from hostile stereotypes and attitudes. The North is largely Muslim, peopled by Arabs and also by non-Arab 'Islamicized' groups. The South is African, divided into different ethnic units, mostly animist by religion, but with appreciable numbers of Christians (some 30,000 Protestants and about 200,000 Catholics, at the beginning of the war), and a small number of Muslims.[29]

The report of the Government Commission of Inquiry into the mutiny of Southern soldiers and the disorders in the Southern Sudan during August 1955 refers to the persistence of the great feeling of hatred, and of fear towards the Northern Sudanese inspired by the slave trade,[30] and cites, as one of the causes of the disturbances, the fact 'that for historical reasons the Southerners regard the Northern Sudanese as their traditional enemies'.[31] Northern attitudes, too, are affected by this past history. Many Northern Sudanese, 'especially from amongst the uneducated class', see the Southerners as of an inferior race, and the traders in the South often referred to, and addressed, them as *abeed*, a constant and contemptuous reminder of the old days of the slave trade.[32] Against this background, it was not surprising that there should have been widespread belief that Northern soldiers, who were being transferred to the Southern Sudan, would be used to exterminate the Southerners.[33]

British policies during the period of Anglo-Egyptian 'Condominium' contributed to this cleavage between North and South. In 1930, the British laid down the following basic principles for the governing of the South:

---

areas. Figures for deaths are given in Kasfir (1976:1) who considers the estimate of half a million or more deaths conservative. Hale (1978:174) cites estimates of 500,000 to 1,000,000 killed in the fighting, in reprisals, and by famine, banditry and disease. O'Ballance (1977:158) considers that the estimate of 500,000 dead has no solid foundation. See also Eprile, 1974:49 for a variety of estimates.

29. See Hale, op. cit., 158ff.
30. Sudan Government, 1956:4.
31. ibid., 81.
32. ibid., 123–4.
33. ibid., 120.

(a) The building up in the Southern Sudan of 'a series of self-contained racial or tribal units' with structure and organization based on traditional usage and beliefs.

(b) The gradual elimination of the Northern Sudanese administrators, clerks and technicians in the South, and their replacement by Southern Sudanese.

(c) The use of English where communication in the local vernacular was impossible.[34]

The application of these principles could only reinforce the barriers to unification. Indeed, there was speculation that the Southern peoples might be united with East African territories. When it became clear that this was not the wish of the East African states, and that in any event, developments in the Sudan were rendering attempts at economic and other separation anomalous, the British reversed their policy. It was now designed 'to act upon the facts that the peoples of the Southern Sudan are distinctively African and Negroid but that geography and economics combine (so far as can be seen at the present time) to render them inextricably bound for future development to the Middle Eastern and Arabicized Northern Sudan: and therefore to ensure that they should, by educational and economic development, be equipped to stand up for themselves in the future as socially and economically the equals of their partners in the Sudan of the future'.[35]

With the rapid movement to independence, however, there was no possibility of Southerners participating as equals in a unified Sudan. The South was educationally backward and economically undeveloped. Political organization was only beginning;[36] there was no national consciousness in the South uniting its different tribes, in contrast to the North, with a nationalist movement led by an educated class.[37] Much of the profit of the cotton boom after the Second World War was spent on development projects, mainly in the North. Sudanization, pursuant to the appointment of a Sudanization Committee in 1954, was a great disappointment to Southerners: of the 800 posts to be Sudanized, only four junior posts of Assistant District Commissioner and two of *Mamur* were given to the South.[38] Inevitably, against a background of past

34. Beshir, 1970:46.
35. ibid., 62–3, and 119–21, which reproduces the British memorandum on the new Southern Policy, dated December 1946.
36. O'Ballance, op. cit., 36.
37. Beshir, op. cit., 70.
38. Albino, 1970:33.

conflict and present division, and in the context of the greater economic, educational and political development of the much more populous North, independence in 1956 meant domination by the North.

The effect was the same as that of a two-tier pattern of domination, with the internal overlords taking over on decolonization. The resultant structure of power could be fairly described, I think, as an internal colonialism by the North over the South. It appeared such to Southerners. Thus the Commission of Inquiry into the disturbances in August 1955 commented that 'the Northern administration in Southern Sudan is not colonial, but the great majority of Southerners unhappily regard it as such . . .'[39] Two of the Southern leaders, Joseph Oduho and William Deng, in their book on *The Problem of the Southern Sudan*,[40] describe their perception of the relations between North and South in chapters devoted to 'Political Subjection', 'Administrative Subjection', 'Educational Subjection', 'Economic Subjection', 'Social Subjection', and 'Religious Subjection'. Albino, another of the Southern leaders, in his book *The Sudan: A Southern Viewpoint*, writes that 'since the Sudan became independent, the Arabs took power from the British, and, because of bitter memories of the past on both sides, sought to behave in a manner which they believed would frighten Southerners into submission. They have a complete monopoly over economic, social, educational, administrative, and military affairs. In short, the Arabs run the whole machinery of government. The South, on the other hand, is a colony.'[41] And in his chapter on 'The Anatomy of Domination' he covers much the same ground as Oduho and Deng, including attacks on Northern attempts to 'Islamicize' the South.

Sudan's 'Secret War' was precipitated by the political conflicts attendant on decolonization, with its crucial problem of redefining the relations between North and South on independence – whether the South was to be incorporated in a united Sudan, and if so under what conditions of regional autonomy, or whether the South was to be accorded the rights of self-determination, and of separation as an independent state. Starting in 1955 with the mutiny in the South, the war continued to 1972, when an agreement was arrived at for a measure of regional autonomy.[42] It was waged with great ferocity, with many atrocities, and much slaughter of innocent people. Southern forces contributed in some

39. Sudan Government, op. cit., 7.
40. Oduho and Deng, 1963.
41. Albino, op. cit., 4.
42. See O'Ballance, op. cit., Appendix B, 163–4, for the terms of the agreement.

measure to the slaughter of their own groups by reprisals against suspected collaborators and by banditry.

Many charges were made of genocide by the North. There were allegations of the systematic liquidation of Southern leadership. A former governor of one of the Southern provinces wrote that 'the charge against the North of "genocide" (an abused and exaggerated word) is true in so far as Khartoum governments, or the Northern soldiers with their connivance, did make a bid to liquidate educated elements and potential leaders as a matter of policy'.[43] I think myself that the charge of genocide against the North is exaggerated, but there can be no doubt that this was a highly destructive conflict, and that it included many episodes of genocidal massacre.[44]

The situation was very different in Nigeria. The structure of Nigerian society on the eve of independence in 1960 could not be described as approximating a two-tier system of domination. Over a period of years prior to independence, the representatives of the different regions and the colonial authorities had worked out a federal constitution, designed to achieve a balanced distribution of power, though weighted at the federal level in favour of the more populous North. In all federal constitutions, there is tension between the principles of unity and of autonomy. This was particularly marked in Nigeria, where the plural structure of the society, and the end of colonial domination, provided the opportunity and encouragement for highly destructive struggles for power.

The pluralism in Nigeria rested on the three regional sections of the federation,[45] each with the dualism of a dominant ethnic group and of ethnic minorities. In the Northern Region, the Hausa-Fulani were dominant with a population of some 15,000,000, in the West the Yoruba, about 10,000,000, and in the East the Ibo, also about 10,000,000. They differed in language, religion and social organization. The North was about 75 per cent Muslim, and almost entirely so in the extreme North; the West was somewhat evenly divided between Islam and Christianity; in the East, perhaps 90 per cent were Christian and 10 per cent animist.[46]

43. Richard Owen, 1970:9.

44. See the following sources: Sudan Government, op. cit.; O'Ballance, op. cit., Ch. 5; Albino, op. cit., 60–63; Eprile, op. cit., Ch. 4; *Grass Curtain*, Vol. 1, No. 3 (December 1970), 6–7.

45. The Mid-West was only established as a fourth region in 1963.

46. I am following, and combining, the accounts given by Lloyd, 1970:1–13, and Kirk-Greene, 1967:3–11.

The Hausa, living in walled cities, centres of trade and administration, have the traditional centralized structures of authority of the emirates. The Ibo are strongly egalitarian, and organized in a large number of small village groups, claiming descent from a common ancestor; they have few titled offices. The Yoruba fall between these two extremes, with kingdoms of some complexity, and social organization based on descent groups.[47] To these differences in religion, language and social organization must be added those of climate, geography and economic development.

British colonial administration contributed to the divisions between the disparate groups they had so arbitrarily brought together, though in the later years policy was directed to establishing a secure basis for federation. The initiatives of the rival ethnic groups themselves also contributed both indirectly and directly to division. Yoruba and Ibo seized the opportunities available to them for western education, and they were more highly educated than the Hausa, whose exposure to western education was limited by British and Muslim conservatism. And in the struggles for position and power, political parties became identified with ethnic groups, superimposing another layer of pluralism on an already highly divided society.

The violently destructive conflicts emerged out of these plural divisions. There were two series of events which have been described as genocide. The first belongs structurally to the situation I have treated as that of the stranger or hostage group. The second arose in the context of the somewhat parallel relationships of ethnic groups in the federated state. The two series of events were interrelated, and in both the Ibos were the victims.

Many Ibos had left their poor and overcrowded region to work in the North. Here they were compelled by Muslim Northern society to live beyond the pale and they built their stranger settlements outside the walls of the towns. In reading accounts of the Ibo settlement in the North, one sometimes gets the impression that the Ibo were all senior civil servants and entrepreneurs. Since there seem to have been as many as 1,000,000 Ibo in the Northern Region, the great majority must have been working class, and in quite modest employment. One commentator describes the Ibo from the East as 'driven by too little land at home and too much industry and ability inside him', and comments that he was to be found all over Nigeria, especially in the North, as the

47. See Lloyd, op. cit., 3.

typical clerk, small shop-owner, hotelier, contractor, mechanic, railway and postal employee.[48]

In January 1966, in a first military coup, two leading Northern politicians and four of its most senior army officers were murdered. This coup and the steps taken towards political centralization were interpreted in the North as an Ibo conspiracy to dominate Nigeria. Following demonstrations by Northern civil servants and students, rioting mobs slaughtered several hundred Ibo. In the military counter-coup of July 1966, and its aftermath, Northern soldiers murdered Eastern officers and men. Persecution of Ibos continued through to the great massacre of Easterners in September and October 1966, when troops and street mobs invaded the stranger settlements in all the major towns in the North, killing, looting and burning. The massacres appear to have been organized.[49] Some 6–8,000 were killed and many thousands wounded and maimed. The Ibo population abandoned its possessions in the North and fled back to the East.

This genocidal massacre was a major cause of the secession of the Ibo, leading in July 1967 to the outbreak of civil war between the Federal Government and the Eastern Region. Biafra was born in massacre and bred in starvation.[50] During the two and a half years of warfare, between 600,000 and 1,000,000 Easterners were killed in battle or massacre, or died of famine or disease. The politics and strategy of starvation were particularly horrifying. There was the heartrending spectacle of utterly emaciated men, women and children, mothers with infants, in the final despair of starvation, with a daily death toll of thousands in the last stages of the war. There was the horror that considerations of sovereignty and of military strategy should take precedence over humanitarian concern for the almost countless innocent victims of this deadly struggle. And there was incredulity that as many as 1,000,000 people might have to die so as to safeguard the unity of an artificially created colonial conglomerate of peoples. It is all the more difficult to accept the conception of the sanctity of the unity of the successor state when one recalls that from the beginnings of the amalgamation of Nigeria, there had been threats and movements of secession by different sections, and that the conferring of a constitutional right to secession had been

48. Kirk-Greene, op. cit., 7.
49. I have been following the account by St Jorre, 1972:44–5, 58–9, 70–71, 74–5, 84–7. Estimates of the numbers killed vary greatly. Southerners from all tribes were attacked. Several hundred Northerners were killed in reprisals in the East.
50. Phrase used by Perham, 1970:234.

seriously debated at the constitutional conference in September–November 1966.[51]

Many Ibo believed that the choice before them was between secession or genocide. Their leaders charged the Federal Government with plans to commit genocide, and these charges were taken up also by responsible leaders in other countries. They were vigorously repudiated.[52] In looking back at this controversy, some observers contend that the most powerful argument against the charge of genocidal intent is provided by the steps which were taken after the war to integrate the Ibos fully into the new twelve-state Federal Republic of Nigeria.

In Pakistan, there was no question of a traditional overlordship being re-established on decolonization. Pakistan was born in the partition of India as an entirely new creation, in which the mode of relationship between the theoretically equal plural sections had still to be defined. The basis of its unity was the brotherhood in Islam, and fear of Hindu domination, 'the resin of a common hatred'.[53] But the initial political and spiritual exhilaration of a new nationalism was beset from the earliest days by the divisive forces of ethnic pluralism.

The main division was between West Pakistan, which was consolidated into the four provinces of Baluchistan, the North-west Frontier, Punjab and the Sind, and East Pakistan, comprising the eastern half of Bengal, a portion of Assam and the tribal areas of the Chittagong Hill Tracts.[54] The differences between these two sections were quite extreme. In culture, language, economy, geography, they were two distinct countries with little communication between them. They were separated by over 1,000 miles. In East Pakistan, some 95 per cent or more spoke Bengali, compared with under 2 per cent speaking Urdu, the official language of the West.[55] In addition to their different cultural heritages, the peoples themselves are physically distinctive. In climate, West Pakistan is dry wheat-growing desert country, while in the monsoon climate of East Pakistan, with its rice, jute and tea, there are the flood dangers from the Ganges and Brahmaputra rivers. The natural economic outlets and trading partners for East Pakistan were in the neighbouring parts of

51. Tamuno, 1970.
52. See O'Brien, op. cit.; Perham, op. cit.; Kirk-Greene, 1971: Vol. II, 46–7, 48–9, 56–7, 81, 331, 83–4, 86, 103–5, 118–21, 401; and St Jorre, op. cit., 282–7, 344–53, 380, 382, 395, 404–8.
53. Mascarenhas, 1971:11.
54. Levak, 1975:284.
55. Bengali was only recognized as an official language after language riots in 1952.

India. West Pakistan turned naturally for its cultural and commercial exchanges towards the Arab Middle East, and East Pakistan towards India and the Asian Far East. Both the West, with a population of some 55,000,000 at the time of the genocidal conflict and the East, with some 75,000,000, were large enough in population and territory to constitute separate states.[56]

The pluralism extended beyond the division between East and West. In the East, there were some 10–12,000,000 Hindus, and many Urdu-speaking Muslims who had migrated to East Pakistan and were known as the Biharis, though only a part came from Bihar. In areas where there were large concentrations of Biharis, hostility and resentment developed between them and the Bengalis.[57] In the West, there was the pluralism of the different populations in the constituent provinces, Punjabi, Baluchi, Pathan, Sindhi.

Given the diversity of peoples, and the problems of setting up a new state, it is not surprising that there were difficulties in arriving at a constitutional accommodation. In 1940, some years before partition, the Muslim League had passed a resolution in terms of which the constituent units would be autonomous and sovereign. But this was later changed to a commitment in favour of a unified sovereign state. There was delay in framing the constitution, and resort to different constitutional arrangements, including the consolidation of the four provinces in the West into a single unit. This seemed to be a solution to problems of parity of representation in the national parliament between the West and the East, but in fact it contributed to polarization.

The main source of polarization lay, however, in a relationship between West and East which the Bengalis saw as colonialism, and which indeed bore many of the marks of a colonial domination. The West wing became increasingly more industrialized and prosperous, while conditions in the East deteriorated. On partition, the per capita income of the West exceeded that of East Pakistan by 10 per cent: this disparity had risen to 30 per cent by 1960, to 40 per cent by 1965, and to 60 per cent by 1969.[58] The bulk of Pakistan's foreign exchange was earned in the East, but largely expended on industrial development in the West. So too, a quite disproportionate share of foreign aid went to the West. Economic domination was secured by political domination, the senior

56. See J. E. Owen, 1972:24, and the International Commission of Jurists, 1972:71.

57. International Commission of Jurists, op. cit., 9.

58. J. E. Owen, op. cit., 25.

military personnel, the senior civil servants, and the central government bureaucracy as a whole, being overwhelmingly West Pakistani. The effect of this wide-ranging discrimination was to nurture the movement for greater regional autonomy in East Pakistan.

The long periods of military dictatorship and of martial law give some measure of the tensions in the creation of the new state. These tensions reached their apocalyptic climax following the Legal Framework Order introduced in 1970 by the then military dictator (or 'Chief Martial Law Administrator'). This laid down the conditions and procedure for the framing of a new constitution. It reaffirmed an earlier pledge to restore democratic institutions, it promised elections in October 1970 with a distribution of seats in the National Assembly proportionate to population, and it defined the constitutional relations between the Federal Government and the Provinces as maximum autonomy for the Provinces, but adequate powers for the Federal Government 'to discharge its responsibilities in relation to external and internal affairs and to preserve the independence and territorial integrity of the Country'. By another Order, the Province of West Pakistan was dissolved into the four provincial divisions of the Punjab, the Northwest Frontier, Sind and Baluchistan.

In the elections, the Awami League campaigned on a Six-Point Programme for almost the maximum possible autonomy for the East, short of total separation. It gained 167 of the 169 seats allocated to East Pakistan in the National Assembly, becoming the majority party, and in the East Pakistan Assembly it won 288 of the 300 seats. There followed negotiations and a campaign of non-cooperation in the East when the President (and Chief Martial Law Administrator) postponed the convening of the National Assembly *sine die*. Negotiations were resumed, and seemed to be moving cordially towards a resolution of conflict. But during the course of the negotiations, the government was in fact mobilizing its military forces in the East; and on 25 March 1971, it struck with devastating force.[59]

It would seem that the government intended to eradicate dissidence in the East by admonitory massacres and massive terror. The International Commission of Jurists describes the principal features of this ruthless repression as 'the indiscriminate killing of civilians, including

59. In these brief comments on the constitutional difficulties and the discrimination against the East, I have drawn on the following sources: J. E. Owen, op. cit., 23–8; International Commission of Jurists, op. cit.; Mascarenhas, op cit., 6–33; Levak, 1974:203–21, and 1975:283–307; Morris-Jones, 1972; Indian Ministry of External Affairs, 1971.

women and children and the poorest and weakest members of the community; the attempt to exterminate or drive out of the country a large part of the Hindu population; the arrest, torture and killing of Awami League activists, students, professional and business men and other potential leaders among the Bengalis; the raping of women; the destruction of villages and towns; and the looting of property. All this was done on a scale which is difficult to comprehend.'[60] It was carried out, I should add, with unspeakable brutality and atrocity, and with the additional horror of torture and extermination centres. As the resistance of the Bengalis mounted, the army responded with massive collective reprisals in the annihilation of Bengali villages. Where non-Bengalis were in a majority, the Biharis attacked the Bengalis, and many Biharis served in the auxiliary forces of the West Pakistan army.[61] Bengalis too engaged in massacre and atrocity against Hindus and Biharis.

On 16 December 1971, the war ended following the intervention of the Indian Army, which sealed the successful secession of the now independent state of Bangladesh. Estimates of the Bengalis killed in Bangladesh vary greatly, with an upper limit of perhaps 3,000,000. Chaudhuri presents a chart, incomplete however, of the worst affected places in eighteen districts, giving figures for the property damaged, the number of slaughter-houses and mass graves discovered, women ravished, skulls and skeletons found, and total killed – in all, 1,247,000.[62] A separate chart,[63] prepared by the United Nations Relief Committee in February 1972, gave a total of over 1,500,000 houses destroyed (with an allowed error of ± 25 per cent). In addition, there were some 10,000,000 refugees in India, largely Hindu, living under conditions of extreme hardship, and with an appalling death rate.

The International Commission of Jurists expressed the view that there was 'a strong prima facie case that the crime of genocide was committed against the group comprising the Hindu population of East Bengal'. It viewed the army atrocities as part of a deliberate policy by a disciplined

60. International Commission of Jurists, op. cit., 26–7.
61. For accounts of the war, see the International Commission of Jurists, op. cit.; Chaudhuri, 1972; Mascarenhas, op. cit.; Payne, 1973; Indian Ministry of External Affairs, op. cit. See also Nafziger and Richter (1976) for an analysis of the role of economic forces and social classes in the conflict. A discussion by Young (1976, Ch. 12) deals with the politics of secession in Biafra, Bangladesh and Southern Sudan from the perspective of cultural pluralism. Nordlinger (1975–6) discusses the same conflicts from the perspective of the role of military governments in communally divided societies.
62. Chaudhuri, op. cit., 199–202.
63. ibid., 148.

force.[64] As to the killing of non-Bengalis by Bengalis, the Commission found 'it difficult to accept that spontaneous and frenzied mob violence against a particular section of the community from whom the mob senses danger and hostility is to be regarded as possessing the necessary element of conscious intent to constitute the crime of genocide'.[65] Throughout this massive catastrophe 'the United Nations failed to use its available machinery to deal with the situation either with a view to terminating the gross violations of human rights which were occurring or to deal with the threat to international peace which they constituted'.[66]

Our final case study is of 'consociational democracy' between religious groups. In the successor state of Lebanon, carved by the French out of its mandated portion of the Ottoman Empire, somewhat unique constitutional arrangements followed independence in 1943. In contrast to the federal solutions in Nigeria and Pakistan, there was a unified legislature and administration with structural balance between the religious sections based on a formula of differential participation. Thus, in terms of a National Pact, the President of the Republic was required to be a Maronite Christian, the President of the Council a Sunnite Muslim, and the President of the Chamber of Deputies a Shī'ite Muslim. Distribution of seats and of administrative positions followed a ratio of 6 : 5 Christians to Muslims, derived from a 1932 census which increasingly ceased to correspond to reality as Muslims multiplied more rapidly than Christians.

This constitutional solution to pluralism was greatly admired. But selection for office by the criterion of religious affiliation maintains, and probably enhances, the significance of religious division, particularly in a society with appreciable geographic concentration of sects and the recognition of religious courts having jurisdiction in matters affecting personal status. And there had been an outbreak of civil war in 1958, between Christians and Muslims-Druzes.

The pluralism extends far beyond the division between Christians and Muslims. Among Christians, the Maronites dominated, getting more than a proportionate share of power as compared with the many other Christian sects. So too, among Muslims, the Sunnites and the Druzes took over a portion of the share of public office due to the

64. International Commission of Jurists, op. cit., 57.
65. ibid.
66. ibid., 98.

Shī'ites, probably the largest of the Muslim sects at the present time.[67] Maronites and Druzes virtually constitute nations,[68] but these major religious communities are themselves fractured by factions, based on clan loyalties, on ancient enmity, on rivalry for power, and on strong-arm domination of an area. Economic differentiation in general favours Christians over Muslims, and Sunnites over Shī'ites, with the rich, how-ever, and the poor, in all these divisions. Political parties, though not necessarily exclusive, find their social basis for the most part in the sectarian factions.[69]

Added to these divisive complexities there is an external dimension of even more incredible complexity, with appreciable orientation of Mus-lims to the Arab world, and of Christians to the West, the differences being reinforced by distinctive educational institutions. And the Arab world itself is no unity, but divided by national interests and inter-national alliances, by conservatism and radicalism, by political move-ments stimulating further political fragmentation in Lebanon, as in the Nasserist movements and the Ba'th Socialist Parties, with changeability in policy, as notably in the Syrian involvement in Lebanon. Then too there are the different policies pursued by the superpowers, and (final, and overwhelming complexity) the establishment of perhaps as many as 300,000 Palestinian refugees in Lebanon (about 10 per cent of the population at the outbreak of the civil war in 1975), organized also in different factions, and mounting commando raids against the Israelis, who respond with massive reprisals in Lebanese territory.

The factionalism and fragmentation might not have been so destruc-tive, but for the domination of the society by the overriding cleavage between Muslims and Christians. And then too the society was a jungle of arms. It was, is, like the Wild West, with almost everyone armed and easy on the trigger – the strong-men with their bodyguards, the political parties, the sects, the factions, with their private militias, and in addi-tion, ordinary armed gangs and bandits. 'Phalangists, Chamounists, monks, moderate Muslims, Nasserists, Ba'thists (Syrian or Iraqi), the left, communists, everyone has his politics and arms. The army and the Palestinians too. States within the state, the very essence of feudalism with its bands of armed men,'[70] and many nations providing arms,

---

67. See Salibi, 1976:18, and Barakat, 1977:26.
68. See Barakat, op. cit., 35–6, and Desjardins, 1976:67ff.
69. See Salibi, op. cit., Ch. II, and Desjardins, op. cit., Ch. VII.
70. Desjardins, op. cit., 126.

money, or permitting the passage of munitions or the transfer of funds –
'Syria, Iraq, Saudi Arabia, Kuwait, the Federation of United Arab
Emirates, Iran, Egypt, Libya, Algeria, Jordan, but also Israel and the
U.S.A., Soviet Russia, several East European countries (notably Bul-
garia which increasingly replaces Czechoslovakia as suppliers of arms)
and even ... the Vatican'.[71]

It was inevitable then that the civil war of 1975–6 should have been
anarchic and annihilating. Its causes lie deep within the structure of
Lebanese society – the divisions and tensions between Muslims and
Christians, the resistance to necessary reforms by the Christian establishment, the greater militancy among Muslims with the growth of Arab
nationalism and the changing structure of international power, class
conflicts, the pressures of poverty and the massing of the poor in
the slums of Beirut. But the detonating cause was the Palestinian
issue.

The Palestinians, largely though not exclusively Muslim, supported
by Soviet Russia, commanding militia of their own, threatened by their
very presence the established relations between Christians and Muslims.
Inevitably, they became involved in the internal affairs of Lebanon.
Dispossessed themselves, they established close relations with the Muslim masses, and with radical movements in Lebanon; and their commando raids on Israel, and Israeli reprisal raids taking a deathly toll of
innocent Lebanese in the South, plunged them even more deeply into
the internal affairs of Lebanon, and posed the intolerable dilemma for
the Lebanese government that suppression of the Palestinian commandos
would antagonize the Muslim Lebanese.

The civil war started as a war between Christian and Palestinian
forces. But it soon moved along the lines of the major confessional
cleavage, though with conflicts also between different sections of the
same general confessional group. In the process the civil war escalated
to the use of heavy artillery, the bloodiest battles following the break-up
of the Lebanese army. And it was waged with a terrible barbarity, with
indiscriminate slaughter, with torture, obscene mutilation, and joy in
atrocity, with devastation of villages, and with genocidal massacres at
al-Karantīnā and al-Maslakh, at al-Dāmūr, at Bayt Millāt, and at Tall
al-Zaʿtar. In the course of the civil war, perhaps as many as 40,000 were
killed and 180,000 injured, the city of Beirut destroyed and a society

71. ibid., 195 (and ff.).

disintegrated to the point that violence persists even in the presence of two peace-keeping forces, Syrian and United Nations.[72]

The examples I have chosen are linked to colonization, to decolonization, and to plural relations in the successor states. There are many other situations leading to the establishment of plural societies – old religious differences associated with regional concentration; uneven development and inequality in participation; or the forced transportation of peoples to other countries under slavery; or ancient conquest and annexation, as with Armenians in the Ottoman Empire; or migrations resulting in the creation of hostage groups. I shall return to some further discussion of structural factors related to genocidal conflict, in the chapter on process, where I discuss the centrally planned, systematically organized genocide against the Armenians in Turkey and the Jews in Germany.

72. For documentation of the above discussion, see Desjardins, op. cit., Ch. II, 38–9, 149, 183–90; Bulloch, 1977: Ch. VI, 106, 115, Ch. VIII, 184; Salibi, op. cit., 109, 124, 146–7, 152–8. Bulloch comments (102) that when the Christian Phalangists overran a mainly Christian Palestinian camp, 'the Phalangist militiamen were reasonably restrained in their treatment of the Palestinians there largely because they were Christians'.

Chapter 5

Warrant for Genocide
Ideological Aspects

Jamais on ne fait le mal si pleinement et si gaiement que quand on le fait
par conscience.
  [Frontispiece quotation from Pascal in Pieter N. Drost, *The Crime of
  State II – Genocide*]

We are thus driven to the unfashionable conclusion that the trouble with our
species is not an excess of *aggression*, but an excess capacity for fanatical
devotion.
  [Arthur Koestler, *Janus: A Summing Up*, p. 14]

Buried within the title of this chapter, 'Warrant for Genocide', is a
liberal assumption as to the nature of human nature or of man in
society. The assumption is that massive slaughter of members of one's
own species is repugnant to man, and that ideological legitimation is a
necessary pre-condition for genocide. Thus Cohn, in his discussion of
the theory of a Jewish world conspiracy as a legitimating ideology for
organized groups of killers of Jews over a period of some eight centuries,
writes that it cannot be said that these groups consisted wholly of
genuine fanatics. On the contrary, they contained many purely destructive types, wanting nothing but a chance to torture and murder, and
looters interested mainly in the property of those killed; and, in the
modern period, they contained opportunists at all levels seeking a better
income, more security, more prestige than they could otherwise have
hoped for. But, he continues, it seems nevertheless 'certain that however
narrow, materialistic, or downright criminal their own motives may be,
such men cannot operate without an ideology behind them. At least,
when operating collectively, they need an ideology to legitimate their
behaviour, for without it they would have to see themselves and one
another as what they really are – common thieves and murderers. And
that apparently is something which even they cannot bear.'[1]
  The liberal assumption seems reasonable enough. The existence of

1. Cohn, 1967:263–4.

84

society presupposes moral restraints on destructive conflicts, and the presence of many multi-racial and multi-ethnic societies, with defenceless minorities and past or continuing tensions, testifies to the effectiveness of these restraints. At the same time, one must allow for the possibility that there are historical situations or periods in which genocide is taken for granted. Either it was customary under certain conditions, in which case tradition would be the legitimation, or it raised no ethical problem which might evoke an ideology of legitimation.

It would seem that the ideology may emerge after the massacres, as rationalization or as justification, rather than as warrant, but generally there would be ideas circulating which encourage the commission of genocide and the mobilizing of murderous mobs and of organized killers. The most widely held theory is that these ideologies act by shaping a dehumanized image of the victims in the minds of their persecutors. We are, of course, again in the presence of the liberal assumption of powerful moral inhibitions against the slaughter of one's own kind. Since the victims are not human, the inhibitions against their slaughter cease to be operative.

There are many examples of the application of this theory to the interpretation of genocide. Colin Legum, in an account of 'The Massacre of the Proud Ibos' in Northern Nigeria,[2] describes the flight of some 600,000 refugees, 'hacked, slashed, mangled, stripped naked and robbed of all their possessions; the orphans, the widows, the traumatized'. He comments on the role of the Ibos in Northern Nigeria and on the tensions between them and the Northerners. He recalls his own concern over the virulent local propaganda which had been directed against the Ibos for years, and a particularly notorious pamphlet in the 1964 elections, caricaturing them in very much the same way that Julius Streicher had caricatured the Jews in *Der Stürmer*. He writes that 'while the peasants complained of exploitation, the educated Northerners spoke of the Ibos as vermin, criminals, money-grabbers, and sub-humans without genuine culture'. He analyses the conditions which produced the mass killings – an alien group of traders, entrepreneurs and skilled craftsmen on the one hand, and on the other, great tensions and the fear of alien domination in the host community. And he concludes that 'in such conditions, political leaders can exploit actual or imaginary grievances against the alien minority. The danger signal is when there is official sanction for talking about a minority group in non-human terms. This process seems essential to provide some kind of justification for dealing

2. Legum, 1966.

with other human beings as one would treat dangerous animals – exterminate them.'

By way of further example, the theory of the demonization of Jews as the context for exterminatory anti-semitism makes use of the relationship between ideological dehumanization and genocide. Or again, in an analysis of the sociology of evil, Coser refers to concentration camp and prison guards who had brutally murdered Jewish, Ukrainian and other prisoners during the Second World War, but who had staunchly maintained that they had been justified in acting as they did because their victims were not 'people like you and me'. 'These concentration camp guards, though they lived in the same physical environments as their victims, nevertheless managed to build so immense a social distance between "them" and "us" that they perceive their victims as not belonging to the same human race.'[3]

Assuming that dehumanization is a significant ideological factor in the genocidal process, how is it to be defined? The most obvious short-hand definition is the denial of human status. However, this merely transposes the problem to defining human status. Is the denial of human status to be equated with the denial of basic human rights? But what are these basic human rights? Definitions of human rights vary with time and place, with historical period and societal context. Dehumanization might be conceived as the relegation of the victims to the level of animals or of objects or to a purely instrumental role. The denial of a common humanity would seem to be an important component of any definition, since it emphasizes the element of exclusion. The concept of dehumanization should certainly incorporate these aspects, and it should be related to the definition of genocide, since we are dealing with the problem of the relationship between genocide and ideologies of dehumanization.

Genocide, in terms of the perspective of this study, is a crime against a collectivity, taking the form of massive slaughter, and carried out with explicit intent. As a crime against a collectivity, it sets aside the whole question of individual responsibility; it is a denial of individuality. All members of the group are guilty solely by virtue of their membership in it. Characteristically, the very old and the very young, the defenceless, those who could not conceivably be seen as combatants, are among the victims of the massacres. The intent, as we have seen, is to destroy a group 'as such'. The introduction of this phrase in the Genocide Convention introduces an ambiguity, but I have assumed that the crime is con-

3. Coser, 1969:107–8.

stituted by deliberate extermination of a group, whatever the further goal – economic progress, or a racially ordered hierarchy, or a utopian society. Otherwise the definition would be meaningless for all practical purposes. Indeed the crime seems more horrifying when extermination is carried out, not in blind hatred, but in pursuance of some further purpose, the victims being cast in a purely instrumental role. This is the ultimate point in the denial of human individuality and significance.

There is a definition of dehumanization by Kelman,[4] which meets the requirement of relating the concept of dehumanization to genocide. He is dealing with sanctioned massacres, by which he means massacres which occur in the context of genocidal policy, and which are directed at groups that have not themselves threatened or engaged in hostile actions against the perpetrators of the violence. He identifies dehumanization as one of the processes by which the 'usual moral inhibitions against violence become weakened'. He comments that inhibitions against murdering fellow human beings are generally so strong that the victims must be deprived of their human status if systematic killing is to proceed in a smooth and orderly fashion, and that to the extent that the victims are dehumanized, principles of morality no longer apply to them and moral restraints against killing are more readily overcome.

Kelman defines dehumanization as the denial of identity and community. 'To accord a person identity is to perceive him as an individual, independent and distinguishable from others, capable of making choices, and entitled to live his own life on the basis of his own goals and values. To accord a person community is to perceive him – along with one's self – as part of an interconnected network of individuals who care for each other, who recognize each other's individuality, and who respect each other's rights.'[5] This is a very idealized and individualistic conception of what it means 'to perceive another person as fully human', and markedly so in a reference to John Donne's 'Any man's death diminishes me, because I am involved in mankind.' However, it helps to bring out some of the essential elements – the exclusion from community (and I would add, the denial of a common humanity), and the rejection of individual significance, with its corollaries of the categorization of the target group in pejorative terms and its aggregation of the victims into the anonymity of a collectivized mass. The ideology would then include a dehumanizing characterization of the target group, and a theory which relates it to licence for genocide.

4. Kelman, 1973:48–9.
5. ibid.

The animal world has been a particularly fertile source of metaphors of dehumanization. These metaphors derive from the culture and characteristics of the group applying them, and, of course, express in no way the qualities of the vilified group. If one wishes to understand why European settlers might use the word *ratons* in reference to Algerians, and Afrikaans settlers in South Africa the term *bobbejaan* (baboon) in reference to Africans, the explanation is presumably to be sought in the urban culture of many of the European settlers and in the rural culture of Afrikaners. Some of these animal descriptions or animal analogies seem specially designed to awaken horror and to elicit fear, as in the image of octopus-like tentacles reaching out. Hunters and gatherers have been a frequent repository of images borrowed from the bestiary. Described as animals, they have often been hunted down like animals, which is not to say that describing others as animals necessarily implies any inclination to massacre them.

The reduction to an object is expressed more in practice than in ideological formulations, though I have encountered its implicit use in race relations. There is subordination to an object in serfdom with its tie to the land, and it is present also in some measure in the South African Pass Laws by which a document becomes a crucial element in the identity of Africans and their enjoyment of some quite elementary human rights. Its most complete expression is in chattel slavery, and above all in the death camps, with the stripping of social identity and the reduction of the victims to numbers.

Demonization in such elaborated forms as a Jewish world conspiracy must be rare, if not unique, though stranger groups are sometimes viewed by their host societies as sorcerers or as endowed with magical powers. At a less demonic level, there is the Shylock image, a composite of exploitative traits, sharp practice and downright dishonesty, clannishness and arrogance. The hostile stereotype of Ibos, sketched in the article by Legum,[6] falls in this category. It is often applied to hostage groups engaged in trade, the so-called middlemen, and it is unfortunately given wider currency in much scholarly writing. Then too, there are various denigrating characterizations of other groups said to be derived from the experience of living together.[7]

Many theories are available to invest these hostile images with des-

6. Legum, op. cit.

7. See my discussion of 'Ideologies of Cultural Difference in Race Relations' and 'Ideologies of Violence among Subordinate Groups', in *Race, Class and Power,* 1974: Chs. 1 and 3.

tructive potential. Above all there are the theories of progress and of evolution. The elimination of hunters and gatherers is said to be an inevitable consequence of progress, a regrettable cost. Colonization was linked to evolution, the conquered peoples being conceived as lower in the scale of evolution with rights and capacities by no means comparable to those of their conquerors. In the march of progress, the unfolding of evolution provided the justification that many peoples are destined for 'the rubbish bins (the trash cans) of history'. In the Nazi phrase, these are 'mistmenschen'.

Ideologies of dehumanization abound in the sacred writings of universal religions, yielding sanction for destructive conflicts, between Christians and Jews, Christians and Muslims, Hindus and Muslims, the Faithful and the Infidels, the Believers and the Heretics. They were waged with great atrocity and genocidal massacre. I referred to the religious wars in the opening chapter. They are by no means remote from our own day. In the nineteenth century there were the *jihads* in Northern Nigeria, in the twentieth century the genocides against Jews, and between Hindu and Muslim in India after the Second World War, and in Bangladesh in the last decade.

Then too there was the genocide against Serbs in the Second World War, which I have not as yet mentioned. This arose out of a long history of conflict between Croats and Serbs, fuelled later in the newly constituted state of Yugoslavia by Croatian resentment of Serbian hegemony and repression, and Serbian resistance to Croatian demands for autonomy. The defeat of Yugoslavia by the Axis powers, the partition which followed, and the establishment of the satellite Croatia provided Croats with the opportunity to slaughter hundreds of thousands of Serbs in a genocide which bore a strong religious stamp, reminiscent of earlier wars against the Schismatics. It was a genocide by Croatian Roman Catholics with Muslim support, against Serbian followers of the Orthodox Church. Some Catholic priests participated in the killings, and conducted the ceremonies of forced conversion by which thousands of Serbs escaped massacre. And there was participation also, or at any rate condonation of the massacres, at higher levels of the Catholic hierarchy. Serbian forces themselves engaged in counter-massacres of non-conformists, especially Muslims.[8]

In Northern Ireland the conflict is often described as being waged between ethnic groups (presumably Scots and English on the one hand,

8. See Paris, 1961, particularly Ch. VII; Seton-Watson, 1955; Vucinich, 1949: 272 and 355–9.

and Irish on the other), or between classes (presumably English–Scots bourgeoisie and 'labour aristocracy' against Irish labouring class). But the lines of conflict are drawn between Catholics and Protestants, and this must surely be accorded some weight, given the long struggle for Catholic emancipation from quite extreme legally imposed disabilities. As recently as 1977, I heard a Mr Ian Paisley, a Protestant strong-man, preaching in his palatial church in Belfast to a packed congregation of the faithful. He took the following text from the Book of Revelation for his sermon: 'and I saw a woman sit upon a scarlet coloured beast, full of names of blasphemy, having seven heads and ten horns. And the woman was arrayed in purple and scarlet colour, and decked with gold and precious stones and pearls, having a golden cup in her hand full of abominations and filthiness of her fornication ...' He delineated with his hands the Whore of Babylon on one side (the right!) and the Lamb of God on the other. He kept turning towards the whore in her purple silks, seeming to caress her invisible form with passion, while making perfunctory gestures in the direction of the Lamb. Yet however much he may have been drawn to the scarlet woman, it symbolized in his sermon the Papacy, and there was no mistaking the hatred, ostensibly against the Papacy, but certainly with effective impact against Catholics in general, though he disclaimed any such intention. The text itself was taken from the revelation of the seven vials of God's wrath, in which dire torment and horrendous slaughter are visited on the idol worshippers and the blasphemers. It all sounded like a revival of the conflicts in the Christian Church at the time of the Reformation, but it still retains vitality for sections of the Protestant population of Northern Ireland.

Religious differences may have significance for the process of dehumanization, even when they do not yield theological formulations. It is striking that the cases of genocide discussed in the last chapter, with a few exceptions such as in Rwanda and Burundi, are marked by religious differences between the killers and their victims. This suggests that religious values (even among those who are not devout and in conflicts quite unrelated to matters of faith) may be ideologically significant at a different level, shaping sentiments of exclusion, and derogatory stereotypes of the followers of other religions. And it suggests too that we underestimate the contemporary significance of religion in genocidal conflict.

Metaphors sometimes serve a function subsidiary to, and analogous with, ideologies of dehumanization. Diseases which strike horror or repel, and which call for radical surgery, are specially favoured. Susan

Sontag, in an analysis of *Disease as Political Metaphor*, writes that modern totalitarian movements, whether of the right or the left, have been peculiarly and revealingly inclined to use disease imagery, the Nazis repeatedly analogizing European Jewry to syphilis and to a cancer that must be excised, while disease metaphors were a staple of Bolshevik polemics. She continues that:

To describe a phenomenon as a cancer is an incitement to violence. The use of cancer in political discourse encourages fatalism and 'severe' measures – as well as strongly reinforcing the popular perception that the disease is necessarily fatal. The concept of disease is never innocent. But it could be argued that the cancer metaphors are in themselves implicitly genocidal. No specific political view seems to have a monopoly on this metaphor. If Hitler called the Jews the cancer of Europe, Trotsky called Stalinism the cancer of Marxism, and in China in the last year the Gang of Four have become, among other things, 'the cancer of China.' John Dean called Watergate 'the cancer on the presidency.'
The standard metaphor of Arab polemics – heard by Israelis on the radio every day for the last twenty years – is that Israel is 'a cancer in the heart of the Arab world' or 'the cancer of the Middle East,' and an officer with the Christian Lebanese rightist forces besieging the Palestine refugee camp of Tal Zaatar in August 1976 called the camp 'a cancer in the Lebanese body.'[9]

In similar vein, there was the Nazi metaphor of the Jew as a dangerous bacillus, to be eradicated at all costs. And by way of further example, there is a curious document purporting to be the minutes of a secret meeting of the Ittihad[10] Central Executive, held early in 1915, at which the extermination of the Armenians was planned.[11] One of the speakers is recorded as comparing the Armenians to 'a canker, a malignance which looks like a small pimple from the outside, which, if not removed by a skilful surgeon's scalpel, will kill the patient'. Later, a different type of metaphor is used, in which the alien nations left from ancient times are likened to malignant weeds, which must be plucked from the roots and cast aside.

It is important to bear in mind the rather obvious point that the ideologies do not work in a vacuum. Sometimes the accounts of American massacres in Vietnam, with their repeated references to the use of the word *gooks* for the Vietnamese, seem to imply that the pejorative term or the hostile stereotype was a highly significant factor in motivat-

9. Sontag, 1978:29–33.
10. The Young Turk Committee for Unity and Progress.
11. Toriguian, 1973:39–46.

ing the massacres. But there may be dehumanization without massacre – this is surely the general case – and presumably massacre without dehumanization. There is a broad context within which ideologies operate – a context of historical relationships, of structural divisions, of material interests, of political objectives. In the context of the Vietnam conflict, it would include the historical relationships within Vietnam itself; the structure of the U.S.A. and its army, the use of the word *gooks* being taken as symbolic of racist attitudes in both American society and its armed forces; the imperialist war between the U.S.S.R. and the U.S.A., fought on the territories of small nations; the process of struggle itself between an army equipped with highly destructive long-range weapons and guerrilla forces merging with the local population; the tactics employed – search and destroy, free fire-zones, defoliation, massive relocation, indiscriminate reprisal, on the one hand, and on the other, the anti-personnel mines, the booby traps, the ambushes, the sniping, the killing and the mutilating. While the ideologies of dehumanization draw on certain general themes, their special content and idiosyncratic forms are shaped by the particular context within which they operate; and it is to this context that one must turn for the analysis of the role of the ideology in a specific historical situation.

Kelman, in the paper referred to above, deals, as we have seen, with sanctioned massacres, which (1) occur in the context of an overall policy that is genocidal in character, being designed to destroy all or part of a category of people defined in ethnic, national, racial, religious or other terms, and (2) are directed at groups that have not themselves threatened or engaged in hostile actions towards the perpetrators of the violence.[12] He adds that there are, of course, historical and situational reasons why a particular group becomes a suitable target for massacres, but that it cannot be said 'in any objectively meaningful sense, that they provoke the violence against them by what they have done. They are not being murdered because they have harmed, oppressed, or threatened their attackers. Rather, their selection as targets for massacre at a particular time can ultimately be traced to their relationship to the pursuit of larger policies. They may be targeted because their elimination is seen as a useful tool or because their continued existence is seen as an irritating obstacle in the execution of policy.'[13]

The distinction seems a useful one, between situations in which there is some threat, however slight, to the interests of those who perpetrate

12. Kelman, op. cit., 31–3.
13. ibid.

or plan or incite the massacres, and situations devoid of such threat. Certainly, there are difficulties in applying the distinction. Where the outside observer may see no threat whatever, objectively considered, the actors themselves may feel threatened. Thus the Christian massacres of Jews at the time of the Black Death were motivated by the grotesque belief that they were causing the plague. No doubt, too, many people believed in the equally grotesque theory of a Jewish world conspiracy. And leaders may deliberately foster quite unrealistic beliefs, exploiting the credulity and fears of their followers in pursuit of their own objectives. Still, one can distinguish between massacres of a weak defenceless hostage group used as a scapegoat, and massacres arising in the course of a conflict in which there is some realistic threat or challenge to the interests of the dominant group in the host society.

Most of the cases of genocide or of genocidal massacre reviewed in the last chapter arose in the course of 'real' conflicts of interest, related to the structure of power. There were the challenges to the structure of domination in movements for national liberation, or for greater regional autonomy, or for secession, as in Algeria, the Sudan and Bangladesh. There were movements to reverse the structure of domination, as in Rwanda and Burundi, or to change the basis of consociation, as in the Lebanon. Or the conflict developed out of the very radical solution of partition, with its threat to livelihood and indeed survival for many millions, as in the partition of India. These are all essentially political struggles. This is not markedly the case in the massacres of hunters and gatherers where the material interests in the exclusive occupation of land predominate. But in the genocides against hostage groups there is often, over and above the interest in loot and expropriation, the further motivation by explicitly political objectives. Ethnic and religious differences converge, in many such cases, with economic and political considerations.

The strength of political factors and the inextricable interweaving of political considerations in so many genocides against racial, ethnic and religious groups, demonstrate the impossibility of separating the racial, ethnic and religious from the political, as seemingly required by the Genocide Convention with its exclusion of political groups from its scope. Can one really interpret the exterminating massacres of Hutu in Burundi in purely ethnic, non-political terms, thereby placing it within the terms of the Genocide Convention; or for that matter, can one interpret it in purely political non-ethnic terms, falling outside the purview of the Convention? The absurdity of this artificial separation between the political and other factors was, of course, foreseen by some of the representatives in the debates on the framing of the Convention. In the context of the present discussion of ideology, there is the further absurdity of this artificial separation in the fact that political ideologies of dehumanization may have great relevance for genocide against ethnic, racial and religious groups.

In German national socialism, ideologies of dehumanization of racial, religious, national and ethnic groups received their most systematic formulation as a theory of society, and as a blueprint for political reconstruction and military expansion. Rejecting traditional western moral and religious concepts about the nature of man and his inalienable dignity as a human personality, national socialism proclaimed the virtues of violence, of storm and of blood; worship of the German 'race people' replaced the concern for the individual and other despised values of Christian humanism. Endowed with the supreme mission to lead and dominate other races, by virtue of the Aryan superiority of their racially pure blood, the German people had the right to subjugate other peoples, to use them purely as means, as expendable slave labour, or indeed to slaughter them. In a grandiose design for (ultimately) world hegemony, Nazi ideology organized other peoples in a hierarchy which defined their right to survival, or the conditions of their incorporation into the living space of the Greater German Reich, or of subjugation as auxiliary lands, or of affiliation.

Jews, Gypsies and Poles were especially stigmatized for genocidal massacres. Jews and Gypsies were deemed totally expendable, in much the same way as the mentally defective whom the Nazis exterminated. In Poland, Nazi policy aimed at the destruction of the Polish élite, the incorporation of parts of Poland in the German Reich, the dissolution of Poland as a state, and the large-scale enslavement of Poles. In contrast to the material benefits in labour, in territory and resources, the Nazis had nothing whatever to gain from the persecution of Gypsies.

As for the persecution of Jews, as distinct from genocide against the Jews, this served the Nazis in many different ways. Given the wide diffusion of anti-semitism, it was a source for support in other countries. Within Germany itself, it functioned as a unifying factor. This may partly explain the contradictory elements in the stereotype of Jews, which would have an appeal for many different categories of the German population. Thus Jews, in Nazi imagery, embodied both capitalism and its arch-enemy communism; and they symbolized demonic power and conspiratorial malevolence, and at the same time, contemptible weakness and diseased degeneracy. Here then was a threat to survival, which called for a unity transcending the class struggle, and it was combined with an easy vulnerability of the victim. In addition, there were the material benefits in expropriation and other forms of robbery, to which we have already referred. Ideologies of dehumanization, combined with geopolitical considerations, and under the constraints of the military situation, shaped the fate of other peoples in the conquered territories.

Marxist doctrine is the very antithesis of German national socialism in its total rejection of all forms of racism, but it incorporates ideologies of dehumanization which have relevance for our problem. There is, in the Communist Manifesto, a thoroughgoing dehumanization of the bourgeoisie. It is described as having drowned the most heavenly 'ecstasies of religious fervour, of chivalrous enthusiasm, of philistine sentimentalism, in the icy water of egotistical calculation; it has resolved personal worth into exchange value; for exploitation, veiled by religious and political illusions, it has substituted naked, shameless, direct, brutal exploitation.' The bourgeois see in their wives mere instruments of production; not content with having the wives and daughters of the workers at their disposal, as well as common prostitutes, they take the greatest pleasure in seducing each other's wives.

The proletarian class of labourers, arising in the process of the development of bourgeois capitalism, sell themselves piecemeal as a commodity. They become an appendage of the machine, increasingly pauperized. As the repulsiveness of their work increases, so their wage decreases, and as the use of machinery and the division of labour increase, so does the burden of their toil increase. But in the proletariat, the bourgeoisie has produced its own gravediggers. The continued existence of the bourgeoisie is no longer compatible with society. Its fall and the victory of the proletariat are equally inevitable. Whereas all previous historical movements were movements of minorities or in the interest of minorities, the proletarian movement is the movement of the immense majority in the interest of the immense majority. The violent overthrow of the bourgeoisie lays the foundation for the sway of the proletariat. In place of the old bourgeois society, there arises an association of people, in which the free development of each is the condition for the free development of all.

We are, of course, in the presence of a Revelation of the Lamb of God and the Whore of Babylon. It is a revolutionary model of extreme

Genocide

and irreconcilable opposition. But is there anything in this picture of increasing polarization, and of the inevitable violent extinction of a dehumanized class of people, which would encourage wholesale massacre? Or to phrase the question in the concrete form in which it has often been debated, could the massacres of the Stalinist regime have derived their warrant from Marxism?

A conservative, or minimal, statement of the killings under the Stalinist regime is to be found in the denunciation of Stalin to the Twentieth Congress of the Communist Party of the Soviet Union by the party's first secretary, Nikita S. Krushchev, at a closed session in February 1956.[14] This denunciation by a former aide and active accomplice of Stalin is as remarkable for what it contains as for what it omits. A major theme, with which the report opens and ends, is the attack on the cult of the individual, raised by Stalin to near deification. To this cult of the person, in conjunction with certain personality defects in Stalin, 'his capricious and despotic character', the report attributes many serious perversions of party principles, of party democracy, of revolutionary legality and the brutal violence of mass repression through the government apparatus, which began precisely 'when socialism in our country was fundamentally constructed, when the exploiting classes were generally liquidated, when the Soviet social structure had radically changed, when the social basis for political movements and groups hostile to the party had violently contracted, when the ideological opponents of the party had long since been defeated politically'.[15]

In Solzhenitsyn's *Gulag Archipelago*, we have a much fuller account of the killings under Stalin. Krushchev's denunciation is delivered from the exalted heights of the Praesidium, Solzhenitsyn's from the depths of the slave camps of the Gulag Archipelago, as he pieced together the events under conditions of the most extreme deprivation, as he experienced them in contact with the victims, and as he reconstructed, in the years following his release, the terrorism and the massacres. It is immediately clear from a comparison of these two denunciations that Krushchev had only touched on the fringe of the killings. And yet Solzhenitsyn does not view his own account as complete. He dedicates his volumes to all those who did not live to tell it, and he asks their forgiveness for not having seen it all, nor remembered it all, nor divined it all. Moreover, his central concern was with the Gulag Archipelago,

14. I am following the text in the edition by Bertram Wolfe, 1957. For discussion of different editions of this speech in English, see Gouldner, 1977–8:32, fn. 68.
15. Wolfe, op. cit., 104.

as it was 'fertilized' by crimes of a political colouration. He seeks to convey to the reader the utterly dehumanized death-dealing brutality of the 'destructive labour camps', 'the slaughterhouses of the Archipelago', 'the polar death house',[16] recalling the slave and death camps of the Hitler regime, which they preceded. He comments that 'Hitler was a mere disciple, but he had all the luck: his murder camps have made him famous, whereas no one has any interest in ours at all.'[17]

Solzhenitsyn traces the terror back to the very inception of Bolshevik rule under Lenin. He is at pains to reject the thesis that the extreme terrorism was a consequence of the personality cult of Stalin. Indeed, he finds the suggestion ludicrous, and repeatedly subjects it to ridicule. Nor does he accept the theory that the Soviet regime merely continued the tradition of Russian despotism, embodied in Czarist rule. Conditioned as we are to the belief in the tyranny of the preceding Czarist regime, it is startling to see from Solzhenitsyn's account how benign it was, compared to the Soviet regime, in its use of mass terrorism and of executions, and in its treatment of political prisoners.[18]

These perspectives are drawn from the accounts of an executioner and a victim. Both have been highly influential. Krushchev's denunciation was followed by a major change in Soviet repression, with the freeing of some 5,000,000 political prisoners,[19] and selective terrorism in place of mass arrests and purges. Solzhenitsyn's writings carry to the widest audiences, in the most deeply human terms, at the intimate level of personal suffering, some impression of the immense anguish of the violent transformation of Russian society. As to the loss in human life, Solzhenitsyn quotes a figure of 66,000,000 – sixty-six million – from the beginning of the October Revolution to 1959.[20] For the decade 1929–39 alone, Gouldner gives an estimate[21] of 20,000,000 shot, or dying of famine or disease or exposure, as the direct result of punitive action by the Soviet government,[22] to which must be added the slaughter in the decade immediately following the October Revolution, and in the decade of the war years. However unreliable the estimates, it is clear that we are in the presence of the major holocaust of our time.

16. Solzhenitsyn, 1974–8, Map, Frontispiece, Vol. II, p. 72; Vol. I, p. 12; Vol. III.
17. ibid., Vol. III, 359.
18. See ibid., Vol. I, 29ff., and Chs. 9–12.
19. Gouldner, op. cit., 5.
20. Solzhenitsyn, op. cit., Vol. II, 10.
21. Gouldner, op. cit., 11.
22. For further estimates of the slaughter in this decade, see ibid., 29, 35, 37.

Genocide

Now the relevant question for this discussion is whether Stalinism had its ideological roots in Marxism (or Marxism-Leninism). We may define Stalinism, in part, as totalitarian control, based on state ownership of the means of production, with despotic monopoly of power, and the systematic use of mass terror.[23] Could this system be regarded as the direct result of the application of Marxist theory by the Stalinist regime? Did the dehumanization of the victims and the warrant for their slaughter have a source in Marxist theory?

The opposing viewpoints on the relationship between Stalinism and Marxist theory are that Stalinism is the inevitable issue of Marxism-Leninism, and on the contrary, that they are quite disconnected.[24] There are many variants on these themes – Stalinism as error, as deviation, as an aborted Marxist revolution, as petrified at the stage of early state capitalism, as a counter-revolutionary Thermidorean reaction and reversion to Russian tradition.

At a wider level of interpretation, the opposing viewpoints may be defined as genetic (Stalinism ideologically inherited from Marxism) versus environmental (Stalinism as social inheritance, as continuation of the old regime).[25] Clearly, both views are extreme. The Stalinist regime was shaped by many 'environmental' factors. There were the traditions of Russian society, including despotic rule, with Stalin often compared to Ivan the Terrible,[26] but more broadly, inclusive of peasant cultures and of urban élite cultures. There was the structure of the society, with its forms of economic development, a small urban proletariat in an overwhelmingly rural society, and sharp cleavages between town and country. There were the historical circumstances of the First World War, of the civil war, of international threat and intervention, of the rise of nazism, and of the Second World War. There were the internal crises, and the often improvisational response to these crises. There were the internal processes which led to personal tyranny, to the growth of the bureaucracy and of secret police, to conflicts between despot and party and bureaucracy and army and police, and to the institutions of mass terror.

Any suggestion of ideological (idealistic) determinism must certainly

23. See ibid., 10–14; Kolakowski, 1977:284–90; and Marković, 1977:299–304, for discussions of the nature of Stalinism.
24. Gouldner, op. cit., 8. Cohen, 1977:3–29, presents a strong argument for discontinuity between Bolshevism and Stalinism.
25. Kolakowski, op. cit., 297.
26. See, for example, Souvarine, 1977:528–32.

be rejected. However, one can hardly deny the significance of ideological factors, even though they were not determinant. The revolutionary changes in Russian society were carried out in the name of Marxism-Leninism, and key concepts of the theory were applied in the framing and implementation of policies.[27]

But the specific interpretation of Marxist theory was not inherent in Marxism. Other interpretations might have been made. The milder form of Chinese terrorism resulted from differences in both interpretation and social context. Gouldner[28] shows that the Chinese communists derived a different model of economic development from the application of Marxist theory to their society and that they had a quite different relationship to the peasantry. Moreover, they operated with a different conception of human nature, and with different assumptions as to personality. Even class enemies were accessible to thought reform and change in consciousness. And the Chinese communists were not exposed to the same acute international threat as the new Soviet regime. In the result, their system of terror spared the Chinese the Soviet holocaust.

Following the Chinese model is, of course, no assurance that the consequences will be comparable, as can be seen from the history of the Khmer Rouge revolutionary regime which took power in Cambodia in 1975. But there were crucial differences in ideology, leaving little room for the re-education of rejected social categories. And the Khmer Rouge leaders felt threatened by counter-revolution – their hold on power was indeed quite precarious – and they confronted an immediate crisis of famine conditions, as a result of the devastation wrought by American bombing and by civil war.[29] In the brief period of their rule, vast numbers met their deaths most brutally by execution and massacre, and as a consequence of the policies pursued for the immediate radical restructuring of Cambodian society.

Leaving aside the question of the relationship between Marxism and the decimation of population under Stalinism, and returning to the more general problem of the influence of Marxist theory, there are elements of this theory which have an affinity for highly destructive conflict. Acceptance of the theory of increasing polarization between proletariat and bourgeoisie, between the emancipatory forces of revo-

27. See the discussion by Kolakowski, op. cit.
28. Gouldner, op. cit., 38–41.
29. See Tan, 1979, for an excellent analysis of Khmer Rouge ideology. The Khmer Rouge regime is discussed further in Chapter 8, below.

lution and the enslaving forces of reaction, readily yields a Manichean vision of a world torn apart in deadly conflict between good and evil. The preoccupation with classes encourages an indifference to the individual and to individual suffering. The belief that being determines consciousness, a cardinal belief in traditional Marxism, readily yields a conception of guilt by social origin; people are guilty for what they are, rather than for what they do. Given the movement to a higher level of civilization, social categories, whose origins or function cast them in a reactionary role, are excluded from, or rendered marginal to, the moral community. In the light of a Messianic faith in a final and definitive upheaval which will lay the foundations for a utopian society, whole groups become expendable for the realization of an ultimate good, and a whole armoury of antitheses and lethal malediction becomes available – enemies of the people, bourgeois nationalists, revisionists, rightists, reactionaries, doomed classes, counter-revolutionaries.

It seems paradoxical to suggest that Marxism incorporates a dehumanizing ideology, conducive to most lethal and merciless conflict.[30] Marxism is, after all, one of the great humanist doctrines of our day, with its vision of a society free from inequality and conflict, in which men may live in full creativity. Yet this combination of the highest ideals with massive slaughter is all too common. Indeed the high ideals often serve as warrant for massacre. Unfortunately there is a great deal of truth in the quotation from Pascal at the opening of this chapter, that men never surrender themselves to evil with more joyous abandon than in the service of a good conscience.

30. One of the many discussions of this problem is to be found in Kovaly, 1974.

Chapter 6

Genocidal Process
The Turkish Genocide Against Armenians

I asked my gendarmes what all the strange little mounds of earth were which
I saw everywhere, with thousands of dogs prowling round about them.
'Those are the graves of the infidels!' they answered calmly.
'Strange, so many graves for such a little village.'
'Oh, you do not understand. Those are the graves of these dogs – those
who were brought here first, last August. They all died of thirst.'
'Of thirst? Was there no water left in the Euphrates?'
'For whole weeks together we were forbidden to let them drink.'
    [Record of an interview with an Armenian physician (Viscount Bryce,
The Treatment of Armenians in the Ottoman Empire 1915–1916, p. 563)]

I will be discussing genocidal process in the context of the Turkish
genocide against the Armenians, and the German genocide against the
Jews and other peoples. But first, I would like to offer some general
comment on the genocidal process. And this will also explain why I am
narrowing the discussion of process to these two genocides.

Part of the problem is that there is no single genocidal process. The
forms of genocide are too varied, with quite different sequences of
action, and great differences in scale, raising different 'logistic' problems. Where the victims are numerous, but dispersed among the general
population, they have to be concentrated for massacre. The disposal of
many bodies is an acute problem; in Turkey, Rwanda, Burundi and
Bangladesh, it was eased by the availability of rivers. The victims themselves may be induced to assist in the process of concentration by
treachery, or forced to cooperate in the preparations for the disposal
of their bodies. Where small numbers are involved, the type of atrocity
can more readily take the form of manual and intimate slaughter.

Technology is an important variable. Farming implements and artisans' tools may be the most available weapons, or there may be a
general availability of modern armament. At the present time, there is
almost certain to be sophisticated arming of the killers by the greater
and lesser international powers, and mechanized equipment for the disposal of bodies, such as United Nations bulldozers designed for devel-

101

opment projects. Even where sophisticated weapons are available, the more 'primitive' manual weapons and operations may be preferred. One reads all too often of the clubbing to death of victims, sometimes with rifle butts, and of the smashing of skulls and other singularly brutal ways of doing to death. Given the state of international morality, it is difficult to credit that there could have been any shortage of ammunition. These methods serve to magnify the terror of the massacres, quite apart from sadistic gratification for the killers. Certain forms of genocide are of course only possible where there is a high development of technology, with an efficient bureaucracy. The atomic bombings of Hiroshima and Nagasaki represent the absolute in white-collar technological genocide.

Some genocides have appreciable spontaneity, others are highly organized. There is probably always a measure of organization. What appears to be spontaneous may of course be organized, as in the inflaming and unleashing of mobs, for example, against the Ibos in Northern Nigeria, or against the Armenians in Turkey or the Tutsi in Rwanda. Related to this distinction is that between genocides which are centrally planned and executed, and those which take somewhat the form of mass social movements, or of a social process with the convergence of different strands, as in the extinction of many hunting and gathering peoples in the course of the advancing industrial exploitation of resources. The same type of genocide may take quite different forms. Thus the East European pogroms range from the seemingly spontaneous action of mobs to organized massacres by military forces, as in the Ukrainian pogroms launched by Petlura at the end of the First World War.[1]

Genocides may explode with sudden violence or take a quite protracted course. There are societies in which genocidal massacres over an appreciable period of time precede the final extermination, as notably the case in the Turkish genocide against the Armenians. By contrast, the genocidal assaults of Hindus on Muslims and Muslims on Hindus in the process of Indian partition erupted with cataclysmic speed, though of course arising out of ancient enmity and renewed political strife.

Somewhat related to differences in duration is the important distinction between genocides in which there is no threat from the victims and those in which there is threat or initiatory violence or reciprocal violence. The issue of actual or potential threat from the victims is a difficult one to determine, since it is necessary to take account of the

1. See Comité des Délégations Juives, 1927, and Torrès, 1928.

perceptions of those who commit the genocide and the deliberate manipulation of fears and prejudices in the ideological assaults on the target group. But the distinction is clear enough between genocides in which the victims are weak and defenceless and do not engage in violence, and those in which the genocides arise out of violent conflict, and in which the victims have some (significant) capacity to resist, or in which, objectively considered, the victims do constitute a serious threat. An example of the latter would be the Hutu majority in Burundi after the massacres of Tutsi in the neighbouring country of Rwanda.

In rare cases, there may be an equal capacity to annihilate, following for example the changing fortunes of war. In India, partition created a situation in which Hindus and Muslims each constituted majorities in different parts of the country, with the capacity to engage freely in reciprocal genocidal massacre. Ian Morison analyses this process in the Punjab in the following terms:

In its recent manifestations, it has appeared rather as a sort of infectious hysteria or mental derangement. The carriers are the refugees. The incubation period is the time it takes a large number of refugees to move from one part of the country to another. It requires a suitable climate in the way of a latent cleavage, usually economic, between the two communities. Auxiliary irritants which accelerate an outbreak are irresponsible politicians and journalists and those gangster elements who profit from anarchy. The outbreak is correspondingly severe if the resistance offered to it by the body politic – namely, the normal machinery of maintaining law and order – is reduced in strength. The initial symptoms vary, depending upon whether the two communities are evenly balanced or one greatly preponderates. In the first case each suffers from a psychosis of fear, a terror that it is about to be attacked; and in the second case the majority suffers from a psychosis of revenge, often both fear and revenge are mixed, and they are soon absorbed in wild and undiscriminatory hostility ...[2]

By way of further example, the Lebanon in 1975–6 presented the phenomenon of the somewhat equal capacity of Christians and Muslims to engage in genocidal massacre. The more usual case of violent genocidal conflict, however, is that in which one of the parties has by far the greater power and the conflict escalates, by a process of polarization, through murder and massacre to genocide.

I have emphasized the differences in the processes of genocide, but there must also be certain regularities. Over and above the atrocity of

2. *The Times*, 19 September 1947, as quoted by Campbell-Johnson, 1951:203.

mass slaughter, there seems to be almost invariably the additional gratuitous atrocity of torture, perpetrated with incredible brutality, and, as appears from many accounts, with hilarious and joyful abandon. Sexual torments and mutilations are common enough. They are certain to be inflicted where the genocidal conflict is between the circumcised and the uncircumcised. Perhaps they are an invariable element, outside of the remote technological annihilations. But accounts often draw a veil over this aspect, as one which cannot be put into words, or as unprintable or unspeakable or indescribable.

It would seem that the élite are by no means immune to the fascination of these forms of torture. In a chilling passage, Desjardins describes how both sides in the Lebanese conflict had tortured, emasculated, torn women apart, with the same hatred, the same savagery. 'Priests tortured, as did devout Muslims. Young girls of the best Christian society, petty bourgeois costumed at Pierre Cardin or Courrèges, admirers of Brassens and Bob Dylan, castrated prisoners; university faculty, advocates of coexistence between the communities, embodying the wisdom of Islam and of Christianity, gouged out eyes and disembowelled women.'[3] If the contending parties are of different religion, even if religious values do not seem to be salient in the conflict, one may expect special torment to be visited upon spiritual leaders, and the desecration of holy places and sacraments, and the 'abomination', to use a Biblical word, of forced participation in sacrilege, as in the enforced eating of the sacred cow.

Ideological dehumanization of the victims is a constant feature, the mass slaughter itself being the denial of a common humanity. It is expressed too in the handling of the victims, in the disposal of their bodies, and in the obscene mutilation of corpses. There are often 'rituals of degradation' which deliberately reject, with brutal contempt, the most deeply held human values, and the deepest sentiments of human attachment. Thus men are tortured before their wives and children, women are repeatedly raped in the presence of their families, children are killed in the arms of their mothers, and prospective victims are forced to slaughter their fellow victims by the most fearful means.

Euphemisms are commonly used by those in authority to describe the genocidal process. Solzhenitsyn[4] refers to the Soviet phrase 'special settlers' for the exiled nations; elsewhere he mentions the versatile category of 'social prophylaxis'. In Nazi Germany, we had such euphemisms

3. Desjardins, 1976:39.
4. Solzhenitsyn, 1974–8: Vol. III, 386.

as 'the resettlement of alien elements', 'evacuation', 'special treatment', 'cleaning-up operation', 'securing the army's rear', 'executive measure', 'liquidation', 'final solution'.[5] For exterminations in warfare, there is the convenient euphemism of military necessity.

However, the regularities I have described are very tenuous and very limited. They hardly touch on the process of massacre. Robert Payne[6] presents a 'schema of massacre', but it is derived from the genocide in Bangladesh and limited to rather specific conditions. In my book *The Pity of It All*,[7] I traced the process of violent polarization between racial and ethnic groups in Algeria, Rwanda, Burundi and Zanzibar, but this also referred to specific conditions. For the most part, I do not think it is possible to write in general terms about the genocidal process. The only valid approach would be to set up a typology of genocides. Dadrian[8] lists the following forms: (1) cultural; (2) violent-latent (that is, genocide as a by-product of other operations); (3) retributive (either punitive or admonitory); (4) utilitarian (I think this overlaps with others of his categories); and (5) optimal (massive, relatively indiscriminate, sustained and aiming at total obliteration). Using some such typology, one might analyse the genocidal process in each type, and under specified conditions. This is a major task, which I could not undertake. Instead, I am limiting myself to some aspects of the genocidal process in two of the major genocides of our era, the Turkish against the Armenians, and the German against the Jews. They share in common centralized planning and bureaucratic organization.

The Armenian genocide is the 'forgotten genocide' of the twentieth century, remembered mainly by Armenians. Yet it was the precursor of the coldly calculated bureaucratic genocide, and particularly horrifying for the orgy of cruelty by which hundreds of thousands, perhaps as many as 800,000 or more, were done to death in the Ottoman Empire during the First World War. And contemporary indifference is in sharp contrast to the deep international concern at the time.

There had been a long, if intermittent and convoluted, involvement of outside powers in the treatment of Armenians and other Christians

5. For discussions of euphemisms, see Hilberg, 1961:216; Dicks, 1972:58, 89; Kelman, 1973:48; and Poliakov, 1968.
6. Payne, 1973: Ch. 6.
7. Kuper, 1977.
8. Dadrian, 1974–5:100–102.

Genocide

under Turkish rule. The Treaty of Paris (1856), at the conclusion of the Crimean War, had incorporated guarantees for internal reforms in the Ottoman Empire. A generation later, following the Russian–Turkish War, the occupation of many settled Armenian areas by the Russians, and representations by the Armenian Patriarchate for protection of Ottoman Armenians, the Treaty of San Stefano (1878) imposed on the Sublime Porte the obligation 'to carry out, without further delay, the ameliorations and reforms demanded by local requirements in the provinces inhabited by the Armenians, and to guarantee their security against the Kurds and Circassians'. When this treaty was revised by the Treaty of Berlin, the reforms previously guaranteed to Russia alone were guaranteed to the European nations (Great Britain, Austria-Hungary, France, Germany, Italy and Russia), with power to superintend their application.[9]

These provisions proved ineffective. In 1894 there was the massacre of Sassun, an old-style massacre of Armenian men, women and children by regular Turkish units and the irregular *Hamidiye* (Kurdish) cavalry, in reprisal for the refusal to pay a tribute to Kurdish chieftains and for rebellious resistance. Under pressure from European powers following riotous and bloody disturbances attendant on an Armenian demonstration in Constantinople, the Sultan signed a Programme of Reforms, which also proved illusory. 'Even before the promulgation of the reform act of October 1895, massacres had begun in Trebizond. In the following months, the Armenian Plateau met with the same fate. Abdul Hamid's actual response to European meddling was the extirpation of between one and two hundred thousand Armenians during 1895–1896.'[10] And the same writer records the disillusionment as 'once again, the nations of Europe, now involved in the struggle for empire, turned away from the tragedy to which they had contributed'. It was not until some five years after the Adana massacres of 1909 that the European powers finally imposed on the Ottoman government an agreement for reforms, and for procedures to ensure their implementation, which seemed to promise relief. But these were set aside with Turkey's participation in the First World War. And the way was now cleared for the final solution of genocide.

Whether the genocide be traced back to the decree in February 1915 for the disarming of Armenians, or to the first deportations on 8 April,[11]

9. Nalbandian, 1963:27–8.
10. Hovannisian, 1967:28.
11. See Toynbee, 1916:638. Lepsius (1919:10–11) gives the end of March 1915 as

106

the ensuing massacres became almost immediately known to the outside world. Already on 24 May 1915, the Entente nations (Britain, France, Russia) charged the Ottoman government with massacres of Armenians over a wide area, and declared that they would hold all the members of the Turkish government personally responsible as well as those officials who had participated in the massacres.[12] Morgenthau, American Ambassador in Constantinople, reports that in April 1915 he was suddenly deprived of the privilege of using cipher for communicating with American consuls, and that the most rigorous censorship was also applied to letters.

Such measures could mean only that things were happening in Asia Minor which the authorities were determined to conceal. But they did not succeed. Though all sorts of impediments were placed on travelling, certain Americans, chiefly missionaries, succeeded in getting through. For hours they would sit in my office and, with tears streaming down their faces, they would tell me of the horrors through which they had passed. Many of these, both men and women, were almost broken in health from the scenes which they had witnessed. In many cases they brought me letters from American consuls, confirming the most dreadful of their narrations and adding many unprintable details.[13]

Morgenthau made repeated, but unsuccessful, representations to leading members of the Turkish government. Dr Johannes Lepsius, a most nobly dedicated and courageous man, whom Morgenthau describes as a highminded Christian gentleman, representative of German missionary interests, had investigated the earlier massacres of 1895–6 and published his account of them. He now arrived in Constantinople, in July 1915, to carry out further investigations.

Back in Germany, he bore witness to the new waves of massacres, and the following year he published his report, a highly confidential report, since he did not wish to embarrass his government in its relations with its Turkish ally. It seems, however, to have been widely disseminated before the German censors formally prohibited the printing and distribution of further copies.[14] In England, in July 1916, Viscount Bryce submitted to the Secretary of State for Foreign Affairs massive

the date for commencement of the deportations, and December 1914 as the date for the calling in of arms in Zeitun, Cilicia.

12. Hovannisian, op. cit., 51–2.
13. Morgenthau, 1918:327–8.
14. See the preface by Pinon to Lepsius, 1918, and Trumpener, 1968: 227, 240.

documentation of the massacres. These documents, edited by Arnold Toynbee, and consisting largely of eye-witness accounts from neutral witnesses, from consular representatives, missionaries, nurses in the Red Cross, German subjects, and survivors, were published later in the year as a government Blue Paper, with a preface by Viscount Bryce and a historical account by Toynbee. And quite apart from the many diplomatic dispatches, and parliamentary debates, and the wide concern in missionary circles, there was the agitation in the European and American press.

These early documents convey some of the horror of this overwhelming catastrophe. They relate the events with an immediacy, and with an emotional involvement, drained from later, scholarly writings. And in presenting this brief description, I shall rely appreciably on these accounts.

The first step in the genocidal process was the emasculation of the Armenian population. It was initiated by the disarming of the many soldiers serving in the Turkish army, followed by the disarming of the civilian population. Morgenthau describes this process.[15] In the early part of 1915, the Armenian soldiers, mostly combatants, were stripped of their arms and transformed into road labourers, and into pack animals, stumbling under the burden of their loads, and driven by the whips and bayonets of the Turks into the mountains of the Caucasus. They were given only scraps of food; if they fell sick, they were left where they had fallen. In many cases, they were dealt with in even more summary fashion, 'for it now became almost the general practice to shoot them in cold blood'. As for the disarming of the civilians, the Armenians understood what their fate would be, if they were left defenceless. Many surrendered their arms, and this was taken as evidence that a revolution was planned, and the bearers were thrown into prison on charges of treason. The punishment of those suspected of concealing arms, or discovered to be concealing arms, was even more dreadful than the massacres of unarmed soldiers.

Morgenthau writes that most of us believe that torture has long ceased to be an administrative and judicial measure, yet he did not believe that the darkest ages ever presented scenes more horrible than those which now took place all over Turkey. 'Nothing was sacred to the Turkish gendarmes; under the plea of searching for hidden arms, they ransacked churches, treated the altars and sacred utensils with the

15. Morgenthau, op. cit., 302–5.

utmost indignity, and even held mock ceremonies in imitation of the Christian sacraments. They would beat the priests into insensibility, under the pretense that they were the centres of sedition.' (There follow descriptions of atrocities perpetrated.)

The emasculation of the Armenian population was completed by the culling of Armenian leaders. Throughout the country, the government arrested and deported the élite, the educated, the deputies, the publicists, the writers, the poets, the jurists, the advocates, the notaries, the civil servants, the doctors, the merchants, the bankers and generally all those with substantial means and influence. This measure was presumably designed to deprive Armenians of leadership and representation so that the deportations might be completed without public clamour and without resistance.[16] The effect was to leave the Armenian population a defenceless and easy prey for the next stage, that of deportation.

The deportations were countrywide. Smyrna and Aleppo were spared the mass deportations of Armenians, as was Constantinople (in which Lepsius reports some 10,000 deportations). The deportations were carefully timed, moving from one region to another. There was variation in their pattern. Some latitude was allowed local authorities, and there were a few officials who resisted the deportations, but they were mostly removed from office, or rendered ineffective by the activities of the local branches of the ruling party. Toynbee reports[17] that in areas of strategic significance, because of proximity to the advancing Russians, the military authority, with the help of the local Kurds, carried out an extermination of the civilian populations. But there were also exterminations of civilian populations in regions removed from the battlefront. In some areas, the movement of civilians bore more nearly the semblance of a genuine deportation; and the men would be spared. There were areas in which the women might be bullied into conversion to Islam; in others, conversion might be disallowed; or the women might be massacred like the men. And there were differences in the use of torture and in the disposal of Armenian property.[18]

Toynbee describes what was a common pattern of deportation.[19] It would start with a call from the public crier that male Armenians forthwith present themselves at the Government Building. This was the usual procedure, though in some cases the warning was given by the soldiers or gendarmes slaughtering every male Armenian they encoun-

16. Lepsius, 1919:29. 18. ibid., 653.
17. Toynbee, 1916:640. 19. ibid., 640–41.

tered in the streets. When the men arrived, 'they were thrown without explanation into prison, kept there a day or two, and then marched out of the town in batches, roped man to man ... They had not long to ponder over their plight, for they were halted and massacred at the first lonely place on the road ... The women and children were not disposed of by straightforward massacre like the men. Their destiny under the Government scheme was not massacre but slavery or deportation.' Usually after a few days, the women and children, and the remnant of men who, through sickness, infirmity or age, had escaped the general fate of their sex, were ordered to prepare themselves for deportation. For the women, the alternative of conversion to Islam (if available) could only be ratified by immediate marriage to a Muslim, and the surrender of children to be brought up as true Muslims. 'Deportation was the alternative adopted by, or imposed upon, the great majority.'

The former Italian Consul-General at Trebizond gives this agonized account of his suffering as a helpless spectator of the deportation from that town.

It was a real extermination and slaughter of the innocents, an unheard-of thing, a black page stained with the flagrant violation of the most sacred rights of humanity, of Christianity, of nationality. The Armenian Catholics, too, who in the past had always been respected and excepted from the massacres and persecutions, were this time treated worse than any – again by the orders of the Central Government. There were about 14,000 Armenians at Trebizond – Gregorians, Catholics, and Protestants. They had never caused disorders or given occasion for collective measures of police. When I left Trebizond, not a hundred of them remained.

From the 24th June, the date of the publication of the infamous decree, until the 23rd July, the date of my own departure from Trebizond, I no longer slept or ate; I was given over to nerves and nausea, so terrible was the torment of having to look on at the wholesale execution of these defenceless, innocent creatures.

The passing of the gangs of Armenian exiles beneath the windows and before the door of the Consulate; their prayers for help, when neither I nor any other could do anything to answer them; the city in a state of siege, guarded at every point by 15,000 troops in complete war equipment, by thousands of police agents, by bands of volunteers and by the members of the 'Committee of Union and Progress'; the lamentations, the tears, the abandonments, the imprecations, the many suicides, the instantaneous deaths from sheer terror, the sudden unhingeing of men's reason, the conflagrations, the shooting of victims in the city, the ruthless searches through the houses

110

and in the countryside; the hundreds of corpses found every day along the exile road; the young women converted by force to Islam or exiled like the rest; the children torn away from their families or from the Christian schools, and handed over by force to Muslim families, or else placed by hundreds on board ship in nothing but their shirts, and then capsized and drowned in the Black Sea and the River Deyirmen Deré – these are my last ineffaceable memories of Trebizond, memories which still, at a month's distance, torment my soul and almost drive me frantic.[20]

The next stage in the genocide was the journey to the final destination, the dreary, desolate waste of the Syrian desert and the Mesopotamian valley. The convoys of the exiles were little more than death caravans. The long journey on foot inflicted terrible physical sufferings. 'Yet,' Toynbee writes, 'these were the least part of their torture; far worse were the atrocities of violence wantonly inflicted upon them by fellow human beings.' And he describes the mobbing by Muslim peasants with the connivance of the gendarmes assigned to the convoys; the outrages against the women; the massacres of the old men and the boys, and of women too by Kurds and 'chettis' (brigands recruited from the public prisons) and gendarmes.

It depended on the whim of the moment whether a Kurd cut a woman down or carried her away into the hills. When they were carried away their babies were left on the ground or dashed against the stones. But while the convoy dwindled, the remnant had always to march on. The cruelty of the gendarmes towards the victims grew greater as their physical sufferings grew more intense; the gendarmes seemed impatient to make a hasty end of their task. Women who lagged behind were bayoneted on the road, or pushed over precipices, or over bridges. The passage of rivers, and especially of the Euphrates, was always an occasion of wholesale murder ... The lust and covetousness of their tormentors had no limit. The last survivors often staggered into Aleppo naked; every shred of their clothing had been torn from them on the way. Witnesses who saw their arrival remark that there was not one young or pretty face to be seen among them, and there was assuredly none surviving that was truly old ...

As for those who were transported by rail from the metropolitan districts and the railway zone, 'the sum of their suffering can hardly have been less'. They were packed in cattle trucks; they were turned out into the open to wait for days or even weeks for rolling-stock; in breaks in the railway line, they were forced across the mountains on

20. ibid., 291–2.

foot; they died by the thousands of hunger, exposure and epidemics 'in the vast and incredibly foul concentration camps' which grew up along the route. 'The portion of them that finally reached Aleppo were in as deplorable a condition as those that had made the journey on foot from beginning to end.' And they were finally marooned with the other exiles in the worst, and most remote, districts at the disposal of the government, 'with neither food, nor shelter, nor clothing and with no able-bodied men among them to supply these deficiencies by their labour and resource'.[21]

Here in the desolate wastelands, the poor surviving remnant were subjected to the final torment of slow death by exposure and starvation.[22] The deportations were merely a cloak for genocide. How can one question Morgenthau's conclusion that if the Turks had undertaken such a deportation in good faith, it would have represented the height of cruelty and injustice, but that in fact they never had the slightest intention of re-establishing the Armenians in this new country. And Morgenthau adds that they knew that the great majority would never reach their destination, and that those who did would either die of thirst and starvation, or be murdered by 'the wild Mohammedan desert tribes'. The deportations really represented a new method of massacre. 'When the Turkish authorities gave the orders for these deportations, they were merely giving the death warrant to a whole race; they understood this well, and in their conversations with me, they made no particular attempt to conceal the fact.'[23]

The concern of the Great Powers seemed more sincere, and the commitment to the Armenian cause more serious, than in the past. The Treaty of Sèvres (August 1920) provided for the recognition of Armenia as a free and independent state. It imposed on Turkey the obligation to ensure equality of treatment for racial, religious or linguistic minorities, and to facilitate to the greatest extent possible the return to their homes, and the re-establishment in their businesses, of the Turkish subjects of non-Turkish race, who had been forcibly driven out after January 1914 by fear of massacre or other pressure. There were Turkish trials of some of those involved in the massacres and the Ittihadist triumvirate of the First World War were put on trial and sentenced to death *in*

21. ibid., 642–5.
22. See, for example, the report by an American eye-witness, quoted in Lepsius, 1919.
23. Morgenthau, op. cit., 308–9.

absentia.[24] Carzou, in *Un Génocide exemplaire: Arménie 1915*, reprints the judgments of the courts relating to murder and massacre in three areas, and these are entirely consistent with the eye-witness accounts.[25]

But this is where the retribution and restitution ended. The trials were of little significance save as confirmation of observers' accounts. And as to the provisions of the Treaty of Sèvres, they were swept aside in the predatory rivalries of the victors, in their unwillingness to assume a mandate over Turkish Armenia, in the Turkish–Armenian war, in the aftermath of the Russian revolution, in the Turkish–Soviet Treaty of Friendship and the Turkish–Greek war, in further massacres of Armenians, in the growth of Turkish nationalism and the resurgence of its military power. In the result, the Treaty of Lausanne in July 1923 makes provision for the rights of minorities to equality of treatment, but for the rest, it ignores the earlier commitments to the Armenians.

Thus ends the Armenian presence in Turkey, reduced from a population of perhaps 1,800,000 to some 32,500 at the present time.

Genocide is pre-eminently a government crime and governments can hardly be expected to plead guilty. The German case is unusual, with its radical change of government, and its acceptance of responsibility for genocide in a massive and continuing programme of reparations. The more usual, perhaps invariable response, particularly if the same government continues in power, is to deny responsibility, first on the ground that there was in fact no genocide, and second by the contention that the victims were themselves the guilty parties and responsible for the loss of life they sustained.

The denial of genocide in the Armenian case includes in part a battle of statistics, based on Turkish estimates of the Armenian population at the time as not more than 1,300,000, thereby greatly reducing the number of those who perished. This is in contrast to the estimate of the American Committee for Armenian and Syrian Relief of a pre-war Armenian population of 1,800,000, or the estimate of Arlen, who wrote in his recent review of the genocide[26] that 'it is possible to say, not precisely but with a general respect for accuracy and plausibility, that in the course of the 1915–1916 massacres and deportations close to one million Armenians – more than half the Armenian population of Turkey – disappeared; which is to say, were killed outright by police or soldiers,

24. Hovannisian, 1971:419–20.
25. Carzou, 1975:233–46.
26. Arlen, 1975:240.

or by roadside massacres, or by forced marches, or by starvation, or by sickness, or by conditions in the concentration camps'. Hovannisian, in an early work,[27] had given an estimate of between 1,500,000 and 2,000,000 Armenians in Turkey at the time of the massacres. But he told me, in a recent discussion, that he thought the population numbers were understated, and that an estimate of over 2,000,000 Armenians was by no means an exaggeration, with 1,000,000 or more victims in the course of, and in the immediate aftermath of, the massacres and deportations.

But the magnitude of the crime of genocide is hardly reduced if the number of victims is, say, 200,000. The statistical argument must therefore be complemented by such assertions as that the deaths were the result 'not only of the transportation but also of the same conditions of famine, disease, and war action that carried away some 2 million Muslims at the same time', and that the army had been given orders to care for the protection and needs of the Armenians during their march and in their new war-time settlements.[28]

As for the second theme, that of the victims as their own executioners, there is the attempted justification that the deportations were a war-time measure, rendered necessary, so the argument runs, by the disloyalty of the Armenians, who were accused of supporting the country's enemies.[29] Now the Armenians were divided between Russian and Turkish territory and Russian Armenians served in the Russian army as Turkish Armenians served in the Turkish. There were also volunteer Armenian units assisting the Russians, the English and the French, and there would seem to be no doubt of the sympathies of the Turkish Armenians for the European Powers to whom they had turned in the past for protection against Turkish rule. But there is substantial evidence, advanced by both Toynbee and Lepsius, against the thesis of Turkish–Armenian disloyalty. And even if this had been true, it would have been argument for the disarming of Armenian soldiers and their conversion into labour battalions, or their internment with other able-bodied Armenians, but no argument for massacres of the men, nor for deportation of the women and children, the aged and infirm, by long and incredibly arduous forced marches, nor for the choice of desolate

27. Hovannisian, 1967:34–7.
28. Shaw and Shaw, 1977: Vol. II, 315–16.
29. An extreme version of the Turkish case will be found in Shaw and Shaw, op. cit., Vol. II. See also the critique of this version by Hovannisian, August 1978, and the Shaws' response, August 1978.

wastes as the destination of the survivors of the death caravans. The whole plan of the deportations, and the testimony of eye-witnesses, are overwhelming evidence of an exterminatory intention to so reduce the Turkish–Armenian population as to dispose of the Armenian Question once and for all. There is as little credibility in this line of Turkish defence as in the defence of the Burundi government that in its slaughter of Hutu (variously estimated as between 100,000 and 200,000), it was punishing, though admittedly with some understandable excesses, only those guilty of massacres and planned genocide against the Tutsi.[30]

The twentieth century is sometimes viewed as initiating a new process in genocide. Toynbee writes[31] that its distinguishing marks 'are that it is committed in cold-blood by the deliberate *fiat* of holders of despotic political power, and that the perpetrators of genocide employ all the resources of present-day technology and organization to make their planned massacres systematic and complete'. He describes the massacres at the instigation of the Sultan Abdul-Hamid II at the end of the nineteenth century as amateurish and ineffective compared with the largely successful attempt to exterminate the Ottoman Armenians during the First World War, and the latter in turn as less effective than the German genocide of the European Jews, 'since the general level of technological and organizational efficiency in Germany during the dozen years of the Nazi regime was considerably higher than it had been in Turkey during the ten years of the C.U.P. regime'. Arlen writes[32] to similar effect that the entire production of the Armenian genocide (of 1915) was based on the imperfectly utilized but definitely perceived capacities of the modern state for politically restructuring itself, which were made possible by the engines of technology. In due course, 'Hitler's Germany was to perfect the process of railway deportation and to develop the gas chamber and the crematoria, and Lenin's and Stalin's Russia was to evolve further the institutions of the concentration camp and secret surveillance ... But in virtually every modern instance of mass murder, beginning, it appears, with the Armenians, the key element – ... which has raised the numerical and psychic levels of the deed above the classic terms of massacre – has been the alliance of technology and communications.'

The Sultan Abdul-Hamid's massacres do not appear to have been all that amateurish and ineffective. They had limited objectives, being

30. See Kuper, 1977: Ch. V.
31. Toynbee, 1969:241–2.
32. Arlen, op. cit., 243–4.

designed as a sort of ambassadorial note to the European powers to refrain from intervention in the domestic affairs of Turkey, and a most bloody warning to the Armenians themselves against seeking the intercession of these powers on their behalf or aspiring to autonomy. They also took a somewhat different form from the later genocide in the sense that they were perpetrated on the spot without resort to such devices as the death caravans of the deportation. Lepsius, in *Armenia and Europe*, in which he reports his investigations in 1896, describes how massacres were announced by a bugle call or other signal and called off at an appointed time (though there was variability in this), and he shows the concentrated nature of the massacres, particularly evident in the tabular statement of occurrences in Asia Minor in 1895, prepared by the Committee of Delegates from the six embassies, and included by Lepsius in an appendix.[33] But whether or not the Sultan's massacres were relatively ineffective, and however much they differed in the immediacy and concentrated nature of their occurrence, they employed many of the same elements as the 1915 genocide, serving somewhat as a pilot project for the later genocide. The organizational base was found in the provincial and local administration, with its officials, its military and its police.

There was similar use made of social forces, generated from the plural structure of the society, and hostile to the Armenians, so that the slaughter had some appearance of spontaneous action by mobs of Turkish peasants and townsmen, and by plundering and massacring bands of Kurds and Circassians. Religious hatreds played their part, with terrible atrocities against priests, the desecration and destruction of churches, and forced conversions. Even the actions of the European nations described by Lepsius as 'a fine piece of moral scene-painting behind which political intrigue wished to hide',[34] resemble the later abandonment of the Armenians to the disastrous consequences of Great Power involvement in their affairs.

The extreme vulnerability of the Armenian minority, and its selection as a target for genocide by the Turkish rulers as they became involved in the cataclysmic conflicts of the First World War, rested on the superimposition of differences in structure and culture, and of issues of conflict with considerable historical depth. The system of administration had served to maintain, perhaps even to enhance, the ethnic and cultural

33. See Lepsius, 1897:280–331. A summary by Lepsius of his analysis of the organization and course of the massacres is given in ibid., 58–61 and 76–85.
34. ibid., 92.

distinctiveness of the Armenians. The *millet* was a unit of Turkish administration for the more effective control of subject populations. It conferred, on the basis of religious affiliation, appreciable autonomy in spiritual matters, in the maintenance of religious seminaries and, later, of other schools, and in the exercise of certain limited judicial functions. The effect in the case of the Armenian subjects of the Ottoman Empire was a convergence of political, ethnic, religious and cultural differentiation, too deep-rooted to be effaced by such reforms as were introduced.

To these differences must be added occupational differentiation. It is quite often referred to in the literature, sometimes in the pejorative characterization of Armenians as a 'mercantile race', whatever this may mean. It is the same characterization as is applied to Jews, or to Chinese in South-east Asia, or to Indians in East Africa, or to Lebanese in West Africa, and seems to be used as a justification for murder, as if this quality in the victim transmuted massacre to justifiable homicide. In the case of the Armenians, it is true that they were active in commerce, a not unusual reaction where subjects are largely denied advancement to positions of leadership in government and warfare. Lepsius writes[35] that the Armenians controlled 60 per cent of imports, 40 per cent of exports, and at least 80 per cent of the commerce in the interior. But some 80 per cent were peasants, and the remainder were not only merchants, but members of the liberal professions and artisans, to the extent that the American Consul at Aleppo reported[36] that in the areas evacuated there was no longer, with some exceptions, a single mason, smith, carpenter, potter, tentmaker, weaver, shoemaker, jeweller, pharmacist, doctor, advocate, not a single person belonging to the liberal professions or engaged in some craft. Yet there was sufficient involvement of Armenians in commerce for this to serve as a source of grievance and as an issue for manipulation.

The administrative framework for the mosaic of peoples who composed the Turkish Empire also served to maintain the distinctiveness of other groups. In the eastern provinces, nomadic Kurdish tribesmen maintained a state of feud with the settled Armenian communities which they periodically ransacked.[37] Abdul-Hamid had used the Kurds as an irregular force of cavalry against the Armenians in the 1895–6 massacres. In the turbulent history of these areas, there had been many

35. Lepsius, 1918 : 328, 277–9.
36. ibid., 280.
37. Arlen, op. cit., 172.

forced movements of population, following the vicissitudes of war, and these had left their bitter residue of antagonistic memories. Of special significance were the many Muslim refugees from previous upheavals (the Shaws cite a figure of over 1,000,000 for the period 1878–97[38]), and more immediately from the Balkan wars and the new Christian regimes of Bulgaria, Serbia and Greece. All these divisions offered a base for the mobilization of social forces murderously hostile to the Armenians.

The divisions and conflicts between subject groups operated within the wider context of the overriding conflicts in Turkish–Armenian relations. It is difficult to estimate the power of the major cleavage of religion. There were areas, as we have seen, in which the Muslim inhabitants or the officials were quite opposed to the deportations, and the Turkish leaders of the Committee of Union and Progress were not themselves religious fanatics. But nevertheless, their declaration that the country was engaged in a holy war in the defence of Islam was deliberately designed to inflame religious passion; and the participation of the Turks themselves in the deportations and the pillage and the massacres, the desecration of churches, the atrocities against priests, the forced conversions, all point to the persistence of ancient religious hatreds. The long history of the intervention of foreign nations on behalf of the Christian subjects of the Ottoman Empire arose out of, and was superimposed on, this fundamental religious cleavage. But this concern of the outside powers was anything but purely benevolent. It was associated with, and no doubt appreciably motivated by, predatory interests in the dismemberment of the Turkish Empire, already far advanced. Engaged in a highly destructive conflict, initiated by disastrous campaigns, the Turkish rulers were now driven from the high hopes with which they had entered the war, to the desperate defence of their borders and dissolving empire. Under these circumstances, anxiety lest the Armenians revolt became the conviction that they were disloyal, and warrant for their genocide.

The provincial and local administrations provided, as we have seen, the organizational base for the genocide. The presence of local branches of the Committee of Union and Progress, the 'many-headed hydra' of the Young Turk Clubs, greatly enhanced the effectiveness of this administrative structure. These branches became the catalysts of genocide, exerting pressure where necessary on reluctant officials, inflaming the hatreds of the populace with tales of Armenian treachery and atrocity,

38. Shaw and Shaw, op. cit., Vol. II, 238–9.

and in general activating the genocidal process. There was some variability by reason of the dependence on local initiative and the variation in such conditions as proximity to the Russian front; and there was some appearance of spontaneity, given a great reliance on the action of mobs and predatory bands. But the country-wide distribution of the destruction of Armenian communities, the timing, the general pattern were the product of a central administrative plan. It proceeded, however, appreciably by indirection, that is to say not by massacres from the centre, but by setting in motion the genocidal process, as a low-cost operation with extensive reliance on local social forces.

Chapter 7

Genocidal Process
The German Genocide Against Jews

And I looked, and behold a pale horse: and his name that sat on him was
Death, and Hell followed with him. And Power was given unto them over
the fourth part of the earth, to kill with sword, and with hunger, and with
death, and with the beasts of the earth.

[*Revelation* 6:8, quoted as frontispiece in *The Holocaust Kingdom* by
Alexander Donat]

Doctor in Killing Centre: 'We are the Dominicans of the technological age.'

[From *The Deputy* by Rolf Hochhuth]

All genocide overwhelms with horror and despair at the human suffering so mercilessly inflicted. Yet in the German genocide against
Jews, many unique elements add to this feeling of overwhelming
horror and despair.

There was the enormous scope of the genocide. Pogroms had
become an integral part of Jewish life in many Christian countries.
Even genocide was not unprecedented, as in the Ukrainian genocide
against Jews at the end of the First World War. But the German
genocide was worldwide in ultimate intention. It was directed not
only against Jews in Germany and throughout Europe, but Nazi
doctrine was exported to, or imported by, countries in other continents.
Though spearheaded by an anti-Christian Nazi movement, the genocide was deeply rooted in Christian anti-semitism, which ensured the
active participation of other European peoples in the European genocides, though with most notable and courageous exceptions, and a
complicity or indifference in the outside world, so that death seemed
to guard all exits.

Then there was the extreme bureaucratic organization of the genocide. This was one of its most dehumanized aspects. We know all too
well the passionate outbursts by murderous mobs under incitement of
their leaders. These fall well within the expected range of human
behaviour. But to use bureaucratic planning and procedures and regulation for a massive operation of systematic murder throughout a whole
continent speaks of an almost inconceivably profound dehumanization.

Who would have believed that human beings would send out mobile killing units for the slaughter of unarmed men, women and children in distant lands? Or that they were capable of organizing, on the model of a modern industrial plant, killing centres which processed their victims for slaughter, as if on a conveyor belt; eliminated waste, gathered in, with careful inventory, their few possessions, their clothes, gold teeth, women's hair, and regulated the distribution of these relics? Or that the killing centres might be combined with slave camps, in which the exploitation of labour was carried to the extreme of rapid expendability, or that such leading German firms as I. G. Farben and Krupp would establish branches in the vicinity of the gas chambers and crematoria?

Yet all this was done, with coordination between the bureaucracies of the state, of the Nazi party, of the military and big business. The civil service infused the other hierarchies with its sure-footed planning and bureaucratic thoroughness. From the army the machinery of destruction acquired its military precision, discipline, and callousness. Industry's influence was felt in the great emphasis upon accounting, penny-saving, and salvage, as well as in the factory-like efficiency of the killing centres. Finally, the party contributed to the entire apparatus an 'idealism', a sense of 'mission', and a notion of 'history-making'.[1]

There was a great proliferation of bureaucratic organization, as new sections and sub-divisions mushroomed for the discharge of special functions, and in the course of its development, the machinery of destruction drew in every segment of organized German society, including organized Jewish society. It was indeed the organized society in one of its special roles.[2] Though engaged in mass murder on a gigantic scale, this vast bureaucratic apparatus showed concern for correct bureaucratic procedure, for the niceties of precise definition, for the minutiae of bureaucratic regulation, and for compliance with the law. The law was, of course, no obstacle, but an instrument of policy; it was promulgated as needed, and judges obligingly assisted in its re-interpretation, by such decisions, relating to employment, for example, as that the racial characteristics of Jews amounted to sickness and death, or that Jews had 'no inner tie' to the performance of labour, so that the ordinary rules would not be applicable, or by a decision

1. Hilberg, 1961:39.
2. ibid., 178, 640. Hilberg's *The Destruction of the European Jews* is the major study of the bureaucratic organization and genocidal process in the annihilation of the Jews in Europe.

relating to unauthorized killing, which was to be punished as murder
or manslaughter if selfish, sadistic or sexual motives were found, but
which did not call for punishment if purely political motives prompted
the killing, if the act was an expression of idealism, unless the maintenance of order required disciplinary action or prosecution.[3]

In what I suppose was conformity with bureaucratic norms, there
was the attempt to control spontaneous killings. It is true that the
mobile killer squads had incited pogroms by the local populations in
Lithuania, Latvia and Galicia, but this was not the accepted pattern.
They detracted from the systematic efficiency of planned annihilation.
It seems too that they may have offended, at any rate at times, against
a sense of the proprieties and human decencies in mass killing. Hannah
Arendt reports[4] that in Romania even the Nazi S.S. (*Schutzstaffeln* –
Security Services) were taken aback, and occasionally frightened, by
the horrors of old-fashioned spontaneous pogroms on a gigantic scale;
they often intervened to save Jews from sheer butchery, so that the
killing could be done in what, according to them, was a civilized way.

Spontaneous action posed a problem also in the German army on
the eastern front, when soldiers were attracted by the operations of
the mobile killing units, and it became necessary for discipline and
morale and overall efficiency to attempt some control over unauthorized killings. The 'ideal' seems to have been that of the dispassionate,
efficient killer, engaged in systematic slaughter, in the service of a
higher cause. It was this 'ideal' that the chief of the S.S. and police
expressed in an address to his top commanders in October 1943.

Most of you know what it means when 100 corpses lie there, or when
500 corpses lie there, or when 1,000 corpses lie there. To have gone through
this and – apart from a few exceptions caused by human weakness – to
have remained decent, that has made us great. That is a page of glory in our
history which has never been written and which is never to be written …[5]

German bureaucratic norms of procedure, industrial norms of efficiency,
Prussian military norms of honour and discipline had converged with
Nazi ideology in an ultimate dehumanization.[6]

3. ibid., 59, 99, 648.
4. Arendt, 1969:190.
5. Quoted in Hilberg, op. cit., 648.
6. There was a carry-over of the dehumanized bureaucratic norm in the trial
of Eichmann for his participation in the holocaust when his Counsel referred to
'killing by gas and similar medical matters' and when questioned, repeated that
'it was a matter of killing, and killing, too, is a medical matter' (Arendt, op. cit.,
69).

The reality of this dehumanization was the antithesis of the dispassionate killer. It found expression in the most sadistic cruelty – in the brutality of the deportations, the running amok in the ghettoes of Poland, the stripping of social identity in the death camps to a number and an object, the gratuitous torments, the terror, humiliation, degradation and torture designed to destroy in the spirit before annihilating in the flesh. The absolute power of the killers, and the total vulnerability of the victims, encouraged the commission of every conceivable atrocity. Steiner sees in the death camps the realization of 'the millenary pornography of fear and vengeance cultivated in the Western mind by Christian doctrines of damnation'. He describes them as a complete, coherent world.

They had their own measure of time, which is pain. The unbearable was parcelled out with pedantic nicety. The obscenities and abjections practiced in them were accompanied by prescribed rituals of derision and false promise. There were regulated gradations of horror within the total, concentric sphere. *L'univers concentrationnaire* has no true counterpart in the secular mode. Its analogue is Hell. The camp embodies, often down to minutiae, the images and chronicles of Hell in European art and thought from the twelfth to the eighteenth centuries ... It is in the fantasies of the infernal, as they literally haunt Western sensibility, that we find the technology of pain without meaning, of bestiality without end, of gratuitous terror. For six hundred years the imagination dwelt on the flaying, the racking, the mockery of the damned, in a place of whips and hell-hounds, of ovens and stinking air.[7]

And the testimony of survivors bears witness to the infernal horror of the death camps, as in this account, quoted by Des Pres in his study of *The Survivor*:

The burning had reached a pitch that night. Every chimney was disgorging flames. Smoke burst from the holes and ditches, swirling, swaying and coiling above our heads. Sparks and cinders blinded us. Through the screened fence of the second crematory we could see figures with pitchforks moving against the background of flames. They were men from the special squad turning the corpses in the pits and pouring a special liquid so that they would burn better. A rancid smell of scorched flesh choked us. Big trucks passed us trailing a smell of corpses.[8]

And Des Pres comments that this was 'Auschwitz in the fall of 1944,

7. Steiner, 1971:55.
8. Des Pres, 1976:172–3.

when the Jews of Hungary were being killed so fast and in such numbers that the usual gas-to-oven process had to be supplemented by pits in which the victims burned alive'.

The Jewish dead are estimated at about 6 million out of a total population of 8.3 million who remained in German-occupied Europe after 1939.[9] Other groups also suffered genocidal massacres on a vast scale. Perhaps as many as 16,000,000 Poles and Russians were slaughtered in captivity, or killed by starvation and exposure in the concentration and labour camps; and Gypsies were freely massacred. But the genocide against Jews was pursued with a relentless determination and persistence. The German definition of Jews in terms of ancestry excluded the possibility of escape through conversion, as had been sometimes possible in Turkey; and death was visited on all, men, women and children, by reason of birth and, with some exceptions, regardless of religion. There was no conception of the saving of Jewish souls, as in the burning of Jews during the Inquisition. There were no military objectives to be gained, no land to be conquered for German colonization, though the evacuation of areas for German settlement in Poland was certainly a consideration. Initially persecution of the Jews had brought political gains in the support of an appealing doctrine, and material gains in the expropriation of Jewish possessions, but in the course of the destruction process, genocide became an overriding end in itself, to which economic priorities were sacrificed (as in the slaughter of Jewish workers), and even military priorities (as in the clogging of lines of retreat for the defeated German armies by the deportations from Hungary in 1944). And the annihilation of Jews continued to the very last, when the war was clearly lost, in the frenzied slaughter of Hungarian Jews, and the deportations from Italy, Greece and Slovakia, and the last-minute death marches. The genocide of Jews was a most complete realization of the annihilation of a people *as such*.

Looking back at the course of the genocide, there is such a logical and systematic progression of stages that it gives the impression of having been planned from the beginning. But the order for the *Final Solution* (annihilation) of European Jewry was only given in about July 1941: the initial policy was to bring about a vast emigration of Jewry. Yet the many preliminary steps since 1933 seemed to point to-

9. See Manvell and Fraenkel, 1967:4–5. Hilberg, op. cit., 767, gives a lower estimate of 5,100,000 Jewish dead.

wards the ultimate holocaust. Hilberg argues[10] that the administrative continuity of the destruction process throughout the period of emigration and of annihilation is to be found in the fact that the introductory steps of definition, expropriation and concentration served not only as inducements to emigration but also as stepping stones to annihilation.

Presumably where the victims are not physically identifiable, as was the case with the German Jews, they have to be legislatively or administratively defined and identified. This was a matter of some complexity, given the numbers of converted Jews, of mixed marriages, and of children to these marriages, the so-called *Mischlinge*. There was much bureaucratic wrangling between the Nazi party working to combat the part-Jew as a carrier of the 'Jewish influence', and the civil service seeking to protect in the part-Jew 'that part which is German'.[11] Jews were finally defined in terms of ancestry as persons with three or four Jewish grandparents, or as persons with two Jewish grandparents, if they belonged to the Jewish religion or were married to a Jewish person on 15 September 1935. Two degrees of *Mischlinge* were established. *Mischlinge*, particularly those of the second degree, with one Jewish grandparent, and the Jewish partners in mixed marriages, continued to pose an obstacle to the *Final Solution*, and they mostly survived the holocaust.[12]

The process of defining Jews was completed at a later date by a system of identification. This provided for personal documents in the form of identification cards, passports stamped with the letter *J*, ration cards marked with *J*, or obliquely with the word *Jude*. It included the assignment of Jewish middle names (Israel for men, Sara for women), save where the first name was an approved Jewish name; and it extended to the conspicuous marking of persons and apartments with the Star of David. Identification proved a powerful instrument of police control, and it paralysed the victims with the oppressive feeling of being continuously under public surveillance.[13]

10. Hilberg, op. cit., 32.
11. ibid., 47.
12. In 1939, there were in the Old Reich, Austria and the Sudeten area 64,000 *Mischlinge* of the first degree, and 43,000 of the second degree, while the total number of intermarriages in the Reich, Austria and the Protectorate of Bohemia and Moravia at the end of 1942 was 27,774 (Hilberg, op. cit., 268, 275). For general discussion of definition, of *Mischlinge* and intermarriage, see Hilberg, op. cit., 43–53, 268–77, and Reitlinger, 1961:186–92.
13. Hilberg, op. cit., 118–21.

The expropriation extended ultimately, as we have seen, to the most wretched possessions of the victims. It was characteristically systematic. Its bureaucratic organization cut across the four major hierarchies of the civil service, the business sector, the military and the Nazi party, with the civil service and the business sector in the forefront. Its targets were the Jewish professions, enterprises, financial reserves, wages, claims upon food and shelter, and finally the last personal belongings, down to underwear, gold teeth and women's hair.[14] Jews were dismissed from the civil service; they were forced out of responsible positions in industry and commerce; 'Aryan' descent became a pre-requisite for active service in the armed forces. Artistic and intellectual creativity came under attack with the ejection of Jewish musicians, artists and writers, with the burning of books, with the driving out from the universities, and with the closing down of legal and medical practices. A process of 'Aryanization' conveyed Jewish business enterprises at low cost to German buyers. Liquidation and compulsory transfer followed on a decree defining Jewish enterprise. Such property as remained was depleted by special taxes, and finally quite simply seized by the state. Impoverished, subjected to forced labour, Jewish workers were assigned a special status, ensuring the minimum of wages for the maximum of work, and industry availed itself of this opportunity for the extreme exploitation of Jewish workers, as it did later in the rapid devouring of labour from the death camps. Discrimination in food rationing, which extended to children and nursing mothers, threatened the surviving Jews with starvation: they would have been annihilated in any event even in the absence of killing centres.

Perfected by the bureaucracies and fuelled by human greed, the process of expropriation extended even into the death camps. Its ultimate expression is in the extraction of economic utility from corpses, and in the passage of an ordinance for the confiscation of the property of Jews 'who take up residence abroad', passed at a time when the deportations were launched in pursuance of the *Final Solution*. Legal validation of the legitimacy of the acquisition of property by murder!

The process of concentration took two forms – social isolation (or exclusion from community) and physical isolation and concentration. Even before the passage of the major Nuremberg laws, Jews were the target of so much vilification and concentrated hate that they were

14. ibid., 54.

already socially isolated. Towns were plastered with abusive slogans. Great hordes of Nazi rabble, the brown-shirted Storm Detachments, roamed the streets, abusing, tormenting and torturing Jews under the benevolent eyes of the police; and in 1933, there had been the widespread and violent boycotting of Jewish firms, and of Jewish doctors and lawyers. The result was the creation, as Rabbi Joachim Prinz of Berlin described it in a speech in April 1935, of a ghetto of a different type from those of the Middle Ages, a ghetto without geographical boundaries.

The ghetto is the 'world'. Outside is the ghetto. On the marketplace, in the street, in the public tavern, everywhere is ghetto. And it has a sign. That sign is: neighbourless. Perhaps this has never before happened in the world, and no one knows how long it can be borne; life without a neighbour. Everywhere life depends upon the 'neighbour' ... That we have lost. The Jews of the big cities do not notice it so keenly, but the Jews of the small towns, those who dwell on the marketplace without a neighbour, whose children go to school each morning with no neighbours' children, it is they who feel the isolation that neighbourlessness means, a fate crueller than any other, and perhaps the fiercest that can be suffered in the social life of man ...[15]

The laws and regulations, the bureaucratic procedures, systematically completed this process. In September 1935, there was a law to exclude Jews from citizenship. Laws were promulgated at the same time 'For the Protection of German Blood and German Honour', forbidding marriage, or relations outside of marriage, between Jews and nationals of German or kindred blood. An earlier law against overcrowding of German schools culminated in total exclusion from these schools. There were restrictions on movement and on access to public amenities and social services, to which must be added the expropriation of businesses, the expulsion from professions, the dismissals from employment, and the devices for identification, rendering visible, by rituals of degradation, the newly established pariah status. And a national Jewish organization, designed to enter into debate on anti-semitism, became a further instrument of social isolation.[16]

Physical concentration was effected by increasing segregation in Jewish houses, and later by deportations to ghettoes and concentration camps in the last stages of the movement to the killing centres. In 1933 when the Nazis came into power, there had been half a million Jews

15. *The Yellow Spot*, 1936:175.
16. Generally, on the process of concentration, see Hilberg, op. cit., 106–25.

in Germany. By 1939, their numbers had fallen to about 210,000, for the most part as a result of forced emigration, but also through violence, as in the organized pogroms of 1938 and in random murder.[17] Of these, perhaps 40,000 survived the holocaust.

The mass murders in the different countries of Europe took a quite varied course, closely related to the nature of German domination – whether absorption into the Greater Reich (Austria, Bohemia, Moravia), incorporation (part of Poland, Luxembourg), occupation (the special regime of the Government General in other areas of Poland, and different forms of occupation in Norway, Denmark, Holland, Belgium, France, Serbia, Greece), 'satellites par excellence' (Croatia, Slovakia), 'opportunistic satellites'[18] (Bulgaria, Romania, Hungary), or ally (Italy until 1943). The significance of German power in determining the course and magnitude of the genocides in different countries is to be seen in the changing fate of Jewish communities when Germany occupied Italy in 1943 and Hungary in 1944, or in the greater vulnerability of Jews in those countries of Western Europe such as Holland in which German control was at its maximum.

But the extent of German domination was by no means decisive. Also significant were the reactions of the local populations themselves and of their rulers – whether they resisted or cooperated, and whether there were quisling governments ready to carry out the genocidal policies. The Danes were quite remarkable in their total and militant non-cooperation. To be sure, Denmark was accorded an unusual measure of autonomy under German occupation. But when the Danish army dissolved and the Danish government resigned, and when the Germans proclaimed martial law and started the deportations to the killing centres, the Danes succeeded, with great courage and personal sacrifice, in ferrying most of the Jews to the promised sanctuary in Sweden.

In Bulgaria, the government had passed discriminatory laws along the lines of the Nuremberg laws, and seemed to be moving towards the death-dealing deportations. Indeed, in the occupied territories of Macedonia and Thrace, the Bulgarians deported 11,343 Jews. How-

17. The figures for losses after 1939 are taken from estimates quoted by Manvell and Fraenkel, op. cit., 4. The authors comment that the figures they have used are those which give the 'gravest assessment' of the losses. Hilberg, op. cit., 670, estimates the Jewish population in Germany in 1939 as 240,000 and the survivors as 80,000 (this figure including 60,000 displaced persons).

18. Descriptions used by Hilberg, op. cit.

ever, there were significant differences in the discriminatory laws, as in the exemptions for converted Jews, and the anti-Jewish policies were pursued in an evasive and procrastinating way. They stopped short of deportation, and were revoked in August 1944 on the eve of the Russian invasion of Bulgaria. The Italians also passed many discriminatory laws, and persecuted Jews, but at a slow pace and with a large section exempt. They too resisted the deportations, protecting their own Jewish population and providing sanctuary in the areas under their control. It was only when the Italians declared war on Germany, and the Germans occupied Italy, that a portion of the Jewish community in Rome and many Jews in Northern Italy were deported. In Holland, there was courageous resistance, with strikes against the first deportation of Jews to concentration camps in Germany. But a number of circumstances combined to bring about a large-scale annihilation of Dutch Jews. The Germans were in total command, they were assisted by a strong Nazi movement in Holland, and they made skilful and deadly use of the Jewish Council.

At the other extreme, 'races' ranked low by the Nazis in their 'racial' hierarchy joined most freely in the massacres. It was from these groups (Ukrainians, Estonians, Latvians, Lithuanians) that the Germans recruited large numbers of auxiliaries to serve in the police and man the killing operations. The satellite government in Croatia rapidly passed a series of Nuremberg laws, and agreed to pay the Germans 30 reichmarks for each Jew deported to the German killing centres, a small outlay for the profits of expropriation. The Slovakian satellite passed the preparatory laws and participated in the deportations, but in a vacillating way and under pressure from the German government. The end result, however, was the large-scale annihilation of Jews in Slovakia. The Romanians, also low in the Nazi hierarchy of peoples, anticipated the Germans as they embarked precipitately, and with a terrible ferocity, on genocide by means of mob pogroms, army massacres, starvation and suffocation in railway trucks, and murder in their own killing centres. But later, after hundreds of thousands of Jews had been killed, Romania changed course, seeking ransom for its Jewish population. At the outbreak of the Second World War, Romania had the third largest Jewish population in Europe, some 800,000, of whom about 400,000 were killed.

The churches could be an influential factor in the reactions of the local population. They might seek to protect converted Jews. Thus the Metropolitan Stephan of Sofia was particularly outspoken on this issue. On 27 September 1942, he delivered 'a sermon pointing out that God had already punished the Jews "for having nailed Christ to the cross" by driving them from place to place and allowing them no country of their own. God had thereby determined the Jewish fate, and men had no right to torture the Jews and to persecute them. This applied especially to Jews who had accepted Christianity. The metropolitan had then succeeded in freeing all baptized Jews from wearing the star. Prime Minister Filov on his own had liberated the Jews in mixed marriages; thereupon, on September 30, Justice Minister Partov demanded that the wearing of the star should not be obligatory and that all expulsions should be halted.' And the Bulgarian government then halted star production by cutting off the electricity supply from the plant producing the badges.[19] In the Catholic Church, by contrast, the Vatican was notable for its cautious diplomacy in registering protests against genocide, and at times for its remarkable reticence, as in the Pope's failure to denounce the deportations in Rome itself.[20]

The structure of the Jewish communities in the different countries also had a bearing on the course of the genocide. These communities varied greatly in numbers, in the vigour of Jewish cultural and religious life, in the degree of assimilation and the extent of intermarriage, and in their economic role and relationship with ruling strata. Effective communal organization, which would seem to offer some defence, often became an instrument of destruction in the hands of the Germans. Indeed, a key step in the destruction process was the formation of a Jewish Council. The presence of immigrant Jews was used as a step in the destruction process, since the host country and the Jewish Council might more readily accept the deportation of foreign Jews, and this initial step might be expected to encourage a hesitant government's later acceptance of the deportation of its own Jewish nationals.

The course of the military campaigns was a crucial factor in the genocide. On the whole, in the West, the German armies did not take part in the killings, though in Serbia the army massacred Jewish men, the women and children being handed over for murder to the mobile killing squads. But leaving aside the question of the direct participation of the army, German military occupation signalled the doom of

19. Hilberg, op. cit., 481.
20. The play by Rolf Hochhuth, *The Deputy*, is devoted to this theme. The issue is controversial. See also Fein, 1979: Ch. IV; and Manvell and Fraenkel, op. cit., Ch. VI.

Jewish communities, as in Italy and Hungary. In the East the German armies became actively involved in the genocide when the Germans invaded the U.S.S.R. Eastern Europe was the most populous area of Jewish settlement, with over three and a quarter million Jews in Poland, and between two and a half and three million in the U.S.S.R., Lithuania, Latvia and Estonia. Here Jews were massacred by the millions, perhaps as many as three million in Poland, and half a million to a million in the U.S.S.R.

Anti-semitism in Poland was already extreme, and the persecution of Jews, including pogroms, already far advanced, when the Germans invaded Poland in September 1939. The Poles themselves had prepared the ground for genocide, and when they were liberated at the end of the war, they fell upon the poor surviving remnant of Polish Jewry in a wave of pogroms.

Because of an initial situation conducive to genocide, and because of the heavy involvement of Nazi party members in the administration of occupied Poland, the Germans were able to move with brutal immediacy to the annihilation of Polish Jewry. The initial step, carried out with lavish disregard for human life, was the concentration of Polish Jews in cities, followed by their confinement in closed medieval-type ghettoes, where they were almost totally at the mercy of their killers. Here they were destroyed economically by the expropriation of property, accompanied by anarchic pillage and brigandry, by the exploitation of Jewish labour, and by the deprivation of food. Given the extreme poverty of Polish Jews, their major resource was labour, and this was ruthlessly expended in labour columns, labour camps and ghetto workshops. They were destroyed in the labour columns and in the labour camps, and they were destroyed in the ghettoes by starvation and by the diseases of extreme overcrowding under insanitary conditions, and by brutality and torment, and by random killings and organized massacres. More than half a million Polish Jews died in the ghettoes.

The decision to exterminate Polish Jews was probably only taken in about spring 1941, during the planning of the invasion of Russia, though the process was of course already well under way. When German armed forces attacked the U.S.S.R. in June 1941, mobile killing units accompanied them, and trapped large Jewish population centres. With the support of the army, Gestapo and police units, and large numbers of Lithuanian, Latvian and Ukrainian auxiliaries, they

131

massacred (according to Hilberg's account,[21] which I am following) about 1,400,000, of whom some 500,000 were Polish Jews.

We have eye-witness accounts of some of the operations of the killing units, as for example the following affidavit read by Sir Hartley Shawcross at the Nuremberg trials.

... An old woman with snow-white hair was holding this one-year-old child in her arms and singing and tickling it. The child was cooing with delight. The parents were looking on with tears in their eyes. The father was holding the hand of a boy about ten years old and speaking to him softly; the boy was fighting his tears. The father pointed towards the sky, stroked the boy's head, and seemed to explain something to him. At that moment the S.S. man at the pit shouted something to his comrade. The latter counted off about twenty persons and instructed them to go behind the earth mound. The family I have described was among them. I well remember a girl, slim and with black hair, who, as she passed me, pointed to herself and said: 'Twenty-three years old.'

I then walked round the mound and found myself confronted by a tremendous grave. People were closely wedged together and lying on top of each other so that only their heads were visible. Nearly all had blood running over their shoulders from their heads. Some of the shot people were still moving. Some lifted their arms and turned their heads to show that they were alive. The pit was already three-quarters full. I estimated that it held a thousand people. I looked for the man who did the shooting. He was an S.S. man who sat at the edge of the narrow end of the pit, his feet dangling into it. He had an automatic pistol on his knees and was smoking a cigarette. The people – they were completely naked – went down some steps which were cut in the clay wall of the pit and clambered over the heads of those who were lying there to the place to which the S.S. had directed them. They lay down in front of the dead and wounded. Some caressed the living and spoke to them in a low voice. Then I heard a series of shots. I looked into the pit and saw that their bodies still twitched or that their heads lay motionless on top of the other bodies before them. Blood ran from their necks.

I was surprised that I was not ordered off, but I saw that there were two or three postmen in uniform near by. Already the next batch was approaching. They went down in the pit, lined themselves up against the previous victims and were shot. When I walked back round the mound, I noticed that another truckload of people had arrived. This time it included sick and feeble people. An old, terribly thin woman was undressed by others, who were already naked, while two people held her up. The woman appeared to

---

21. Hilberg, op. cit.

be paralysed. The naked people carried her round the mound. I left with my foreman and drove in my car back to Dubno.

On the morning of the next day, when I visited the site, I saw about thirty naked people lying near the pit – about thirty to fifty metres away from it. Some of them were still alive; they looked straight in front of them with a fixed stare and seemed to notice neither the chilliness of the morning nor the workers of my firm who stood around. A girl of about twenty spoke to me and asked me to give her clothes and help her escape. At that moment we heard a fast car approach and I noticed that it was an S.S. detail. I moved away to my site. Ten minutes later we heard shots from the vicinity of the pit. Those Jews who were still alive had been ordered to throw the corpses into the pit, then they themselves had to lie down in the pit to be shot in the neck.[22]

This account, and other accounts, convey so horrifying a picture of the total dehumanization of the killers as to shatter utterly any simple faith in the fundamental goodness of man. Yet there is the absolute contrast in the humanity of the victims, seeking to bring comfort to their fellows in the moment of their own annihilation. And one is torn with anguish by the despair, the helplessness and the isolation of a people so overwhelmed by relentless enemies, so denied help by their own countrymen, and so abandoned by the seeming indifference of the outside world.

Gas killing vans were introduced into the operations of the mobile units, and this technology was then elaborated in the installations of the killing centres. Here Jews from different countries of Europe, and also many other peoples, were massacred in their millions. The death dealing would start in the railway trucks in which the victims were packed, often for days on end, with little or no food and drink. Arrived at their destination, they would be received with terrorizing brutality. They might be sent off immediately to the gas installations in a factory-type, conveyor-belt process, as in the following summary of an extended account by Nyiszli.[23]

Outside, says Nyiszli, the men on night-shift were handling a convoy of Jews, some 3,000 men, women and children, who had been led from their train into the hall 200 yards long and prominently labelled in various languages, 'Baths and Disinfecting Room.' Here they had been told to strip, supervised by the S.S. and men of the Sonderkommando. They were then led into a second hall, where the S.S. and Sonderkommando left them.

22. I have used Reitlinger's version of the English translation, 1961 : 219–20.
23. Nyiszli, 1960 : Ch. VII.

Meanwhile, vans painted with the insignia of the Red Cross had brought up supplies of Cyclon B crystals. The 3,000 were then sealed in and gassed.

Twenty minutes later the patented mechanical ventilators were turned on to dispel the remaining fumes. Men of the Sonderkommando, wearing gas masks and rubber boots, entered the gas chamber. They found the naked bodies piled in a pyramid that revealed the last collective struggle of the dying to reach clean air near the ceiling; the weakest lay crushed at the bottom while the strongest bestrode the rest at the top. The struggling mass, stilled only by death, lay now inert like some fearful monument to the memory of their suffering. The gas had risen slowly from the floor, forcing the prisoners to climb on each other's bodies in a ruthless endeavour to snatch the last remaining lungfuls of clean air. The corpses were fouled, and the masked men washed them down with hoses before the labour of separating and transporting the entwined bodies could begin. They were dragged to the elevators, lowered to the crematoria, their gold teeth removed with pliers and thrown into buckets filled with acid, and the women's hair shaved from their heads. The desecrated dead were then loaded in batches of three on carts of sheet metal and fed automatically into one of the fifteen ovens with which each crematorium was equipped. A single crematorium consumed 45 bodies every 20 minutes; the capacity of destruction at Auschwitz was little short of 200 bodies an hour. No wonder Hoess was proud. The ashes were removed and spilled into the swift tide of the river Vistula, a mile or so away. The valuables – clothes, jewels, gold and hair – were sent to Germany, less what the S.S. and the Sonderkommando managed to steal. Nyiszli estimates each crematorium amassed some eighteen to twenty pounds of gold a day. It was melted into small ingots and sent to swell the resources of the Reich in Berlin.[24]

If they were briefly spared – though this seems hardly the appropriate word for the torments awaiting them – they might be assigned to some labour unit, or to special revolting tasks, such as the digging up of corpses from mass graves for cremation to hide the evidence, or to the Sonderkommandos for the processing and disposal of corpses, or to camp labour, or clerical work or medical duties. And they were killed for the most part in the gas chambers, but also by shooting and by hanging, by being beaten or kicked to death, by every conceivable and inconceivable form of torture, by medical technology, including injections into the heart and a variety of medical 'experiments', by starvation and disease, and by sacrificing themselves, at the end of human endurance, on the electrified wires of their prison.

Some 3,000,000 Jews were murdered in the killing centres. Nearly

24. Manvell and Fraenkel, op. cit., 144–5.

2,000,000 were from Poland. Polish Jewry was almost totally anni-hilated. All told, there may have been as many as 7,000,000 victims of all groups in the different concentration camps.

Thus was reached the terminal point in a long process which had started in Germany, even before Hitler's assumption of power in 1933, with an incessant barrage of vilifying propaganda and brutal assaults. From the immediate passage of discriminatory laws in 1933, we can trace an ordered progression to genocide (though the intent developed much later); and the genocide was maintained with fanatical per-sistence to the very end when the German armies were already defeated.

The genocide, as we have said, was distinguished by its bureaucratic legalistic systematic nature. It shared the element of central bureau-cratic planning with the Turkish genocide against the Armenians. There were many other features in common, as in the activating of hostile local forces, the deadly use of the deportations by train and of the marching and labour columns, the starvation, pillage, atrocity. But the German genocide was altogether more radical, more thoroughgoing, more devastating. It was more radical in its conception of Jews as a race, whereas religious conceptions were not without relevance in the Turkish case, permitting some escape by forced conversion. It was infinitely more systematic, seeking to control spontaneity in the organ-ized planning, though allowing infinite scope in the killing centres for self-expression in torture and auxiliary death-dealing. By contrast the Turks made great use of spontaneity, both unorganized and organ-ized. They freely massacred as did the Germans, but they also relied appreciably on creating conditions calculated to destroy. The Germans too created conditions of deprivation which would have destroyed their victims in the course of time by a sort of 'natural' process. But they preferred to take the killing into their own hands; and it was their unique contribution in the history of genocide to establish and operate killing centres with an international catchment area.

I have emphasized, in my discussion of the structural basis of domestic genocides, the plural nature of the societies in which they are carried out. I have thought of this as a tautology. In the Turkish case, the plural structure of the Turkish Empire is clear enough. It is by no means so obvious in Germany, where Jews were highly assimilated and in process of being absorbed, as shown by the extent of inter-marriage and conversion. But they could hardly be described as integrated into the society. Emancipation in the latter part of the nineteenth century was quite recent, particularly when viewed against centuries of rejection, massacre, expulsion and persecution; and the social advance of Jews coincided with new waves of anti-semitism and the spread of 'scientific' racism. It was in this context of an ancient and persisting anti-semitism that the humiliations of defeat and of the peace treaties, hardships of reparations, inflation and economic depression, found release in the annihilation of German Jewry.

Material benefits would certainly have been an inducement, as shown by widespread and ready participation in the expropriation of Jewish industry, commerce and property, and in the exploitation of Jewish labour, and as shown too by the extensive extortionate corruption of German personnel in the concentration camps.[25] With a Jewish population of over half a million, many occupied as lawyers, doctors, scholars, writers and artists, and appreciably concentrated in commerce, Jewish assets offered an attractive prize.[26] But there are almost invariably appreciable material benefits to be derived from genocide, so this can hardly be a sufficient explanation. If it were, there would be very few surviving minority groups. Still material considerations would have contributed to the acceptance of a genocidal policy, which derived its main appeal from a deeply rooted anti-semitism.

It was this same deep-rooted anti-semitism which secured for the Germans a ready cooperation in many countries of Europe. In other countries of Europe, however, evasion or non-cooperation or active resistance frustrated the design for the total annihilation of European Jewry. In explaining national differences in the massacres of European Jews, Helen Fein shows the primary significance of the extent of German control, and the relevance of successful pre-war anti-semitic movements for both the level of cooperation with the Germans in isolating Jews, and the toll of deaths exacted. As for the role of the churches, 'the majority of Jews evaded deportation in every state occupied by or allied with Germany in which the head of the dominant church spoke out *publicly* against deportation before or as soon as it began'.[27]

One can partly explain the German genocide by recounting the course of events and invoking structural and ideological antecedents

25. See Kogon, 1973, on the corruption in the concentration camps.
26. See Marcus, 1934: Chs. VIII and IX, for a discussion of Jewish economic life and the myth of economic dominance.
27. Fein, op. cit., 67.

and current frustrations and conflicts. But the problem still remains of understanding the genocide. Many analysts have tried to answer the question – how was it possible for so civilized a nation to perpetrate so horrendous a genocide, a nation moreover which had given birth to such great philosophers and musicians – as if great philosophers and musicians cannot be ruled by passionate and socially destructive hatreds. They refer to the fact that the genocide was a gradual process, moving step by step, with earlier induction encouraging progressive involvement. They comment on the bureaucratic process, planning and action at lower levels being fragmented by office and function, and proceeding with the customary banality of the daily routine. They draw attention to the legality of the whole process, legitimated by legislation, administrative regulation, judicial interpretation, and general acceptance. And they emphasize the secrecy of the killing operations – the camouflage language of 'the final solution', 'special treatment', 'deportation', 'resettlement' and the removal of the camps from general observation.

Yet millions were active in the final stages of a genocide which called for massive organization and the participation of many agencies: and millions of others must have had direct knowledge of the genocide. One can readily understand that the gradual nature of the process, the legitimation and bureaucratic organization would have facilitated involvement. But one is left with the troublesome thought that there may not have been much resistance at all to involvement in genocide, that it is by no means foreign to man-in-society, and that many features of contemporary 'civilized' society encourage the easy resort to genocidal holocausts.

Chapter 8

Related Atrocities

But accusing foreigners cannot acquit the present leaders of Kampuchea : their inflexible ideology has led them to invent a radically new kind of man in a radically new society. A fascinating revolution for all who aspire to a new social order. A terrifying one, for all who have any respect for human beings.

[François Ponchaud in *Cambodia Year Zero*, p. 16]

But about the silent, treacherous Plague which starved fifteen million of our peasants to death, choosing its victims carefully and destroying the backbone and mainstay of the Russian people – about that Plague there are no books. No bugles bid our hearts beat faster for them. Not even the traditional three stones mark the crossroads where they went in creaking carts to their doom.

[Aleksandr Solzhenitsyn, The Peasant Plague, in *The Gulag Archipelago*, Vol. III, p. 350]

There are certain crimes which have some affinity with genocide, such as the large-scale slaughter of hostages taken from the opposing group, or the shooting down or bombing of passenger planes, or the striking at the soft underbelly of England by bombs in underground trains or subways. But it would be straining the meaning of genocide to apply it to acts of terrorism against unarmed civilians, and in this chapter I want to concentrate on crimes analogous to genocide, which might have been defined as such under the United Nations Convention if the original inclusion of political groups had prevailed, or if economic strata had been included among the protected groups.

I referred in Chapter 2 to the arguments advanced by the Soviet representatives and their supporters against the inclusion of political groups in the definition of genocide on the grounds that this would be contrary to the scientific, historical and etymological meaning of the term, which was linked to fascist and Nazi ideologies and applicable only to racial and national (religious) groups: and that moreover membership in a political organization was a matter of choice, and political groups were too transient and unstable to enjoy protection under the Genocide Convention. Some of the comments on the distinctive nature of political groups were quite alarming, and the course of the debate was such as to provoke from the representative of the United States the acid comment that 'contrary to the opinions expressed by the representatives of Poland and the Soviet Union, his delegation believed that the right to live could not be challenged even on grounds of political belief'.[1] (We may note in parenthesis that this was hardly the position taken by the United States in Vietnam.) Counter-arguments attacked the historical, scientific and etymological arguments, rejected the linking of genocide with the historical accident of nazism-fascism, and denied the conception of political groups as too transient for protection. If they were identifiable and stable enough for extermination, they must also have the necessary identifiability and stability for protection; and slaughter on political grounds was increasingly superceding destruction for reasons of national or racial or religious hatred.

Looking back over the cases discussed in earlier chapters, it is clearly impossible for the most part to disentangle the political aspect from the racial, national or religious. Many of the conflicts were also conflicts between political groups with political objectives. The genocides or genocidal massacres in Rwanda, Burundi, Zanzibar and Algeria arose in the course of struggles for power. In Bangladesh, the Sudan and Lebanon this struggle took the form of a struggle over the conditions of incorporation. The same striving for change in the conditions of incorporation was an element in the Turkish genocide against the Armenians, who had sought, from time to time, the intervention of outside powers to secure reforms or a greater measure of autonomy. In India, the massacres on partition arose in the aftermath of political conflict. The massacres in the process of colonial conquest or the suppression of colonial unrest by admonitory or administrative or exemplary massacres were means to the establishment and maintenance of political domination. It is only the genocides against hunting and gathering groups and against hostage groups which were committed largely outside the course of political struggle. Yet even in the case of the German genocide against the Jews in Germany, the persecution of Jews was an integral and significant element in the political strategies of the German government. But while there were political advantages to be gained from the persecution of Jews, the Nazis must have feared that genocide would be politically counterproductive, since they sought to keep it hidden from the German people.

1. U.N. *ECOSOC*, Session 7, 26 August 1948, 725.

However, leaving aside the question of the interweaving of the political with the racial or ethnic or religious conflict, I want to inquire in this chapter into the nature of some of the more 'purely' political or economic class massacres, and to raise the question whether they constitute analytically a distinctive category of crimes. I shall refer to three case studies – Soviet Russia under Stalin, the slaughter of Communists in Indonesia, and the massacre of its own nationals by the Cambodian government.

I discussed in Chapter 5 Khrushchev's denunciation of Stalin at the Twentieth Congress of the Communist Party of the Soviet Union in February 1956. He enumerated, among the acts of brutal violence, the annihilation of military cadres in the years 1937–41. Then he referred to the 'monstrous' acts in rude violation of the nationality policy of the Soviet state. In mass deportations, 'not dictated by any military considerations', whole nations were moved from their native lands – the Karachai in 1943; the entire population of the Autonomous Kalmyk Republic in the same year; the Chechen and Ingush peoples in March 1944, with liquidation of their autonomous republic; and all Balkars in April 1944, their name being expunged from the Kabardino-Balkar Autonomous Republic. 'Not only a Marxist-Leninist', he declared, 'but also no man of common sense can grasp how it is possible to make whole nations responsible for inimical activity, including women, children, old people, Communists and Komsomols, to use mass repression against them, and to expose them to misery and suffering for the hostile acts of individual persons or groups of persons.'[2] We shall have to look elsewhere, however, for an account of this misery and suffering, since the deportations are dealt with quite briefly in this report, the main preoccupation being with the crimes against Communist Party cadres.

These were indeed formidable, and committed not only against ideological opponents, but also against conforming members of the party. Khrushchev reported that of the 139 members and candidates of the Party's Central Committee, elected at the Seventeenth Congress, 98 persons (70 per cent) were arrested and shot, mostly in 1937–8. They were honest Communists, against whom accusations had been fabricated. The same fate met the majority of the delegates to the Seventeenth Party Congress. Of 1,966 delegates with either voting or advisory rights, 1,108 were arrested on charges of revolutionary

2. Wolfe, 1957:190, 192.

crimes.[3] From 1954 until the February 1956 meeting, the Military Collegium of the Supreme Court had rehabilitated 7,679 persons, many of them posthumously.[4] The report commented on the 'barbaric tortures'[5] by which confessions were extorted, and the use of the concept 'enemy of the people', which made possible cruel repression, violating all norms of revolutionary legality.[6]

Solzhenitsyn offers a much more comprehensive account of the crimes of the Stalinist regime. The slaughter of Communist Party members, particularly the upper echelons, which was a major preoccupation in Khrushchev's denunciation, is seen by Solzhenitsyn in the perspective of three main waves and a never-ending flow of smaller waves. The first main wave of 1929 and 1930 'drove a mere fifteen million peasants, maybe even more, out into the taiga and the tundra ...' where 'they sank down into the permafrost'.[7] 'There was nothing to be compared with it in all Russian history. It was a forced resettlement of a whole people, an ethnic catastrophe.'[8] Ostensibly directed to the liquidation of the *kulaks* as a class, its victims were in fact all strong peasants in general, who were stripped of their possessions and driven with their families, 'to the last scrapings' of their children, into the northern wastes, to the same common destruction.[9] This wave is of no concern to Khrushchev in his denunciation; he approves the policy towards the *kulaks* and peasant collectivization in the most casual way conceivable, without pity for its victims.

The second wave is that denounced by Khrushchev, the annihilation of Communist cadres in 1935–8. Solzhenitsyn comments that in all the accounts, the wave of 1937–8 is portrayed as consisting chiefly of Communist leaders, whereas in fact millions were arrested, and important party and state officials could not possibly have represented more than 10 per cent.[10] There were assignments of quotas for arrest in every city, district and military unit. Among those arrested were 'spies' abroad; and ethnic groups, such as Koreans from the Far East, Leningrad Estonians and Latvian riflemen; and socialists 'all sentenced together and driven off in herds to the slaughterhouses of the

3. ibid., 124.
4. ibid., 154.
5. ibid., 122.
6. ibid., 106.
7. Solzhenitsyn, 1974–8 : Vol. I, 24.
8. ibid., 54.
9. ibid., 55–6 ; see also Vol. III, 350ff.
10. ibid., Vol. I, 70.

Archipelago'; members of the intelligentsia; 'piles of victims, hills of victims'.[11]

The third wave was from 1944–6, 'when they dumped whole *nations* down the sewer pipes, not to mention millions and millions of others who (because of us!) had been prisoners of war, or carried off to Germany and subsequently repatriated'.[12] This wave extends over a longer period, going back to the 1930s with the mass arrest of Koreans from the Far East, and to 1939, when 30,000 Czechs were sent off to the northern camps. It included the 'social prophylaxis' of occupied territories, the nationalities which had transgressed or had been designated as treacherous (Kalmyks, Chechens, Ingush, Karachai, Balkars, Kurds, Crimean Tatars and finally Caucasian Greeks). This list of exiled nations is more extensive than that given by Khrushchev. The wave included also Russian prisoners of war, civilian fugitives of all ages and of both sexes, 'perfidiously returned by Allied authorities into Soviet hands',[13] and 'a big wave of genuine, at-long-last, enemies of the Soviet government'.[14]

There were further waves from the Baltic States in 1940, and in 1941 when the Soviet armies in retreat 'seized as many well-to-do, influential, and prominent people as they could, and carried or drove them off like precious trophies, and then tipped them like dung onto the frostbound soil of the Archipelago'. Later, when the Soviet armies returned in 1944, they imprisoned people in droves. 'But even this was not deportation of whole nations', the main epidemics of banishment hitting the Baltic States in 1948–51. 'In these same years the Western Ukraine, too, was being scraped clean ...'[15]

And then there was the endless stream of little waves – the liquidation of members of other political parties, waves of intellectuals, students, tens of thousands of hostages taken off and destroyed,[16] counter-revolutionaries, exploiting classes, for concealment of social origin, for former social origin, technical intelligentsia, the 'late stragg-

11. ibid., 70–74.
12. ibid., 24–5.
13. ibid., Vol. I, 77–85 and Ch. 4, and Vol. III, 388ff. A detailed case study of the treatment of Russian prisoners of war and civilian refugees will be found in Tolstoy, 1977. (See also Reuben Ainsztein, 1978, for a critique of this study.) Solzhenitsyn's account of the mass deportations is not limited to those whose destination was the Gulag Archipelago.
14. Solzhenitsyn, op. cit., Vol. I, 85.
15. ibid., Vol. III, 391.
16. ibid., Vol. I, 29.

lers after the bourgeoisie – the NEPmen', subversives, all manner of
class enemies, a wave of 'cosmopolite' Jews, and a continuous flow
of religious believers, pouring into the Gulag from its earliest days
through the years following Khrushchev's denunciation.

Siberian penal camps and exile were well established under the
Czars, but on a relatively modest scale. The new rulers enormously
developed and extended these institutions, so that when they came to
the planning of the deportation of whole nations from the North
Caucasus and the Crimea, they had considerable experience on which
to draw and an established infrastructure. The deportations had been
preceded by earlier purges – and a deportation of 30,000 to 40,000
Crimean Tatars – during the collectivization of agriculture. There were
purges, too, for bourgeois nationalism and in the suppression of risings,
while the campaigns against Islam and Buddhism had resulted in the
virtual elimination of religious leaders, mosques and lamaseries.[17] Solzhenitsyn writes that when it came to the deportation of whole nations,
the precious experience gained in previous deportations had been so
widely spread and thoroughly assimilated, 'that they no longer counted
in days or even hours, but in minutes. Practice proved that twenty
or thirty minutes was time enough between the first bang on the door
at night and the last scrape of the householder's heel on his threshold
as he walked into the darkness toward the lorry. Those few minutes
gave the awakened family time to ·dress, take in the news that they
were being exiled for life, sign a document waiving all property
claims, collect their old women and children, get their bundles together,
and leave their homes when the order was given.'[18] The whole process
was infinitely more efficient than the Turkish deportation of
Armenians.

There was some variation in the procedure, the time allowed, the
manner of announcement, the brutality of enforcement. The general
pattern, according to Solzhenitsyn's account,[19] was for armed divisions
to 'enter the doomed people's locality by night and occupy key positions. The criminal nation wakes up and sees every settlement ringed
with machine guns and automatic rifles.' On Red Army Day, 23
February 1944, the men among the Chechens were invited everywhere
to meetings at the village Soviet buildings. The Chechens were held
at gunpoint, the deportation decree was read and the people loaded on

17. Conquest, 1970:97–9.
18. Solzhenitsyn, op. cit., Vol. III, 393.
19. ibid., 388.

to lease-lend Studebakers from the American allies, each family being allowed a maximum of twenty kilograms of luggage. Not only were they deported from their native land, but from other cities and regions of the Soviet Union.[20] A similar fate befell the Ingush. In May 1944, the entire Tatar population of the Crimea was deported, the men being separated from the women and children and sent to serve in work battalions. All Crimean Tatars in the Soviet armed forces were demobilized and assigned to construction units.[21] One source[22] reports accounts that the Crimean Tatars were given only fifteen minutes to collect what belongings they could carry, and that in some cases only five minutes were given, and no belongings or food allowed. The Karachai were deported when the overwhelming majority of the men were serving in the Red Army.

Deportations were by cattle truck and freight cars under conditions reminiscent of the German deportations. From the railway stations the exiles might 'still have to make their way like Volga boatmen (as the Crimean Tatars did up the river Unzha – what more suitable place for them than those northern marshes?), towing rafts on which gray-bearded old men lie motionless, 150 to 200 kilometers against the current, into the wild forest ...'[23] Their destinations were Kazakhstan, Siberia, Central Asia, the Northern Urals and the Northern European areas. In the special settlements to which they were consigned – *special settlement* being the Soviet euphemism for penal exile – they were subjected to extremely harsh conditions of living, and reduced, as Nekrich writes, 'to the status of disenfranchised and persecuted beggars'.[24] Repressive laws imposed continuous surveillance and restraints on freedom of movement under a system of pass laws; and they were discriminated against in employment, which consisted mostly of heavy labour in agriculture, logging, construction, mining and industry.

Predictably, the exiles died in droves. The total number of deported Chechens, Kalmyks, Ingush, Karachai and Balkars (i.e. from the Northern Caucasus and Kalmykia) and of Crimean Tatars in 1943–4 was somewhat more than 1,000,000.[25] Of these the majority were women and children – some 85 per cent of the Crimean Tatars in the

20. See Nekrich, 1978:58–60, who writes that only in Moscow did two Chechens manage to remain during the period of deportation.
21. ibid., 31 and 109.
22. Conquest, op. cit., 105.
23. Solzhenitsyn, op. cit., Vol. III, 388.
24. Nekrich, op. cit., 124.
25. See estimates by Nekrich, op. cit., 138, and Conquest, op. cit., 64–6.

special settlements of Uzbekistan, and somewhat similar percentages of from 70 per cent to 81 per cent in a number of other special settlements. 'So the wrath of the state descended primarily on women and children.'[26] There are few reliable figures of the number of deaths, which were particularly heavy during the transportation and in the early years of settlement. In repudiating the charge that 46 per cent of Tatars had perished during the deportation, the Soviet procurator, in a court case in 1968, presented two official documents, from which it appears that 17.7 per cent of the Tatars who arrived in Uzbekistan died between July 1944 and January 1946.[27] This high figure may very well be an understatement. For overall estimates of the population losses, one must fall back on calculations derived from the census. Nekrich[28] offers the following minimal estimates of losses to 1959 – Chechens 22 per cent, Kalmyks 14.8 per cent, Ingush 9 per cent, Karachai 30 per cent and Balkars 26.5 per cent. This represents an average loss of over 20 per cent or almost one quarter of a million people. Medvedev[29] gives a higher estimate of as many as 40 per cent of the deported Chechens, Ingush, Crimean Tatars, Kalmyks, Volga Germans and others perishing from hunger, cold, and epidemics in the uninhabited places in the east to which they were shipped by the trainload.

The official grounds for deportation were betrayal of the fatherland and assistance to the Germans. But Khrushchev, in his denunciation of Stalin, pointed out the absurdity of holding whole nations responsible for the hostile acts of individual persons or groups of persons; and the deportations were carried out when there was no military necessity for them, since the enemy was being rolled back everywhere under the blows of the Red Army. Moreover, following the denunciation, the decree in November 1956, 'On the Restoration of the National Autonomy of the Kalmyk, Karachai, Balkar, Chechen, and Ingush Peoples',[30] condemned the deportations as arbitrary and lawless.[31] The

26. Nekrich, op. cit., 115–16.

27. ibid., 112–14; see also Conquest, op. cit., 161–2.

28. Nekrich, op. cit., 138.

29. Medvedev, 1977:227.

30. The restoration of national autonomy did not apply to the Crimean Tatars. The decree withdrawing the wholesale charges against 'citizens of Tatar nationality formerly resident in the Crimea' was only handed down in September 1967, and did not provide for the restoration of national autonomy. (See Nekrich, op. cit., 173ff.)

31. Nekrich, op. cit., 136.

objective does not seem to have been the physical annihilation of these nations. This could easily have been accomplished, though at some cost in the antagonizing of allies and other nations and religious groups; and there is evidence also of a contrary intention in the fact that instructions were given to local officials to make some provision for the special settlers. Be that as it may, there can be little doubt of the intention to annihilate these peoples as national entities. They were moved far from their ancestral homes, and constitutionally deleted from their previous administrative divisions. In the revision of history, in maps and new editions of official documents and encyclopedias and in the renaming of towns, this obliteration was carried into the past, present and future in a process Conquest describes as 'The Memory Hole'.[32] And in their areas of exile, they were denied education, and facilities for publications, in their native languages.

There can be no doubt, too, of the intention to punish whole nations, conceived as collectivities, permitting no exemptions for individuals, so that even devoted party members became victims of the deportations. And the punishment, taking the form of an attempt to dissolve all sentimental ties to country and community and home, by brutal uprooting and confinement under conditions inimical to survival, inevitably exacted a heavy toll of deaths. From a different point of view, the whole operation may be seen as a colonization, with the driving out of the native peoples and the resettlement by one's own nationals, in the present case by Russians and other approved settlers – an operation having the further function of securing border areas.

I have not mentioned all the punitive deportations of nations: there were also the strategic preventive deportations. An extended account of the actions against national groups, national religious groups, and other religious groups will be found in a publication of the Institute for the Study of the U.S.S.R., *Genocide in the U.S.S.R.*, though even this account is by no means complete. However, these actions against national and religious groups fall within the purview of the United Nations' definition of genocide. This is true also of the culling of leadership strata, as in the Baltic States. But my particular concern in this chapter is with large-scale massacres of political groups and also of social and economic classes, not included in the United Nations' definition of genocide; and I shall start with the annihilation of peasants.

32. A phrase borrowed from George Orwell, *Nineteen Eighty-Four* (New York: Harcourt, Brace and Co., 1949, p. 40).

The decision to liquidate the *kulaks* as a class was taken by the Central Committee of the Communist Party in January 1930, and it was given legislative form by the Central Executive Committee of the Soviets and the Council of People's Commissars the following month. The term *kulak* was ill-defined. Solzhenitsyn tells us[33] that *kulak* originally denoted a miserly dishonest rural trader who grows rich through the labour of others and through usury and as a middleman, but that after the revolution, by a transfer of meaning, it came to be applied to all those who in any way hired workers, even if only when temporarily short of help from their own families. In practice, however, the victims of the liquidation were not only *kulaks* strictly defined, and not only the rich, but also middle and even poor peasants – indeed the most efficient and productive stratum of the peasantry, and all those who opposed collectivization, or incurred the enmity of the local activists and were persecuted as *podkulachniks,* the aiders and abettors of *kulaks.*

The liquidation of the so-called *kulaks* may be seen, from different perspectives, as a continuation of the Civil War, carrying the revolution to a new level of collectivization and state ownership; or as class warfare between the rulers and the peasantry; or as the imposition of internal colonialism, effected by a transfer of property from the peasants to the state, the exacting of unfavourable rates of exchange, and the consolidation of a despotic form of power through ownership and control of the means of production. Whilst collectivization was accepted Communist Party policy, the decision to engage in a crash programme of forced collectivization was controversial within the Party. It was precipitated by crises resulting from the resistance of the peasantry, the failure of a strategy of inciting the poor and middle peasantry against the *kulaks,* difficulties in the procurement of grain for the cities, and the need to extract the capital required for industrialization by exploitation of the peasants.

The conception of the peasants as petty bourgeois,[34] and hence not part of the same moral community, and the conception of the *kulaks* as irreconcilable enemies, gave licence for the most ruthless violence. Forced collectivization was carried out to the accompaniment of large-scale slaughter and massive deportations. These deportations took a form with which we are all too familiar – the deployment of armed forces, the bureaucratic involvement, and indeed in the present case

33. Solzhenitsyn, op. cit., Vol. I, 55.
34. See the discussion by Gouldner, 1977–8, 41.

the great elaboration of new lumpen-bureaucracies, the merciless up-rooting and dispossession, and the condemnation to lethal conditions of transportation and resettlement. Whole families were uprooted, whole nests burnt out; 'and they watched jealously to be sure that none of the children – fourteen, ten, even six years old – got away: to the last scrapings, all had to go down the same road, to the same common destruction.' They were banished 'to the haunt of wild beasts into the wilderness, to man's primitive condition ... Only the peasants were deported so ferociously, to such desolate places, with such frankly murderous intent: no one had been exiled in this way before, and no one would be in the future.'[35] Estimates of the numbers who perished range from about 5,000,000 to 15,000,000, and this is without taking into account the many millions of peasants starved to death in the artificially induced man-made famine of 1932-3.

It is difficult to see how the deportation and slaughter of peasants differ from the murderous deportation and slaughter of national, ethnic, racial or religious groups. The victims are collectivities, guilt is appreciably by social origin,[36] even young children being deported, and murderous intent explicit enough in the vilification of the *kulaks* and in the choice of the most desolate wastelands for their exile.

The Great Purge, with which Khrushchev was so concerned in his denunciation of Stalin, took a particularly heavy toll of 'politicals'. Medvedev seeks to convey some of the enormity of this purge in the following passage.

Between 1936 and 1938 Stalin broke all records for political terror. The proscriptions of Cornelius Sulla killed several thousand Romans. Tens of thousands perished in the reigns of tyrannical emperors like Tiberius, Caligula, and Nero. The cruelest of all the inquisitors, Tomás de Torquemada, is said to have burned 10,220 living people and 6,860 pictures of absent or dead heretics, and sentenced 97,321 people to such punishment as life imprisonment, confiscation of property, and wearing the garment of shame called *sanbenito*. The *oprichnina* of Ivan the Terrible killed some tens of thousands; at its height ten to twenty people were killed daily in Moscow. In the Jacobin terror, according to the calculations of an American historian, 17,000 people were sent to the guillotine by revolutionary tribunals. Approximately the same number were condemned without a trial or died in prison.

35. Solzhenitsyn, op. cit., Vol. I, 55; Vol. III, 362-9.
36. Forced collectivization coincided with renewed attacks on the churches, and many peasants attempting to resist the destruction of their churches were deported, which is to say, by reason of their religious beliefs (Medvedev, op. cit., 209).

Exactly how many 'suspects' were imprisoned by the Jacobins is not known; the best estimate is 70,000. In nineteenth-century Russia several dozen were executed for political reasons and several hundred, or at most several thousand, 'politicals' died in prison and exile.

The scale of the Stalinist terror was immeasurably greater. In 1936–39, on the most cautious estimates, four to five million people were subjected to repression for political reasons. At least four to five hundred thousand of them – above all the high officials – were summarily shot; the rest were given long terms of confinement. In 1937–38 there were days when up to a thousand people were shot in Moscow alone. These were not streams, these were rivers of blood, the blood of honest Soviet people. The simple truth must be stated: not one of the tyrants and despots of the past persecuted and destroyed so many of his compatriots.[37]

These estimates seem indeed to be most cautious. Conquest,[38] in an appendix devoted to the analysis of the casualty figures, gives a 'conservative solution' for the end of 1938, which does not include 'criminals'.

Already in gaol or camp January 1937	c. 5 million
Arrested January 1937–December 1938	c. 7 million
	c. 12 million
Of which executed	c. 1 million
Died in camp	c. 2 million
	c. 3 million
In captivity late 1938	c. 9 million
Of which in prison	c. 1 million
In camps	c. 8 million

Gouldner[39] cites comparable estimates of some 8,000,000 arrested of whom perhaps 10 per cent were killed, and Solzhenitsyn[40] quotes figures emanating from former high and middle-ranking officials in the secret

37. Medvedev, 1971:269.
38. Conquest, 1968:532.
39. Gouldner, op. cit., 37.
40. Solzhenitsyn, op. cit., Vol. I, 438.

police of half a million 'political prisoners' having been shot throughout the Soviet Union during 1937 and 1938.

The terror ranged widely over Russian society. It drew in millions who could not possibly be described as politically engaged. But they were nevertheless arrested as enemies of the people or as counterrevolutionaries or as Trotskyite Rightists or other useful rubric or under the loose definitions of political crime in the Criminal Code, and they were tried in a perfunctory travesty of legal procedure or otherwise disposed of. It was a terror directed against the populace as a whole, designed to suppress all opposition or potential opposition to the power and policies of the central authority. And it fell with particularly lethal violence on the remnants of former opposition parties and on Communist Party and state cadres, whose members were either executed outright or consigned to prisons or labour camps. Some of these camps can only be described as extermination centres – Kolyma, where outside work for prisoners was compulsory until the temperature reached $-50°C$ and the death rate among the miners in the goldfields was estimated at about 30 per cent per annum; Norilsk, the centre of a group of camps more deadly than Kolyma; and Vorkuta, with temperatures below zero Centigrade for two-thirds of the year and especially deadly for prisoners from southern Russia, who quickly succumbed to the extravagant cold, the exhaustion of hard labour and the starvation diet.[41]

Clearly, the annihilations of politicals would have fallen within the definition of genocide, if protection had been extended to political groups. They differ, however, from many of the genocides discussed in this book. Social contacts of the arrested, their friends, wives, husbands, children and other relatives were exposed to persecution and punishment, and families might be used as hostages to extort confessions, but the slaughter of political groups did not take the form of a root and branch extermination.

In Indonesia and Cambodia, the political opposition was sufficiently identifiable and sufficiently stable to serve as the target for slaughter.

41. See the discussion of the labour camps by Conquest, 1968:Ch. 10; also all three volumes of *The Gulag Archipelago*. In the 'Memoirs of a Bolshevik Leninist' in Samizdat, 1974:171, there is reference to the use of gas chambers for disposing of Oppositionists. Tolstoy, op. cit., 398, comments on this reference that 'for once Marxist ingenuity had anticipated capitalist science: gas-chambers equivalent to those at Auschwitz had been in operation at Vorkuta as far back as 1938'.

But the facts in the Indonesian case are somewhat shrouded in controversy.

The controversy in Indonesia is not whether massacres of Communists took place following an attempted coup in October 1965, but whether the Indonesian Communist Party was involved in the planning of the coup, and if so, in what measure. The events themselves had all the appearance of a revolt by middle-ranking officers against the military supreme command, that is to say, of an internal army conflict. The declared justification for the revolt, the so-called September the 30th Movement, was an alleged plan by a Council of Generals to seize power from the Indonesian President. Three generals were killed in the course of kidnapping, and three generals murdered at the Air Force base, where the conspirators had established themselves. Key points were occupied in the capital and in other cities. The Indonesian Communist Party was compromised in a number of ways. Some of the auxiliaries of the Party who were being trained at the Air Force base became involved in the action; and the chairman of the Party had been taken by the conspirators to their base. Moreover, an unfortunate, somewhat confused editorial in the Party's daily newspaper approved the declared objective of preventing an army coup against the President and the Republic, though dissociating itself from the September movement, by describing it as an internal affair of the army.

In assessing the evidence, the Central Intelligence Agency of the United States Government had no doubt of the responsibility of the Communist Party, declaring that its central role in planning the coup had been well established.[42] But the paranoid perspective of the C.I.A. is a poor guide to the real world, and there is much to suggest a contrary interpretation.[43] In any event, even if the Communist Party had planned the coup, this would in no way justify the large-scale massacres of members of the Party and its affiliated organizations. However, whatever the facts may be, the army, in repressing the coup, imposed its own interpretation of Communist Party guilt. In this it was assisted by a virulent press campaign giving gruesome accounts of alleged Communist

42. See the excerpt from the C.I.A. report of 1968, 'Indonesia 1965, the Coup that Backfired', in *Hearings Before the Sub-committee on Future Foreign Policy Research and Development of the Committee on International Relations*, 1976: 226–36.

43. See for further discussion of this issue, Lev, 1966:103–10; Anderson and McVey, 1971:89–116; Wertheim, 1966:115–27; Palmier, 1973:251–62; Budiardjo, 1976:217–18.

atrocities in the form of sexual and other mutilations; and it derived support also from enmities towards the Party, deeply embedded in the broader context of Indonesian society, enmities which had emerged in violent confrontations in the past.

The background to the massacres was largely a struggle for power between the Communist Party and the army. Among the various estimates of the rapidly growing strength of the Party with its affiliated organizations, I have taken that of Amnesty International,[44] an estimate of 10,000,000 in a total population of perhaps 120,000,000, 'that is, one-quarter of the adult population'. In this struggle, the Communist Party, having failed to establish a militia of its own, was quite vulnerable. It was in conflict too with a powerful religious group, the Muslim *Nahdatul Ulama* Party; and class conflict was interwoven with this religious and ideological opposition. A peasant union, affiliated to the Communist Party, and impatient with delay and sabotage in implementing land reform legislation, had instituted 'one-sided actions'. At about the same time, the Communist Party had mounted a campaign against the 'seven devils of the rural areas', including in this category perfidious landowners. This inevitably alienated the *Nahdatul Ulama*, which in Central and East Java mainly represented the well-to-do land-owner class.[45] In other areas too, where the Communist Party represented the interests of the rural proletariat, it became involved in class struggle with the great landowners. Wertheim argues that 'the extreme cruelty and the mass scale of the murdering, as well as its regional distribution and the accompanying impact on the implementation of the land reforms, could not be explained without taking account of the basic class-struggle character of what happened'.[46]

Estimates of the number of Communists and affiliates slaughtered range from about 200,000 to over 1,000,000. Amnesty International, in a controversy with a former United States ambassador to Indonesia, wrote that 'Admiral Sudomo, the chief of Indonesian state security, has openly admitted that "during the bloody 'people's revenge' after the unsuccessful coup, an estimated half a million actual or suspected Communists were killed".'[47] The 'people's revenge' was not the spontaneous independent mass reaction the phrase suggests. On the contrary, the army engaged actively in the operation, participating directly in the

44. Amnesty International, 1977:23.
45. Wertheim, op. cit., 120.
46. ibid., 125.
47. Amnesty International, 1978.

massacres, and indirectly by organizing and arming civilian killers. The pattern of this cooperation varied in different parts of the country, as shown in the accounts by Seymour Topping[48] and John Hughes.[49] Topping reports that the military executed Communists by shooting, while civilians beheaded their victims or disembowelled them with knives, swords and bamboo spears, often with ritual forms of extreme cruelty. In Central Java, where the Communists made a stand, members of the nationalist and religious parties joined the army as executioners. In East Java, army-trained squads from the youth organization of the religious party took part in the massacres. In West Java, there were no major Communist political centres outside the capital and no mass killings.[50] In Bali, the killings were particularly frenzied, and whole villages were wiped out. Here the arrival of paratroopers restored some order and restraint in the killings. Here too, Topping reports, 'young black-clad executioners bow before chanting Hindu priests who cleanse them of the taint of the blood of tens of thousands slaughtered on the island paradise. Such gestures of contrition during religious festivals are meant to placate the gods; they are not expressions of conscience for the victims. The executioners march proudly in parades and their black garments have become the vogue for many youngsters.'[51]

Communists were readily identified from party lists of members, and, particularly in villages, by intimate knowledge of political affiliation. Of course the massacres extended beyond known affiliation, and gave the opportunity to settle private scores, and to draw in other categories, as in the killing of Chinese merchants and their families in North Sumatra.

The massacres were accompanied by great waves of arrest, and by detention for years without trial. One official statement gives the numbers arrested immediately after the coup as 600,000; a second estimate cites 750,000 arrested since the time of the coup.[52] In the handling of those arrested, there was a quite summary and extremely crude attempt to assess degrees of responsibility by categorizing the prisoners as directly involved in the abortive coup or indirectly involved or as prisoners for whom indications or reasonable assumptions exist of

48. Topping, 1966:16.
49. Hughes, 1968: Part II.
50. Topping, op. cit., 16.
51. ibid.
52. Amnesty International, 1977:41.

direct or indirect involvement;[53] but the principle of collective responsibility by reason of past association was still retained.

In the slaughter of the Communists, the criterion of past affiliation had a finality and immutability quite comparable to massacre by virtue of race and it was based on a similar imposition of collective responsibility. Again the major distinction from the racial or ethnic massacres was that the political massacres did not extend to the same extent to members of families.

Cambodia had been a battleground in the war between North and South Vietnam and their supporting super-powers, and it had also been torn apart by a revolutionary civil war. When the revolutionary forces of the Khmer Rouge finally assumed power, they inherited a devastated country. They sealed it off from the outside world, and it remained largely isolated, until the invasion and occupation by Vietnamese and rebel Cambodian troops in January 1979. Accounts of the new regime were therefore derived from some very early observations, from radio and other communications by the government, and above all from the reports of refugees, recounting their personal experiences.

There may be a tendency, as some commentators argue, for refugees to exaggerate the torments they have endured or witnessed, but I am often conscious of the reverse, the inability to communicate extreme horror, so that the words convey only a pale reflection of indescribable suffering. The circumstances, and different ideological commitments, gave scope for controversy; and in an early study the revolutionary regime was presented as most humanitarian, a position one of the authors later defended, though with appreciable modification, before a sub-committee of the United States Congress.[54] However, the overwhelming weight of evidence was of massive slaughter, brutal exposure of the population to deadly conditions of living, and the imposition of an extremely cruel and despotic regime.[55]

---

53. ibid., Ch. 4 and Appendix 1.

54. See Hildebrand and Porter, 1976, and evidence of Gareth Porter before the Sub-committee on International Organizations, 13 May 1977.

55. See the following sources: Barron and Paul, *Peace with Horror*, 1977; Ponchaud, *Cambodia Year Zero*, 1978; Debré, *Cambodge: La révolution de la forêt*, 1976; *Hearings before the Sub-committee on International Organizations of the Committee on International Relations* (U.S. House of Representatives, 95th Congress, 1st Session, 13 May and 26 July 1977); Shawcross, 'The Third Indochina War', 1978, 'Cambodia: Nightmare without End', 1978, correspondence with

In March 1978, the Commission on Human Rights of the United Nations initiated action inviting the comments and observations of the Government of Democratic Kampuchea, in response to documents submitted, 'relating to the human rights situation in that country'. And pursuant to this decision, the Sub-Commission on Prevention of Discrimination and Protection of Minorities prepared an analysis (ECN./ 4/1335, dated 30 January 1979), based on submissions from the Governments of:

(1) Canada, including a unanimous motion by the Canadian Parliament, expressing horror at the genocide committed by the Government of Democratic Kampuchea;

(2) Norway, forwarding a Preliminary Report of a public hearing held in Oslo;

(3) The United Kingdom, transmitting a report it had prepared on 'Human Rights Violations in Democratic Kampuchea';

(4) The United States of America, submitting a substantial compilation of materials, including reports of interviews with refugees, statements by officers of the executive and legislative branches, among them the President, texts of resolutions by the American House of Representatives and proceedings before a congressional sub-committee;

(5) Australia, forwarding a short, quite diplomatic, statement of concern;

and statements and letters from two non-governmental organizations, Amnesty International and the International Commission of Jurists.[56]

After commenting on the evidence submitted, the Sub-Commission provided the following summary of the allegations:

(i) that the forcible and precipitate evacuation of the population of Phnom Penh and other cities and towns ordered by the Kampuchean authorities immediately upon assuming power, in the absence of adequate arrangements by the authorities to provide food, water and medical care to the

---

Porter, 1978, and *Sideshow: Kissinger, Nixon and the Destruction of Cambodia,* 1979; Eads, 'The Prison Camp State', 1977; and Quinn, 'Cambodia 1976: Internal Consolidation and External Expansion', 1977. For critical reactions to the reporting on Cambodia, see Chomsky and Herman, 'Distortions at Fourth Hand', 1977, and *After the Cataclysm: Postwar Indochina and the Reconstruction of Imperial Ideology,* 1979; Chomsky, 'The Western Press and Cambodia', 1977; and Rousset, 'Cambodia: Background to the Revolution', 1977.

56. Summaries of these submissions will be found in E/CN.4/Sub.2/414/Add. 1–10.

evacuees while in transit or at their destinations, caused the loss of many lives particularly among the aged and the young and among the many sick and wounded persons who could not endure the rigours of the evacuation; (ii) that within the first few days after the assumption of power by the Kampuchean authorities on 17 April 1975, a large number of former military officers, senior officials, policemen, intelligence agents, country officials and military police were executed in various parts of the country as part of a systematic campaign of extermination, and that in a very large number of cases the wives and children of such categories of persons were also executed; (iii) that many persons belonging to such categories who had initially succeeded in concealing their identities or former occupations were subsequently systematically sought out and were also executed, especially since early 1976;

(iv) that although the treament of lower level personnel associated with the previous regime, such as minor officials, non-commissioned officers, soldiers, headmen, and members of paramilitary units, appears to have been different from region to region, many personnel in such categories were also executed either immediately following the take-over or subsequently, particularly since 1976;

(v) that so-called 'intellectuals' such as doctors, engineers, professors, teachers and students, have also been summarily executed, especially since 1977;

(vi) that many ordinary persons have died as a result of being forced to perform exhausting manual labour, under a strict regime, without being provided with sufficient food, rest or medical care;

(vii) that many ordinary persons whose attitudes had not been deemed satisfactory by the new authorities, or who had committed minor infractions (such as being late for work, losing their tools, etc.) have also been frequently punished by execution after one or two verbal admonishments;

(viii) that during 1977 and 1978 large numbers of Kampuchean administrative and military personnel of various levels and their families were also executed in a series of internal purges, and that in a number of instances even the villagers and peasants who had been working under the authority of such purged officials were also executed.

This bare summary is deliberately phrased in neutral terms. One must turn to the supporting reports of interviews and to other accounts to gain some impression of the suffering under this most radical and precipitate revolution. The capital Phnom Penh had been swollen by refugees to perhaps as many as 3,000,000. Its inhabitants and those of other towns were driven out in a gigantic mass migration, and exposed, with much loss of life, to extreme hardship, accompanied by summary executions, in the journey to their new work sites. Indeed, the whole country was turned into an agricultural work site, in which the people laboured ceaselessly on irrigation works, on the cultivation of rice and on other agricultural pursuits. Here their new rulers subjected them to what the Sub-Commission described as 'draconian discipline' in both work and private life. Sentimental ties were dissolved in the separation of families, the indoctrination of children, the continuous surveillance, and the ubiquitous presence of spies in a system of collectivized labour and communal living. Exhaustion, from the extremely arduous work, malnutrition from minimal diets, starvation and disease took a heavy toll of lives; and to this must be added the ravages of the revolutionary terror, with its purges of prescribed categories, and later its purges of party cadres, and with the easy resort to executions, carried out most brutally, for slight infringements of discipline, or for complaints or criticism. It seems impossible at the present time to estimate with any degree of reliability the number of deaths sustained by a population of about 7,000,000 as a result of the massive executions and other policies of the revolutionary government.

The submissions to the Sub-Commission, referred to above, were all made by nations in the Western orbit. However, Soviet Russia was also actively engaged. At about the time of the Sub-Commission's meeting, the Soviet weekly on world affairs, *New Times* (No. 37, September 1978), under a sub-heading *Policy of Genocide*, reported charges by refugees of the persecution of both ethnic Vietnamese and Cambodian revolutionaries trained in Vietnam, the Vietnam radio station declaring that nearly all the latter had been eliminated. On 2 November, *Izvestia* carried a full-scale attack on Kampuchea, which it said was being described, after three years of the present regime, as a 'vast concentration camp', a 'gigantic prison' and a 'state of barracks socialism', where rivers of blood flow and a ruthless and systematic policy of genocide is being carried out with respect to the country's own people. A special course, aimed at the construction of a historically unprecedented society, had been proclaimed – a society without cities, without property, without commodity-money relations, without markets and without money, without families. Those who are dissatisfied with the new regime are being 'eradicated', along with their families, by disembowelment, by beating to death with hoes, by hammering nails into the backs of their heads and by other cruel means of economizing on bullets. Responsibility for this 'monstrous situation', according to *Izvestia*, and for a cultural revolution which destroyed the old intelligentsia and the student class, eliminated doctors and technical specialists, and completely wrecked the educational system, stems from the importa-

157

Genocide

tion of the wild ideas of Mao Tse-tung.[57] And in January 1979, Soviet Russia raised the charge of genocide in the Security Council of the United Nations in its defence of the invasion of Kampuchea by its Vietnamese ally.

The comments and observations of the Kampuchean government were not available to the Sub-Commission. In an earlier communication the government had rejected allegations of human rights violations, claiming on the contrary to have achieved a steady improvement in the living conditions of the people.[58] Now, in response to the invitation to present its case, the Sub-Commission received the following telegram from the Minister of Foreign Affairs of the Kampuchean government:

WE REJECT SUB-COMMISSION DECISION AS IMPUDENT INTERFERENCE IN INTERNAL AFFAIRS OF DEMOCRATIC KAMPUCHEA. BY THAT DECISION SUB-COMMISSION SUPPORTS THE ACTIVITIES OF TRAITORS TO THEIR COUNTRY AND THE MANOEUVRES OF AMERICAN IMPERIALISTS AND THEIR PARTISANS WHO AFTER COMMITTING IMMEASURABLE CRIMES AGAINST THE PEOPLE OF KAMPUCHEA MASSACRING MORE THAN A MILLION INHABITANTS OF KAMPUCHEA AND DESTROYING 80 PER CENT OF KAMPUCHEA CONTINUE TO DEFAME DEMOCRATIC KAMPUCHEA TO WHITEWASH THEIR CRIMES. UNITED PEOPLE OF KAMPUCHEA IS MASTER OF ITS OWN DESTINY AND AFTER THREE YEARS OF EFFORTS HAS SUCCEEDED IN SOLVING FUNDAMENTAL PROBLEMS, IS SELF-SUFFICIENT IN FOOD, IS BUILDING AND DEFENDING THE COUNTRY IN COMPLETE INDEPENDENCE AND SOVEREIGNTY AND RELYING ON ITS OWN STRENGTH WITHOUT RECOURSE TO ANYTHING FROM THE IMPERIALISTS. AS IN THE PAST PEOPLE AND GOVERNMENT OF DEMOCRATIC KAMPUCHEA WILL MAKE MINCEMEAT OF ANY CRIMINAL MANOEUVRES OF THE IMPERIALISTS AND THEIR PARTISANS. THEY WILL NOT TOLERATE ANY AFFRONT TO THE SOVEREIGNTY OF KAMPUCHEA. MINISTER OF FOREIGN AFFAIRS OF DEMOCRATIC KAMPUCHEA, 16 SEPTEMBER 1978.

The government of Kampuchea had every justification for its indictment of American imperialists. They had supported the extremely corrupt and oppressive regime of the republican government, providing it with massive military aid; and in their determination to destroy the bases of the Vietcong within the borders of Cambodia, and in their

57. See *The Current Digest of the Soviet Press*, Vol. XXX, no. 34 (20 September 1978), 17, and Vol. XXX, no. 44 (29 November 1978), 12. It should be noted with reference to the *Izvestia* account that there was some restoration of urban life.
58. E/CN.4 1335, 30 January 1979, p. 23.

158

pursuit of their enemies into the interior, they had dropped half a million tons of bombs on the Cambodian countryside, destroying its economic infrastructure and its agricultural productivity. They had left the new rulers with a most desperate food crisis and the overwhelming task of immediately restoring the cultivation of rice in a war-shattered country. They bear a heavy responsibility for many of the subsequent developments under the revolutionary government.

They had also contributed to an intense hatred of the West. But this was only one of many conflicts with the outside world, deeply rooted in the history of the society. There was the threat from more powerful neighbours, Vietnam and Thailand, with whom Cambodia had ancient territorial disputes. Shortly after the coup by which the previous government took power, Cambodians had slaughtered hundreds of Vietnamese residents, and the South Vietnamese had exacted revenge when they invaded Cambodia under American auspices. The towns themselves were centres of foreign influence with large numbers of Vietnamese and Chinese, representing the private capitalism of small merchants, traders and workshops. Cambodians were almost totally excluded from the mercantile and commercial sectors. Antagonism between town and country thus took on a xenophobic cast. As for relations with the new regime in Vietnam, the Cambodian revolutionary leaders felt betrayed by the Vietcong, so that there was an additional strain of embitterment; and the two countries were soon embroiled in territorial disputes and a vicious propaganda war, which culminated in the Vietnamese invasion of Cambodia.

The country too had been ravaged by many years of civil war, waged mercilessly and with great atrocity, and the people had been subjected to massive bombing raids by the Americans. In this crucible of terror, the surviving revolutionary troops, many of them teenagers, had become hardened soldiers, trained to kill by whatever means.

It is against this background that some of the ideological commitments and revolutionary practices can be understood.[59] The distrust of the outside world, the xenophobia, was expressed partly in the destruction of western artifacts, in the burning of books, and in the attacks on the educated. It was expressed also in the ideological commitment to self-sufficiency, the unwillingness of the rulers to solicit or even receive help from the outside, and the determination to rely only on their own

59. See the excellent analysis by Tan, 1978:3–10, of the social and ideological roots of Khmer Rouge ideology. For further discussions of ideology, see Shawcross, 1979:Ch. 24; Heder, 1978; Rousset, 1977; Pol Pot, 1977.

resources in the building of the new society. The commitment to total revolution in the creation of an egalitarian rural society had as its counterpart the complete destruction of the old society. The towns too harboured the enemies in the civil war, so that, whether or not the deportations were to be explained in part by the need to bring the townspeople to the food, they were certainly dictated also by concern for the consolidation of power.

This need to consolidate the bases of power, and the hatreds aroused in the civil war, converged with other social forces in the slaughter of selected social strata, and in the relentless pursuit of survivors in the closed communes. Here they could hardly evade the ultimate exposure of their social past. Social origins and past social functions took on a clearly identifiable and ineradicable stigma, quite comparable to racial distinctiveness. And the appreciable extension of guilt to members of the family was perhaps encouraged, as Lek Hor Tan suggests,[60] by 'a tragic aspect of the traditional Cambodian penal system that political criminals or "traitors" *and their whole families*' were executed together.

But the course of revolutionary praxis was not predetermined by past events. It was also a matter of choice in the selection of ideological commitments, and of the means to realize the revolutionary objectives. And final responsibility for a regime of massive murder rests with the revolutionary government of Democratic Kampuchea.

60. Tan, op. cit., 9.

Chapter 9

The Sovereign Territorial State
The Right to Genocide

Technically, of course, I had no right to interfere. According to the cold-blooded legalities of the situation, the treatment of Turkish subjects by the Turkish government was purely a domestic affair.

[Henry Morgenthau, *Ambassador Morgenthau's Story*, 1918: 328-9]

Même l'ONU a fait la sourde oreille. Un de mes amis khmers me confiait avec amertume, le jour de Noël 1975: 'En France, il existe des sociétés protectrices des animaux; il existe des usines de fabrication d'aliments pour chines et chats. Les Cambodgiens sont-ils donc moins que des bêtes, puisque personne ne daigne les défendre.'

[François Ponchaud, *Cambodge année zéro*, 1977:230]

The U.N. is first and foremost an organization of *states*, not of nations, and since most states are, in fact, threatened by the claims of nations, it is little wonder that the U.N. is pro-state and anti-nation.

[Pierre van den Berghe, in a personal communication]

The main thesis of this chapter is that the sovereign territorial state claims, as an integral part of its sovereignty, the right to commit genocide, or engage in genocidal massacres, against peoples under its rule, and that the United Nations, for all practical purposes, defends this right. To be sure, no state *explicitly* claims the right to commit genocide – this would not be morally acceptable even in international circles – but the right is exercised under other more acceptable rubrics, notably the duty to maintain law and order, or the seemingly sacred mission to preserve the territorial integrity of the state. And though the norm for the United Nations is to sit by, and watch, like a grandstand spectator, the unfolding of the genocidal conflict in the domestic arena right through to the final massacres, there would generally be concern, and action, to provide humanitarian relief for the refugees, and direct intercession by the Secretary-General. Moreover, some of the steps presently taken by the United Nations in the field of human rights may have the effect of inhibiting the resort to massacre; and there are

161

indications of changing attitudes in the United Nations, though this may be too optimistic an assessment. In the past, however, there was small comfort to be derived from the Genocide Convention, or from the commitments of the United Nations, by peoples whose own rulers threatened them with extermination or massacre.

The almost perennial complaint is that the world remains indifferent to the genocide or the genocidal massacres, and that the United Nations turns a deaf ear. I suppose it may be unrealistic to expect the representatives of the nations, great and small, gathered in imposing session on world affairs, to be unduly concerned over charges of the imminent extermination of a small Indian people in Paraguay. Arens reports[1] that the complaint filed for the Aché Indians by the International League for the Rights of Man resulted in a light flurry of verbal interest among some human-rights-oriented 'experts' and delegates in United Nations corridors, but that no formal action was taken; and that the plea by the Anti-Slavery Society of Great Britain in August 1974 did not succeed in securing a recommendation for even an investigation of conditions in Paraguay. But reactions were by no means totally negative. Some years later, in closed meeting during its thirty-fourth session (February/March 1978), the United Nations Commission on Human Rights did decide on action in respect of a number of countries, including Paraguay. While the nature of the action was not disclosed, it appears from a report of the United States government[2] to have been a recommendation for intercession with the government of Paraguay by the Secretary-General. Moreover, the Inter-American Human Rights Commission of the Organization of American States had adopted a resolution in May 1977 calling attention to reports of serious abuses and requesting the government of Paraguay to take measures to protect the rights of the Aché Indians. There has been some response by the government to these expressions of international concern.[3]

In the Burundi genocide, the situation was very different from the extermination of small bands of hunters and gatherers, deemed expendable in the march of 'progress'. The Hutu were a large settled population of peasants, the massacres took place on a vast scale, and they

1. Arens, 1976:147, 150.
2. Reports on *Human Rights Practices in Countries Receiving U.S. Aid*, by the Department of State to a Joint Committee of the U.S. Congress on Foreign Relations, 8 February 1979, p. 317.
3. ibid.

were immediately known to the outside world, given the presence of diplomatic representatives, missionaries and expatriates. Again, there were many charges of indifference by the outside world. But I would rather describe it, not as indifference, but as a curious mixture of condemnation, of support and of inaction, which permitted the massacres to take their seemingly uninhibited course over the years.[4]

The attempted coup and the massacres by Hutu were on 29 April 1972. Tutsi counteraction was immediate, the suppression of the revolt being followed by the systematic slaughter of selected Hutu strata, with of course much general slaughter. The Belgian government, as the former mandatory power, was most directly concerned. As early as 19 May 1972, the Belgian Prime Minister had informed his cabinet that according to the information at his disposal Burundi was confronted with a veritable genocide; and the Foreign Minister had declared before the Senate Foreign Relations Committee on 24 May that the Belgian Ambassador in Burundi was instructed to express Belgian concern and hope for the restoration of order and peace: accounts in the French press 'found their echo in the French National Assembly on 2 June, when deputies urged the government to take energetic action "to bring an end to the massacre in Burundi" '.[5] But in fact, France lent support to the Burundi government, as did China and North Korea.[6] The U.S.A., on 1 May, declared Burundi to be a disaster area, and engaged in humanitarian relief and diplomatic approaches. Members of the diplomatic corps in Burundi, with notable exceptions, made representations. In his Sunday address on 28 May, Pope Paul referred to the bloody battle of brothers against brothers of the same nation, and on 29 May the Papal Nuncio in Burundi presented the government with a remarkably diplomatic (and insipid) letter of protest on his own behalf and that of other diplomats.[7]

4. The following sources give more extended treatment of the genocide and international reactions: Du Bois, *To Die in Burundi*, 1972, Part II; Lemarchand and Martin, *Selective Genocide in Burundi*, 1974; Lemarchand and Greenland *Les Problèmes du Burundi*, 1974; Kuper, *The Pity of It All*, 1977; Morris, *The United States and Burundi: Genocide, Nickel and 'Normalization'*, 1974; Melady, *Burundi: The Tragic Years*, 1974; Bowen, Freeman and Miller, *Passing By: The United States and Genocide in Burundi*, 1972, 1973, and U.S. Committee on Foreign Affairs, *International Protection of Human Rights*, 1974; Weinstein, *Burundi: Alternatives to Violence*, 1975; and Weinstein and Schrire, *Political Conflict and Ethnic Strategies: A Case Study of Burundi*, 1976.

5. Du Bois, op. cit., Part II, 2–3.

6. Lemarchand, 1975:14–15.

7. See Melady's account and copy of the letter, 1974:15–20, 107–8.

There was also activity in the United Nations. The Secretary-General expressed the United Nations' concern to the representative of Burundi at the United Nations. In the last week of May, he offered assistance for the launching of a United Nations aid programme. On 22 June the first of two small U.N. missions arrived in Burundi, and on 4 July, the Secretary-General reported to a press conference in Geneva that the humanitarian mission had confirmed the enormous suffering; though precise figures could not be obtained, different sources estimated the number of the dead as between 80,000 and 200,000.[8]

Apart from the active concern of the Secretary-General of the United Nations, the various diplomatic approaches, and the provision of humanitarian relief, no serious steps were taken to halt the massacres in either 1972 or 1973. At its meetings in 1973, the Sub-Commission on Prevention of Discrimination and Protection of Minorities forwarded to the Commission on Human Rights a complaint against Burundi of consistent patterns of gross violations of human rights. But when the Commission met in 1974, it effectively shelved the matter by appointing a new working party to communicate with the government of Burundi, and to report back to the next annual meeting of the Commission. The structure and ideology of the United Nations, particularly its protective stance in relation to the sovereign rights of the territorial state, stood in the way of effective action. Moreover, there had been the catastrophic experience of earlier intervention in the Congo. But a major preliminary obstacle was presented by the Organization of African Unity, given the policy of the United Nations and of western diplomats that this body should be primarily responsible for mediating in the conflict, and for initiating appropriate policy.

Whatever representations may have been made privately by members of the Organization of African Unity, its official releases were supportive of the Burundi regime. The Secretary-General of the O.A.U., on a brief visit to Burundi on 22 May 1972, accompanied by the Tanzanian Prime Minister and the President of Somalia, announced that his presence signified the total solidarity of the O.A.U. with President Micombero of Burundi. The O.A.U. summit meeting in Rabat the following month adopted a resolution to the effect that the Council of Ministers was convinced that, thanks to Micombero's saving action, peace would be rapidly re-established, national unity consolidated and territorial integrity preserved. Lemarchand suggests that since most African states are, to a greater or lesser extent, potential Burundis,

8. Du Bois, op. cit., 7–8.

none would wish to establish a precedent that might prevent it dealing with similar crises by means of its own choosing. There would also have been the overriding preoccupation with action against the racist regimes of Southern Africa, and resentment against any involvement which might deflect from that purpose, or reflect on the domestic policies of African states. Whatever the explanation for the attitude of the O.A.U. towards the Burundi massacres, one can well understand the anguish of the victims, confronted with the seeming indifference of African rulers. It is conveyed in the following letter written on 8 September 1972 by the *Mouvement des Etudiants Progressistes Barundi* in Belgium, to heads of African states meeting in Tanzania:

Tutsi apartheid is established more ferociously than the apartheid of Vorster, more inhumanly than Portuguese colonialism. Outside of Hitler's Nazi movement, there is nothing to compete with it in world history. And the peoples of Africa say nothing. African heads of state receive the executioner Micombero and clasp his hand in fraternal greeting. Sirs, heads of state, if you wish to help the African peoples of Namibia, Azania, Zimbabwe, Angola, Mozambique and Guinea-Bissau to liberate themselves from their white oppressors, you have no right to let Africans murder other Africans ... Are you waiting until the entire Hutu ethnic group of Burundi is exterminated before raising your voices?

According to a U.S. report, there was more active concern by a few African heads of state following the ethnic violence in April–May 1973.[9] Perhaps this may have restrained, in some small measure, the fury of genocidal massacre. But one cannot help wondering whether more lives might have been saved if there had been no Organization of African Unity, and whether there might have been more effective humanitarian intervention in the absence of both a United Nations Organization and a Genocide Convention.

I have not yet referred to Uganda, where a murderous regime was establishing itself at about the same time as the massacres in Burundi. The killings in Uganda started immediately after a successful coup by Amin in January 1971, but did not become internationally notorious for some years. The first issue which evoked international involvement was the decision by Amin, in August 1972, to expel the Ugandan Indians on ninety days' notice. They numbered some 75,000, of whom

9. In the above comments, I have made use of the following sources: Du Bois, op. cit., Part II, 1; Lemarchand, 1975, 15; Kuper, 1977, 100; U.S. Congress, *International Protection of Human Rights*, 1974, 72.

about a third were Ugandan citizens. Some exemption was accorded the citizens, who might choose between expulsion or banishment to remote and arid areas, where they could occupy themselves as farmers. There was appreciable international 'concern', the British government being directly affected, since the non-citizens were mostly British Indians. The President of Zaire sought some modification of the policy, and the Presidents of Tanzania and Zambia denounced the expulsions. For the most part, however, African leaders remained silent; there was doubtless appreciable approval. But the issue was taken up in the United Nations by the appropriate body, the Sub-Commission on Prevention of Discrimination and Protection of Minorities, and a proposal made on 22 August 1972 that the Sub-Commission send a telegram to the President of Uganda, expressing its 'concern', and asking that particular attention be given to the humanitarian aspects of the situation affecting non-citizen Asians. Objections were immediately raised that the Sub-Commission had no mandate to send telegrams to heads of state, and the proposal was rejected. In its place, the Sub-Commission passed a resolution recommending that the Commission on Human Rights consider the applicability to non-citizens of the present international legal protection of human rights, and the measures that would be desirable in this field. I have included, in Appendix II, a copy of the report of the proceedings, so that the reader may gain some impression of the deliberations of the international guardians of human rights, and of one of the techniques for denying help to the victims, while extending protection to the executioners – the technique of transforming a concrete and urgent practical issue into a problem of general principle for abstract consideration. Needless to say, the expulsions took their uninhibited course. The victims were brutally treated, a few were killed, and they were systematically stripped of their possessions, which were distributed to, or seized as booty by, soldiers and other supporters of the regime.[10]

In the meantime, the slaughter of Ugandans by a military usurper was becoming more widely known. It was carried out mainly in the consolidation of despotic power, and it extended to almost every conceivable category of victim – ethnic, as in the massacre of Acholi and Lango soldiers in the Ugandan army; political, in the annihilation of

10. See Patel, 1972; Martin, 1974:164–9; the International Commission of Jurists, 1974:3–9; and the Sub-Commission on Prevention of Discrimination and Protection of Minorities, E/CN. 4/1101:E/CN. 4/Sub. 2/332, dated 28 September 1972.

the supporters of the ousted president, and of political opponents in general, real and fancied; the educated élite; religious leaders, and their followers too, notably Catholics; and much indiscriminate killing, random, whimsical, impulsive, with massacres also of entire villages. The killers came from sections of the army, and from security forces, consisting mostly of Southern Sudanese mercenaries, of members of Amin's own ethnic group, the Kakwa, and generally of Nubians inside Uganda. Godfrey Lule, who had been Minister of Justice under Amin, described the Nubians and the newly recruited Sudanese as exercising 'a foreign tyranny more vicious than anything dreamed of by European imperialists or modern white minority governments in Africa'.[11]

Early in 1973, the former Minister of Education, who had served for two years under Amin, sent a long memorandum to African heads of state and government of the Organization of African Unity, giving details of the atrocities of mass murder, and concluding with the complaint that too many nations regarded what was happening in Uganda as an internal matter. 'Is systematic genocide,' he asked, 'an internal matter or a matter for all mankind?'[12] In May 1973, the ousted President of Uganda wrote to the O.A.U. at Addis Ababa, charging that the nature of the outrage on humanity, practised by Amin and his agents, was in fact genocide. Later, in 1974, there appeared David Martin's full-scale study of the regime, and in May 1974, the International Commission of Jurists submitted a report to the Secretary-General of the United Nations on *Violations of Human Rights and the Rule of Law in Uganda*, in which they charged the suspension or violation of most of the fundamental human rights, the breakdown of the rule of law, the placing in abeyance of basic freedoms, the arrest, detention, torture and killing of thousands of civilians, and the establishment of a reign of terror. The submissions included an indictment by a former Ugandan Foreign Minister. Between 1974 and 1976, the Commission submitted, in all, five complaints of human rights violations to the Secretary-General of the United Nations, and in January 1977, Amnesty International submitted to the Commission on Human Rights similar charges of grave violations.[13]

11. Kyemba, 1977:7.

12. The text of the memorandum is given in the reports of the International Commission of Jurists to the United Nations on *Uganda and Human Rights*, 1977:109–20.

13. See Martin, 1974; Emerson, 1975:220–21; International Commission of Jurists, 1974 and 1977; and Amnesty International, 1977.

The Secretary-General of the United Nations did call on Amin to conduct an investigation, hardly an effective measure, but as for the Commission on Human Rights, it successfully parried the charges against the Ugandan regime. At its meetings in 1977, the need for action became even more critical, since its Sub-Commission on Discrimination had recommended that the Commission institute an inquiry under open procedure into the violations of human rights in Uganda.[14] The Ugandan Minister of Justice represented his country as a fully fledged member of this Commission. He recounts in a foreword to a denunciation of the regime by a former cabinet minister,[15] that the Commission discussed, in private session, in 1977, evidence submitted by an internal Ugandan Commission of Inquiry, charging that Amin's various terror units had engaged in wanton killing; and that he was instructed by Amin to deny everything. This, he says, he could not do. 'I would not have been taken seriously. Instead I told the U.N. Commission that more time should be given for consideration of the report's allegations.' In the result, the Commission decided to keep the matter under review, that is to say, it decided to defer consideration to its meetings in the following year.

The proceedings of the Commission on Human Rights are so tortuously camouflaged that it is difficult to know with certainty what transpires. But it would seem that the representatives of the United Kingdom and Canada must have reacted against the secret evasion of the Ugandan issue, since in March 1977 they submitted resolutions,[16] in open session, calling for an inquiry into the human rights situation in Uganda. In a thoroughly disreputable debate,[17] and on a Cuban resolution supported by the automatic majority of African, East European, Middle Eastern and Asian countries, their attempt to secure an investigation was soundly defeated.

In 1978, there were further developments, as a result it seems of a démarche. In December 1977, the five Nordic governments had jointly sponsored a U.N. General Assembly resolution of concern over repeated gross violations of human rights in Uganda. They had expressed the hope that the Organization of African Unity would 'give appropriate consideration to these violations with a view to their cessa-

14. Most of the sorry tale is given by the International Commission of Jurists in the introduction to its 1977 publication of reports on Uganda.
15. Kyemba, op. cit., 5–6.
16. E/CN. 4/L. 1348 and 1349.
17. E/CN. 4/SR, 1423.

tion', and they had asked the Commission on Human Rights to consider the human rights situation in the country. According to an account by Ullman, the proposed resolution 'aroused intense controversy within the U.N.'s 50-member African group, with some members even willing to support it. But the majority urged – and the Nordic sponsors agreed – that in exchange for a commitment that the Human Rights Commission would take up Uganda once again in March 1978, the resolution would not be publicly debated or pressed to a vote.'[18] At its March 1978 meeting, the Commission on Human Rights did decide on some form of action, but the nature of the action was not disclosed, in conformity with the rules governing proceedings *in camera*.

The Organization of African Unity was even more reticent and protective, though three African states refused to send delegations to the twelfth annual summit meeting in Kampala, presided over by Amin as chairman of the organization for 1975-6: and two African presidents took a persistently hostile stand against the regime.[19] A particularly disquieting item of news was that Amin received a rousing ovation when he attended the summit meeting at Libreville in 1977. I do not believe that this expressed approval of his regime of terror, but that it was rather approbation for his reversal, as it were, of colonial humiliation. I think, too, that there may have been a certain ambivalence in the relationship of the delegates to him. It is certainly a marked feature of many of the western commentaries. Even in their authors' denunciations of Amin, they are often quite meticulous in describing him as General Amin, or as Marshal or President. Perhaps they are only wanting to be formally correct (to a usurping tyrant slaughtering his countrymen). But it seems to me that there is also affection in the use of such names as Idi Amin or Idi Amin Dada or Marshal Idi Amin Dada. Be that as it may, Amin continued for all practical purposes under the protection of the Organization of African Unity and the United Nations Commission on Human Rights, until he invaded Tanzania and was overthrown in April 1979 by a counter-invasion of Tanzanian and supporting Ugandan forces.

Is it exaggerated to describe the actions of the United Nations Commission on Human Rights and the Organization of African Unity as

18. Ullman, 1978:530.
19. In June 1977, a Commonwealth conference passed a resolution condemning the massive violation of human rights in Uganda. Several African representatives took a leading role in this denunciation (*Washington Post*, 16 June 1977).

having the effect of a condonation of the mass slaughter of Ugandan citizens?

In the case of Cambodia (Democratic Kampuchea), there would appear to have been an expeditious response by the Commission on Human Rights. I referred in Chapter 8 to the decision of the Commission, on 8 March 1978, to invite comment by the government of Democratic Kampuchea; this would then be considered by the Commission, together with other available information, at its next session in the following year. At this session in 1979, the Commission had before it a careful analysis prepared by the Chairman of the Sub-Commission on Discrimination. The institution of any action at all, and as speedily as within a period of three years, was quite remarkable. But in terms of the needs of the people of Cambodia, it constituted interminable delay and inhuman indifference. After all, the forced evacuation of Phnom Penh in April 1975 was immediately known to the outside world, and refugees' accounts soon gave abundant testimony to the harshness of the regime and its brutal destruction of human life. Yet the procedures followed were of such a leisurely and administratively protracted nature, that Cambodia had been invaded and conquered by the time the Commission could initiate further action. Moreover the resolution of March 1978 seems virtually to have been forced on the Commission by extreme pressure. There were the submissions by the governments of Canada, Norway, the United Kingdom, the United States of America and Australia, and by two major non-governmental organizations, with supporting documentation, which I assume could not easily be dismissed by the majority of the members. And the debate itself supports this interpretation.

The original resolution proposed by the United Kingdom delegation asked simply that a study of the human rights situation in Democratic Kampuchea should be made with the cooperation of the government of that country and of any other government, non-governmental organization or individual who might be able to provide objective and reliable information on the situation. In support of the resolution, the representative of the United Kingdom argued that the Commission 'had not hesitated to examine the situation in certain countries, such as Chile and South Africa, under other procedures. There were, however, other gross violations of human rights which were as bad as, if not worse than, the cases just mentioned, and which the Commission never considered ... If the Commission continued to turn a blind eye to those situations, it was in danger of discrediting itself, and the United Nations generally, in the eyes of world public opinion.' He then commented on the reports of systematic and arbitrary executions and other flagrant violations of human rights involving thousands of deaths, and systematic brutality at the whim of the authorities, with the slaughter in many cases of entire families. 'All those atrocities had aroused the conscience of the world, but the Commission had disregarded them for political reasons.' If the Commission was to fulfil its functions, it would have to bring the allegations into the open by instituting a full and impartial investigation.[20]

The proposed resolution was innocuous enough, but it aroused opposition of a most disquieting nature. A compromise was arrived at (seemingly in the corridors with much diplomatic frou-frouing) which resulted in the revised resolution to which I have already referred, an almost totally debilitated resolution. The adoption of this resolution may have represented progress and created an important precedent for the Commission, as the United States representative commented; but to the outside observer it appears simply as a stalling operation, with a polite face-saving bow in the direction of the supporters of the original proposal.

In March 1979, during the annual meetings of the Commission, Mr Boudhiba, Chairman of the Sub-Commission on Prevention of Discrimination and Protection of Minorities, presented the report on Kampuchea which the Commission had requested. He concluded that the situation constituted 'nothing less than autogenocide', and that the events described in the documents were 'the most serious that had occurred anywhere in the world since nazism'.[21] The representatives of Australia, Canada, Sweden and the United Kingdom tabled a motion, which, in its revised form, would record the Commission's view that, on the basis of the evidence available, gross and flagrant violations of human rights had occurred in Democratic Kampuchea, and which would note the Commission's decision to keep the situation under review at its next meeting (in 1980) as a matter of priority.

Neither the original nor the revised resolution, though deliberately moderate in tone, were debated. Yugoslavia, acting on behalf of the sponsors (Benin, Egypt, Pakistan, Senegal, Syria and Yugoslavia) tabled a draft decision to postpone consideration of the report on Kampuchea to the next session in 1980. This was carried by a large majority. As for the revised resolution, which carefully refrained from reference to the

20. E/CN. 4/SR. 1466/Add. 1.
21. E/CN. 4/SR. 1510, p. 7.

Sub-Commission's report, it was guillotined on a motion by the Chairman of the Commission, carried by an overwhelming majority, that the Commission should decide not to vote on the resolution. Only Australia, Austria, Canada, France, West Germany, Sweden and the U.S.A. opposed this motion.

The issue was not controversy over the facts. There seemed to be fairly general agreement that the government of Democratic Kampuchea had committed gross violations of human rights. The Soviet representative, using the occasion to attack both the U.S.A. and China, described the Kampuchean government as a 'cut-throat regime' which had established a system of slavery of a new type, and had subjected the people of Kampuchea to 'generalized genocide' (presumably in the sense of genocide against *all* strata, the distinction between political and ethnic slaughter seemingly abandoned in this, as in much other contemporary, discussion). The issue was rather one of *realpolitik* connected with the invasion of Cambodia by Vietnam. In any event, whatever the motivations of the members, the Commission had succeeded in evading even a mildly phrased condemnation of the Cambodian regime.[22] Once again, the Commission had 'risen above principle'.

It was left to the successor Cambodian regime, installed by the Vietnamese, to initiate action, and in August 1979 the new government instituted criminal proceedings against the former Prime Minister and Deputy Prime Minister – *in absentia* – on charges of genocide. The indictment cited massacres by the accused and their associates of nearly all the officers, soldiers and officials of the previous administration, along with their families, and a systematic plan to eliminate ethnic minorities, including a large number of Thai and Cham, and also all those who opposed the regime. It detailed the forced evacuation of the towns; the unprecedented apparatus of repression, reducing the population to a state of slavery; the abolition of all social relations, forcing the population to focus on only one central point of authority; the elimination of Buddhism and Islam, the abolition of culture and education, the systematic killing of religious converts and intellectuals; 'corrupting adolescents in order to make them torturers'; and the destruction of the economy. There was evidence of massacres, executions, torture, mass graves, and survivors' accounts to support the indictment,

22. For these discussions see the reports of the proceedings of the Commission in March 1979, and in particular: E/CN. 4/SR. 1510, pp. 5–8; 1515/Add. 1, p. 4; 1516, pp. 3–5; 1517, *passim*; 1519, pp. 6–18.

and the accused were found guilty of genocide by the People's Revolutionary Tribunal.

But the crimes of the regime proved no barrier to continued participation in the General Assembly of the United Nations. In September 1979, a majority of 71 (against 35, with 34 abstentions) voted to continue the assignment of the Cambodian seat to the ousted government. Among nations supporting the resolution were governments that had previously denounced the regime before the Commission on Human Rights – Australia, Canada, the United Kingdom and the U.S.A. One can only ask – is genocide a credential for membership in the General Assembly of the United Nations? Meanwhile, the Cambodian people were threatened with near extinction by famine and disease, in another chapter in the politics of starvation, reminiscent of the Biafran tragedy in the last stages of the Nigerian civil war.

In Bangladesh, as in Uganda and Cambodia, slaughter pursued its relatively uninhibited course, until invasion by a foreign power, with supporting local forces. The massacres, starting in March 1971, took place under the full gaze of the outside world, with observer reports, and charges of genocide, filtering through to the world press. Yet the United Nations General Assembly and Security Council were only 'seized' of the matter, and then from a quite different aspect, in December 1971 following the escalating of the conflict between India and Pakistan into open warfare, and the invasion of Bangladesh by India. As for the Sub-Commission on Prevention of Discrimination and Protection of Minorities, meeting in August 1971, it speedily disposed of a written request by twenty-two international non-governmental organizations that the Sub-Commission examine the available information and recommend measures for the protection of human rights in East Pakistan. A plea presented in person by the representative of the International Commission of Jurists similarly fell on deaf ears. Only one member is reported as having argued that the Sub-Commission should not remain silent. I found it almost unbearable to read this discussion by a United Nations body of one of the major genocides of the twentieth century; it was so procedural and so devoid of human compassion.[23]

The Secretary-General of the United Nations had been deeply concerned. In July 1971, in a memorandum to the President of the

23. Reports of the proceedings are to be found in the second volume of the summary records of the twenty-fourth session, pp. 69–79, 139–47, and 165–70.

Security Council, he drew attention to the tragic situation in the India-Pakistan sub-continent, and its possible consequences as a potential threat to peace; but no Security Council action resulted from this approach. Indeed, the only effective action taken by the United Nations in relation to the massacres was the mounting of a massive programme of humanitarian relief which continued after the cessation of hostilities. Some perspectives on the failure to take action, arising out of the alignment of the great powers – with the U.S.A. and China supporting Pakistan and Soviet Russia supporting India – and the considerations shaping the United States policy of delicate diplomacy behind the scenes, are given in the United States Congress Hearings before the Sub-Committee on International Organizations and Movements.[24]

I have not dealt with all the cases of genocide or genocidal massacres since the Second World War, discussed in preceding chapters. Sometimes the massacres were so precipitate, as in the massacres of Ibo in Northern Nigeria or of Arabs in Zanzibar, that there was no possibility of preventive action by the United Nations. In Rwanda, United Nations missions had the unfortunate effect of further polarizing relations between Tutsi and Hutu. In Vietnam, there were obstacles to the involvement of the United Nations, and its role was both marginal and intermittent.[25] The Secretary-General had good cause to record, in his introduction to the Annual Report for 1971–2, his deep concern that the United Nations, created in the aftermath of a world war to safeguard international peace and security, should appear to have no relevance to what was happening in Vietnam. And we recall that charges of genocide against the United States were heard by a privately instituted tribunal. In the Sudan, there was seeming indifference to the struggle of the Southern Sudanese, in contrast to the Algerian revolutionary forces, who succeeded in internationalizing their war of liberation. The Turkish genocide against the Armenians preceded the United Nations by many years, and here the contribution of the U.N. was to give the genocide a gentle push down the memory hole.[26]

I have also not mentioned the recent cases of Equatorial Guinea and East Timor. In March 1978, the Commission on Human Rights decided, under its confidential procedures, on some unspecified form of action relating to Equatorial Guinea. Here a dictator of about ten years' standing had been engaged in slaughtering, torturing, repressing and pillaging his people. In August 1979, he was overthrown in a coup, then

24. U.S. Congress, 1974:381–2, 415–32, 913–29.
25. See the discussion by Rajan and Israel, 1976:114–43.
26. See Appendix 2, p. 215.

tried before a military tribunal, found guilty (of genocide, multiple murders, treason, the violation of human rights, and the misuse of public funds) and executed. In East Timor, there had been an invasion of the country by Indonesia in December 1975, and massive slaughter of its inhabitants. The government of Indonesia failed to comply with repeated calls by the United Nations to withdraw its armed forces from East Timor, so as to enable the people of the territory freely to exercise their right to self-determination. In a statement presented to the Fourth Committee of the U.N. General Assembly,[27] Noam Chomsky contrasts the protective stance of the U.S.A. and the West towards the atrocities of the Indonesian occupation with their denunciation of the Khmer Rouge regime in Cambodia.

I have also not mentioned the recent expulsion of Chinese by the Vietnamese government, with great loss of life through the denial of refuge in adjoining countries, and by drowning, starvation and disease. This recalls the many other expulsions of minority groups in recent years, and the danger that, with increasing pressure of population on resources, mass expulsion may become a regular feature of the international scene.

The major and important contribution of the United Nations has been in the provision of humanitarian relief for the survivors of the genocidal conflicts. And I should add also the contribution of its peacekeeping forces, which have no doubt averted many massacres. But taken as a whole, the United Nations performs a quite negligible role in the direct prevention or punishment of the crime of genocide, and the Genocide Convention is virtually a dead letter. In the comments which follow, I seek to explore some of the reasons for this failure.

The performance of the United Nations Organization in the suppression of the crime of genocide is deeply disillusioning, particularly against the background of the humanitarian ideals which inspired its founding, and which the organization continues to proclaim – ideals in which the suppression of war, of crimes against humanity and of genocide were quite central. But of course the United Nations is not a humanitarian, but a political, organization, and its humanitarian goals are at the play of political forces, pressure groups and blocs, in an arena where delegates pursue the divisive interests of the states they represent. Added to this, its ideological commitment to the protection of the sovereignty of the state, with the corollary of non-intervention in its domestic affairs, stands in the way of effective action against 'domestic'

27. A/C. 4/33/SR. 30, dated 1 December 1978.

(internal) genocide. And above all, it is the rulers of the states of the world who gather together at the United Nations, and it is mainly, though not exclusively, the rulers who engage in genocide.

We discussed in Chapter 2 the political conflict in the debate on the Genocide Convention, which resulted in the emasculation of its provisions in two important respects – the exclusion of political groups as potential victims of genocide, and the elimination of effective enforcement procedures. I have stressed, and documented, the rather obvious argument that political division within a society has been, and continues to be, a significant source of systematic massacre, and that there is no valid theoretical reason for denying political groups the protection of the Genocide Convention. Political groups are as vulnerable and identifiable as ethnic groups; moreover, what seems to be a purely ethnic conflict usually has a political dimension, as for example in Burundi, and the seemingly purely political may be interwoven with ethnic antagonisms, as to some extent in both Indonesia and Cambodia. One can only suppose that many of the governments represented in the debates on the Convention did not wish to be denied the right to dispose of their political opponents, by radical means if necessary, and with the minimum of outside interference.

But the issue of the exclusion of political groups from the protection of the Genocide Convention is somewhat academic, since the protection, as matters stand at the present time, is quite spurious. The initial draft of the Convention incorporated the principle of universal enforcement, and made provision for both national and international jurisdiction. It was watered down by the exclusion of the principle of universal enforcement and by other modifications, and now provides for trial by a competent tribunal of the state in the territory of which the act was committed, 'or by such international penal tribunal as may have jurisdiction with respect to those Contracting Parties which shall have accepted its jurisdiction'. Where there has been a change of government, action within the state against the former rulers becomes feasible, and I have referred to two such cases, Cambodia and Equatorial Guinea. In the ordinary course, however, the effect of the present provisions is that the rulers, the main universe for genocidal murderers, would be expected to prosecute themselves or to submit to the jurisdiction of an international penal court, which does not exist, though more than thirty years have passed since the framing of the Genocide Convention.

A somewhat different perspective on these issues, from within the United Nations, will be found in a *Study of the Question of the Preven-*

tion and Punishment of the Crime of Genocide.[28] After surveying the conflict of views on the extension of protection to political and other groups, the Special Rapporteur expressed the opinion that it would not be desirable to include these groups in any new international instruments that might be adopted on genocide, 'in that a consequence of such inclusion would be to prevent some States from becoming parties to the new instruments'. He also believed that other international instruments effectively protect political groups.[29] The discussion of this issue in the report is brief and perfunctory. A much more thorough study is accorded the issue of sanctions. Here the Special Rapporteur recommends that consideration be given to the framing of new international instruments, which, in the absence of an international criminal court, would provide for universal enforcement, but that consideration be given also to the establishment of an international criminal court. He seems to have been driven in these recommendations to the abandonment of expediency, which influenced his approach to the inclusion of political groups. The record was too negative for compromise. He expresses the opinion[30] that the Genocide Convention has not been an obstacle to the perpetration of that crime, and states[31] that apart from the punishment of Nazi war criminals, national laws concerning genocide have not been applied. He comments[32] that a number of allegations of genocide have been made since the adoption of the 1948 Convention, but that 'in the absence of a prompt investigation of these allegations by an impartial body, it has not been possible to determine whether they were well-founded. Either they have given rise to sterile controversy or, because of the political circumstances, nothing further has been heard about them.'

The barrier to the effective implementation of the Genocide Convention lies not only in the emasculation of the enforcement procedures. It is deeply embedded in the structure and performance of the United Nations as a whole, and of the bodies primarily 'seized' with complaints of human rights violations. These bodies are the Commission on Human Rights, and the Sub-Commission on Prevention of Discrimination and Protection of Minorities. The Deputy Director of the Human Rights Division explained to me that the complaints might be classified

28. E/CN. 4/Sub. 2/416, dated 4 July 1978.
29. ibid., 21–3.
30. ibid., 185.
31. ibid., 166.
32. ibid., 184.

Genocide

in three categories – those handled within confidential procedures, those sent for processing, also within the confidential procedures, but published by the authors, and complaints made directly to the Commission by governmental representatives or by observers. As regards the third category of open complaint, he recalled only one recent case, where a charge of genocide had been made against Democratic Kampuchea. Because of the confidentiality of closed meetings and the diplomatic style of reporting in the open meetings, it is not easy to unravel the proceedings of the Commission, or to know how much of the discussion has surfaced. I have some sympathy with a comment in a recent article that 'the reader should be warned that the story of the Commission is frustratingly difficult to follow. This is as the Commission intends. In almost total secrecy it has constructed a bureaucratic and procedural maze. Working groups and *ad hoc* groups have proliferated, delay has been institutionalized and the aim has been not to protect the victims but the oppressors.'[33]

The Commission devoted itself appreciably to the elaboration of norms for human rights behaviour. This was in sharp contrast to its approach to the *violation* of norms. Indeed, it started most inauspiciously by abdicating responsibility in terms of a resolution to the effect that it had 'no power to take any action in regard to any complaints concerning human rights'. Incidentally, this resolution was approved by its parent body, the Economic and Social Council. Complainants would receive the encouraging response that the matter had been noted for consideration in accordance with the procedures laid down, and 'further that the Commission on Human Rights has no power to take any action in regard to any complaint concerning human rights'.

It was not until some twenty years later, in 1967, that the Commission became intensively active in the mounting U.N. campaign against South Africa. In that year, it appointed an Ad Hoc Working Group of Experts to investigate charges of torture, an investigation the experts extended into a sort of preparatory examination into genocide. In the same year, the Council approved the decision of the Commission to give annual consideration to the *Question of the violation of human rights and fundamental freedoms, including policies of racial discrimination and segregation and of apartheid, in all countries, with particular reference to colonial and other dependent countries and territories.* The following year, the Commission enlarged the mandate of the Ad Hoc Working Group to include the remaining white settler dominated

33. Shawcross, Terry and Pringle, 1976.

178

societies in Southern Africa, and in 1969, it established a special Working Group of Experts to investigate complaints against Israel that it had violated the Geneva Convention of 1949.

In 1970, in response to resolutions of the Commission and Sub-Commission, the Council established a new procedure, authorizing the Sub-Commission to appoint a working group to consider communications (i.e. complaints) 'with a view to bringing to the attention of the Sub-Commission those communications, together with replies of Governments, if any, which appear to reveal a consistent pattern of gross and reliably attested violations of human rights and fundamental freedoms within the terms of reference of the Sub-Commission'. If the Sub-Commission refers to the Commission any situation which does appear to reveal such a pattern of gross violations, the Commission may decide on a thorough study or an investigation by an *ad hoc* committee. These actions remain confidential until such time as the Commission decides to make recommendations to the Council. Clearly, this is a category under which action may be taken in respect of charges of genocide; or action may be taken under the earlier resolution, which established procedures for public consideration of allegations of human rights violations.[34]

In 1974, the Commission sent a telegram to the government of Chile calling for an immediate end to its violation of human rights, and in 1975, it appointed an Ad Hoc Working Group to report on the situation in Chile, which had now joined South Africa and Israel as objects of particular concern. These three countries predominate overwhelmingly in the proceedings of the Commission and Sub-Commission on human rights violations. Indeed, in the different bodies of the United Nations, there is such a volume of resolutions and of reports and of denunciations as to justify the common description of the three countries as constituting the pariah group, or the unholy trinity, in the U.N. They serve also, in the view of the Canadian representative at the meeting of the Commission on 15 February 1978, as lightning rods for many other states where violations of the rights of the individual seemed to have become a matter of custom.[35]

The Commission on Human Rights consists of members who rep-

---

34. I have used the following sources in the above account: *ECOSOC*, Resolutions 728F (XXVIII), dated 30 July 1959; 1235 (XLII), dated 6 June 1967; and 1503 (XLVIII), dated 27 May 1970; United Nations Action in the Field of Human Rights (E. 74. XIV. 2, 1974); and Sohn and Buergenthal, 1973: 539–43, 789ff.

35. E/CN. 4/SR. 1442, dated 17 February 1978.

resent their governments and are accountable to them. Members of the Sub-Commission on Discrimination and Protection of Minorities, on the other hand, serve as experts in their individual capacities and not as representatives of their governments. But this is only in theory; they too are nominated by their governments and, no doubt, many respond to the interests of these governments. In practice, both the Commission and Sub-Commission are heavily politicized. By this, I do not mean to imply that these bodies do not include highly principled members, deeply dedicated to the promotion of human rights. But there is a sharp tension between a universal ethic and the power interests of sovereign states. And there are many divisions within the United Nations – between capitalist and socialist countries, between the wealthy industrialized nations and the struggling Third World, and between regional alliances – which serve as the basis for voting blocs, exposing the most tragic issues to 'regional and ideological protection rackets' and to the 'disguised barter of one atrocity for another'.[36]

The subordination of human rights issues to quite naked political interests, which I have documented in a few cases, has provoked repeated comment in the Commission and Sub-Commission. An important speech along these lines was that made at the opening of the thirty-fifth session of the Commission, on 12 February 1979, by the Acting Chairman, Mr Keba M'Baye, President of the Supreme Court of Senegal, and a long-standing member of the *ad hoc* working group of experts on Southern Africa. The meeting was held shortly after the celebration of the thirtieth anniversary of the Declaration of Human Rights, and Mr M'Baye reviewed the world situation – the continued atrocities of war; the Third World, as exploited victims of the egoism of the rich countries, stagnating in underdevelopment and given over to despair and rancour; fear, poverty, torture; violations of the right of peoples to self-determination; massacres, punitive expeditions, the malpractices of *apartheid*; thousands of African and Asian children killed every day by malnutrition and disease; the continued persecution of national or foreign minorities in a world which claimed to aspire to the civilization of the universal; and mass deportation of foreign minorities serving as scapegoats for despotic and unpopular regimes. It was a sad commentary on the current state of human rights.

Mr M'Baye then moved to his criticism of the Commission, reported in the proceedings as follows:

36. Phrase used by Shawcross, Terry and Pringle, op. cit., and comment quoted by Arens, op. cit., 150.

Meanwhile, the members of the Commission on Human Rights had arrived at Geneva with set recommendations and arguments. Each representative had received instructions which he was in most cases unable to modify and which reflected his Government's position and policy on each issue. What of the common ideal of universal human rights and the humanitarian principles which justified members' presence at the session? He had to admit that he had not yet become accustomed to the systematic defence of rigid policy positions, dictated by ideological differences and economic interests, in an organ which aspired to the universal and whose aim was to uphold human dignity. Clearly, representatives were not responsible for that situation, for they were the servants of their Government. Equally clearly, there was little prospect that matters would change for the better in the near future. The Commission did the best it could within the narrow limits imposed on it. Thanks to the spirit of cooperation which had prevailed at the thirty-fourth session, the Commission had been able to organize its work rationally and achieve progress in the promotion of human rights. But promotion alone did not suffice, and a major effort was needed in the field of protection.

It was his hope that future generations would benefit from a Commission of which each member received the single instruction to defend the economic, social and cultural requirements and civil and political freedoms and rights of man. That day would mark the victory of the Universal Declaration of Human Rights, which would no longer be used as a pretext to ease consciences or to disseminate propaganda. Neither would it be possible to plead non-interference in the domestic affairs of States in order to arrogate the right to persecute and starve others. Finally, underdevelopment would not be able to serve as a pretext for the oppression of an entire people. When that day came, cooperation would be genuine, just, based on the principle of solidarity and equality and sustained by a common determination to combat poverty in order to build a world in which each individual could exercise his right to development and find happiness. All efforts would be aimed at securing genuine international peace and concord in a new economic order in which justice bred prosperity.[37]

The speech makes reference to a central ideological commitment of the United Nations, respect for the sovereignty of the state. It is enshrined in Article 2(7) of the United Nations Charter, which provides that 'nothing contained in the present Charter shall authorize the United Nations to intervene in matters which are essentially within the domestic jurisdiction of any state or shall require the Members to submit such matters to settlement under the present Charter; but this principle shall not prejudice the application of enforcement measures under Chapter VII'. The former colonial territories have good reason

37. E/CN. 4/SR. 1477, dated 20 March 1979.

to fear intervention, and the injunction against such intervention is elaborated in the General Assembly's *Declaration on the Inadmissibility of Intervention in Domestic Affairs of States and Protection of their Independence and Sovereignty*.[38] The protection of domestic jurisdiction is almost inevitably invoked by any state charged with violating the human rights of its subjects. But Chapter VII of the Charter, vesting the Security Council with the right to impose sanctions against any threat to the peace, already constitutes a substantial modification of the principle of non-interference in the internal affairs of a state. And the recognition of such international crimes as genocide or crimes against humanity similarly implies limitations on the powers of the sovereign state. Human rights are a matter of legitimate international concern. Yet the United Nations remains highly protective of state sovereignty, even where there is overwhelming evidence, not simply of minor violations, but of widespread murder and genocidal massacre. It is no wonder that it may seem to be part of a conspiracy of governments to deprive the people of their rights.

A second central ideological commitment is to the right of peoples to self-determination. It appears in the first article of the Charter, and in many resolutions of the General Assembly, notably in 1952, in a resolution entitled *The Right of Peoples and Nations to Self-determination*, and again in 1960, in the *Declaration on the Granting of Independence to Colonial Countries and Peoples*.[39] The right to self-determination, to freedom from alien subjugation and exploitation, was an inspiring, crusading call in the world movement for decolonization. But the situation is quite changed in the successor states to the former colonial societies, most of which are multi-ethnic. Now a political movement by an ethnic group to realize the 'inalienable' right to self-determination is seen as a reprehensible attack on the sovereignty and territorial integrity of the state – secession, not liberation. In a debate on Bangladesh at the Commission on Human Rights, the representative of Pakistan interpreted this distinction as follows:

... it was the established jurisprudence of the United Nations that, while the principle of self-determination governed the liberation of territories under colonial rule or in dispute between Member States, it could not be extended to areas that were recognized as integral parts of the territories of Member States. Any such extension on the ground of ethnic, linguistic

38. Resolution 2131 (X), December 1965.
39. See the discussion by Sohn and Buergenthal, op. cit., 535–9.

or racial composition of the people, or of economic disparities within a country, would give rise to such a multiplicity of disputes and cause such anarchy and strife as to destroy the present international order. Such a development would be disastrous even from a purely human point of view, particularly for the newly independent states of Asia and Africa. Pakistan was only one among the many multi-racial, multi-linguistic or multi-religious states which would then be exposed to the dangers of fission and disintegration.[40]

I can well appreciate that there could be anarchy if every group, however small, sought to exercise the right of self-determination. There is certainly a need to define the self which would be entitled to claim the right to self-determination, the conditions for the exercise of that right, and the forms such exercise might take.[41] But as it is, some of the most destructive and genocidal conflicts have been waged precisely in the repression of claims for greater autonomy or for independence by large, distinctive, regionally separate peoples. And one has to ask whether the slaughter of millions in Bangladesh, Biafra, the Sudan and now in Eritrea can possibly be justified by the interests of the Territorial State in the relatively unrestrained exercise of its internal sovereignty and in the preservation of the domains it has conquered or inherited? Or is there a need for the United Nations to abandon a dehumanized scale of values which effectively condones the sacrifice of human victims to the Territorial State?

The general argument in this chapter is that the United Nations provides no protection against genocide, and that the Commission on Human Rights, though vested with a primary responsibility, actually condones the crime by delay, evasion and subterfuge. A weapon available to the Commission is the urgent condemnation of gross violations of human rights, and the exposure of those responsible to the opprobrium of international public opinion. But it is precisely this step that the Commission is reluctant to take. It uses the confidential procedures to hide, in the maximum secrecy it can attain, its own, often disreputable, deliberations; and through the same procedures, it protects its fellow rulers, as a club or a clique might protect its delinquent members. Yet the United Nations is the most appropriate body for protection against, and punishment of, genocide, and the problem is what developments and pressures might render it somewhat effective,

40. E/CN. 4/Sub. 2/SR. 625–35, dated 29 October 1971.
41. These problems are analysed in Lee C. Buchheit, 1978.

and how to bridge the immense distance which presently separates proclaimed ideal from actual practice.

Given the structure and performance of the United Nations, it is perhaps naive to anticipate significant change. Yet there are indications of imminent change. Two new U.N. covenants have now come into force, the International Covenant on Economic, Social and Cultural Rights and the International Covenant on Civil and Political Rights. An optional protocol, attached to the second covenant, enables individuals in a state which ratifies the protocol to have recourse to a Human Rights Committee. As for the Commission on Human Rights, it has somewhat improved its procedures, and it has finally begun to initiate action beyond the boundaries of its three scapegoat nations. There could be appreciable further progress if some of the suggestions were taken up for a more efficient division of functions, and for the appointment of a High Commissioner for Human Rights, or a High Commissioner for the Prevention of Genocide and Torture.

Some significance is also to be attached to the fact that in two countries, Cambodia and Equatorial Guinea, the successor regimes actually instituted proceedings against the former rulers on charges of genocide. As countries overthrow tyrannical and murderous rulers, who seem to be more abundant than ever, we may anticipate that the representatives of the new regimes are likely to show greater moral and militant concern for protection against massacre and genocide. Thus it would seem that the intervention of the new President of Uganda, at the summit meeting of the Organization of African Unity in July 1979, must have contributed to the belated decision to write an African Charter of Human Rights, and to establish an African Commission on Human Rights.

The very acts and omissions of the United Nations in the field of human rights have stimulated protective action in regional intergovernmental, and in international non-governmental, organizations. The Council of Europe has been reasonably effective in the protection of human rights against violation. The Inter-American Human Rights Commission receives, and acts on, petitions from individuals; it has carried out a number of investigations. Steps are being taken to establish an African Commission for the protection of human rights on that continent. The international non-governmental organizations try to fill, as well as they can, some of the vacuum left by the United Nations in the area of human rights, and they act continuously as a pressure group. Their activities remain invaluable, not only as agencies with independent specialized functions, but also as conscience in an unconscionable organization, and as focal points for international public opinion. Their continued recognition and participation in the U.N. is, of course, highly vulnerable to repressive punitive action. This became all too clear when a representative of the World Conference on Religion and Peace had the effrontery to comment on the denial of religious tolerance by certain countries, whose membership within the majority coalition in the U.N. had secured them a degree of practical immunity from criticism.[42] Dictators, accustomed to the systematic suppression of human rights in their own countries, are not likely to view sympathetically the unfriendly exercise of freedom of speech by the representatives of relatively powerless organizations.

Regardless of the actual and potential contribution of the United Nations, the regional inter-governmental associations, and the international non-governmental agencies, the first, and perhaps main, line of defence against domestic genocide lies within the countries themselves. And in the concluding chapter, I turn to the discussion of the non-genocidal society.

42. Liskofsky, 1975:896–900. The author writes that in passing a resolution in reaction to this intervention, the Commission on Human Rights, 'which is expected to promote human rights, including freedom of expression, appeared eager to silence those who spoke out within the U.N. against human rights violations'. The original resolution and the final modified resolution passed by the parent Economic and Social Council are given on pages 911–14.

Chapter 10

The Non-Genocidal Society

He collapsed beside his carpet-slippers
Without a murmur, shot through the head
By a shivering boy who wandered in
Before they could turn the television down
Or tidy away the supper dishes.
To the children, to a bewildered wife,
I think 'Sorry Missus' was what he said.
   [Michael Longley, 'Wounds', in *An Exploded View*]

You can't get permission to come into Durban as a cook in an urban area, as a waiter, as a garden boy, as a driver, as a delivery boy. There is the law. You must not cross the Tugela. Somebody came to me and asked me about it. He said he was crying with all the difficulties to try and come to Durban over a period of six months. And I said to him you will cry, my dear son, till you cry no more. They say to us that they want to *canalize* the native labour ... The first time I read of that expression, I can't tell you my feelings.
   [Interview with African leader, South Africa, 1959, in Leo Kuper, *An African Bourgeoisie*, 1965]

Sean MacBride, in a speech condemning the present world phase of unprecedented violence and cruelty, and the near total breakdown in public and private morality, cited the following recent cases of 'massive massacres amounting to genocide' – Indonesia, 1965–7; Chile, 1973; Kampuchea, 1975–6; East Timor, 1975–6; Uganda, 1976–8; the Argentine, 1978–9; the Central African Empire, 1978–9; and Equatorial Guinea, 1977–9.[1] Strangely enough, he omitted the most lethal of the contemporary genocides, Bangladesh in 1971; and he made no reference to Burundi in 1972–3. Though the reader may not define all these cases as genocide within the terms of the United Nations Convention, it remains a formidable list of contemporary massive massacres, with a death toll of many millions.

And these genocidal massacres seem likely to continue, given the state of international relations, the parasitic preying on the internal

1. Speech at the 12th International Council Meeting of Amnesty International, 1979.

strife of smaller nations, the easy availability of weapons for mass destruction, the ready resort to terrorism, and the encouragement of precedent and of relative immunity. Yet internal genocide against racial, ethnic and religious groups could hardly have been a routine feature of societies in the past, since the homogeneous society is rare in our own times, which is to say that effective restraints against genocide must have operated in most societies over most of their histories.

In viewing these restraints, there are clearly certain structural conditions which exclude domestic genocide, such as those described by Egypt in the following account of its society. Egypt had ratified the Genocide Convention at an early date, but did not find it necessary to adopt legislative measures relating especially to genocide, 'since no national, ethnic, racial or religious group exists in the structure of Egyptian society, making the crimes sanctioned by the Convention inconceivable'.[2]

Egypt happens to be a fairly homogeneous society in terms of racial, ethnic or religious groups. But the official accounts nations give of themselves, and the provisions they make in their constitutions, often bear little resemblance to either, their societies or their routine practices. Thus, the constitution of Burundi declares that it draws its 'inspiration from the Universal Declaration of the Rights of Man and the Charter of the United Nations'; and one recalls with equal amazement the complaint by the representative of Burundi, in an open session of the United Nations Commission on Human Rights, 'that he was surprised at the United States' representative's references to the human rights situation in his country. Burundi had a homogeneous population with no minorities. The United States, whose representative obviously had his own peculiar view of human rights, had a number of minorities and minority problems. Why should it attack those countries which were simply engaged in the process of national development?'[3] The United States' representative had mentioned the deaths of several hundred thousand in Burundi in the course of a few months.

I have referred to these self-images, not as descriptions of the societies in question, but as offering a model of structural conditions which exclude the possibility of domestic genocide, unless the term is extended

2. United Nations, *Study of the Question of the Prevention and Punishment of the Crime of Genocide*, 1978:141.
3. E/CN. 4/SR. 1518, p. 18, dated 14 March 1979.

beyond racial, ethnic and religious groups to include the slaughter of political groups and social classes. These structurally homogeneous societies are, of course, the very antithesis of the plural societies described in the genocidal accounts throughout this book as the arena of genocidal conflict.

Where racial, ethnic and religious groups live together in the same society, the differences between them may not be specially significant in social life, or at any rate not a source of deadly conflict. There may be a readiness to absorb strangers and to offer them access to the resources of the society, as was the case in many African societies in the process of pre-colonial nation-building. Or there may be legal guarantees of the rights of minorities, rendering unnecessary special legislation against genocide, as claimed by Soviet Russia, which had ratified the Genocide Convention in 1954.

Thus the Soviet memorandum explained that a system of guarantees, designed to ensure the free development of national, ethnic and religious groups, had existed in Soviet law long before the adoption by the United Nations of the Genocide Convention. 'Equality of rights of citizens of the U.S.S.R., irrespective of their nationality or race, in all spheres of economic, government, cultural, political and other public activity is an indefeasible law.' Criminal sanctions buttress this provision, as also the provisions of the Constitution against hostile propaganda, restriction of rights and other discrimination. 'The question of freedom of worship has been settled in an equally consistent manner.' Freedom of worship and freedom of anti-religious propaganda are recognized for all citizens, and guaranteed by the separation of church from State and school, and by protection under the criminal law. An important role in the prevention of 'so-called national and cultural genocide' is played by the system of rules which makes it possible to ensure the development of the national culture of all the people living in the U.S.S.R. Each of the equal Soviet Socialist Republics, voluntarily united in the U.S.S.R., has the right to regulate its national culture. And finally, Soviet procedural law confirms the equality of citizens before the law. 'Thus, Soviet legislation provides all the necessary guarantees for fully implementing the provisions of the Convention on the Prevention and Punishment of the Crime of Genocide.'[4]

The Western parliamentary democracies place more emphasis on individual rights and political participation – universal franchise, freedom of association and of speech and movement, integrity of the per-

4. United Nations, op. cit., 142–4.

son, due legal process and equality before the law, and equality of opportunity. In one model of the non-genocidal parliamentary society, restraints on destructive conflicts are seen to arise from a complex web of social relationships, and of interdependence, cutting across the racial, ethnic and religious divisions, and from a parliamentary system responsive to competitive pressure groups and competitive party politics. Thus, trade unions, for example, chambers of commerce, churches, sporting associations etc., bring together people of different ethnic groups, loyalty to the voluntary associations fragmenting, in varied contexts, the potentially divisive hostility of exclusive ethnic commitment. This is a model with special appeal in highly industrialized societies, which can offer their members a good standard of living.

There is a further model of the non-genocidal society in which the ethnic, or other divisions, are frankly accepted, and ethnic (or racial or religious) identity used as the basis for a balanced accommodation, either in terms of the constitution, or *de facto*, by virtue of understandings in the conduct of the affairs of the nation. This was the solution attempted by the British in Northern Ireland in 1974, a constitutional power-sharing between Catholics and Protestants, but it was defeated by a strike of Protestant workers. It was also the greatly admired balanced representation of religious groups in Lebanon, described in Chapter 4. Though in the case of Lebanon, there was the powerful disruptive impact of forces external to the society, its collapse is some indication of the inherent dangers in a system which emphasizes the religious or other divisions. Yet there are many societies which have successfully achieved an accommodation based on the recognition of group distinctiveness in the public domain, as for example, Switzerland, Belgium and Holland. In theory, the successful accommodation of religious and ethnic groups in these 'consociational democracies' depends appreciably on the role of élites – their readiness to resolve conflicts peacefully, their willingness to compromise in the adjustment of competing interests.[5]

These models operate with restraints arising from structural arrangements, societal processes and ideological commitments. They are presented in ideal form. And it may be more informative to look at the problem of restraints in societies, which have many of the characteristics we would associate with the probability of genocidal massacres on a large scale. I have chosen as examples Northern Ireland and *apartheid*

5. Esman, 1977, presents some case studies of consociational democracy and critical discussion of the theory. See also Van den Berghe, 1969.

South Africa. But before turning to these societies, I need to discuss what type of massacre would seem to indicate a weakening of restraints against genocide.

I will take as a starting point the following episode during the deportation of the Chechens, as described in Nekrich's book, *The Punished Peoples*.

The chairman of one of the village Soviets, the eighty-year-old Tusha, assisted in the removal of his fellow villagers, his own family being shipped off as well. Only his daughter-in-law remained with him, with her child at her breast. Addressing a Georgian officer, Tusha said in his broken Russian, 'Me born here, me here die. Me no go anywhere!'

Tusha spread his arms out and stood before the gates of his home. The daughter-in-law understood. She cried out and, pressing her child to her breast, took hold of her father-in-law. She pulled him and pulled him toward our group, crying out all the while, 'Daddy, Daddy, come on! They'll kill you.' It all happened in an instant. The officer gave an order to a Russian soldier standing with his automatic at the ready.

'Shoot! All three!'

The soldier blanched and trembled. He said, 'The man I will shoot, but not the woman and child.'

A TT pistol flashed in the officer's hand. Before the soldier had finished his last word he lay on the ground, shot through the head. Within the same instant, the officer had killed Tusha, his daughter-in-law, and her child. They drove us in haste down the path to the roadway. There trucks were waiting for us. Those who lagged along the way were shot. That is the way it was.[6]

Nekrich adds the following comment:

Did this nameless Russian soldier know that the moment he refused to kill that woman and child he saved the honor of the Russian people?

It is not likely that he thought so. He was simply behaving like a human being. And his entire person rebelled when they tried to turn him into an animal. He was left there in the mountains, lying by the old man, the woman, and the child, a symbol of human brotherhood and its inseverable bonds. Someday at that place a monument will be erected to Mankind.

The comment is startling. Indeed, it was so startling that a scholar reviewing the book by Nekrich for the *New York Review of Books*[7] was constrained, quite unconsciously I am sure, to re-edit the account as the story of a soldier who had refused 'to kill an old Chechen, his daughter-in-law and her baby in the course of the rounding up'. There can be no doubt of the heroism of the Russian soldier in defying his

6. Account by a Chechen writer, Nekrich, 1978:58–9.
7. 17 August 1978:37.

officer's order, and he paid for it with his life. But he was, after all, ready to murder an eighty-year-old man, quite as defenceless as the woman and her baby. How could this possibly be interpreted as consistent with the honour of the Russian people?

Yet on reflection, the comment by Nekrich does not make quite the same shocking impact. The attitudes of soldier and officer are poles apart. In the action of the soldier, there would seem to have been the influence of some ancient chivalry towards women and children, whereas the officer was immediately disposed to engage in a root and branch extermination. The soldier was held back by powerful restraints, inhibiting indiscriminate slaughter and protective of future generations. By contrast, the officer acted in total rejection of ties of common humanity, and in total disregard for the guilt or innocence of his victims.

Throughout this book, I have referred to a variety of genocidal massacres in the struggle for power. There are centrally planned and executed massacres, and others which seem to be the spontaneous action of enraged mobs. The victims may be a selected category, such as the men in a village suspected of sabotage or held as hostages, or the victims may be any and every member of the target group. All these types of massacre may indicate the breakdown of restraints against genocide, and the possibility, or likelihood, of escalation to genocide under certain conditions. But I will take as a specially sensitive indicator of the breakdown of these restraints, massacres which do not distinguish on the basis of age or sex or personal guilt. And I will use this indicator in my discussion of Northern Ireland and *apartheid* South Africa, which I have described as marked by many of the characteristics we would associate with some likelihood of massive genocidal conflict. Indeed, many observers would describe these societies as already engaged in genocidal conflict.

I have described the plural society as the arena of domestic genocidal conflict, and both Northern Ireland and South Africa are plural societies of an extreme type. The pluralism derives from ancient conquest and colonization. In Northern Ireland, a society which inexorably produces Protestants and Catholics,[8] the social basis of the pluralism is religious difference as socially elaborated over centuries. In South Africa it is racial difference as systematically exploited under *apartheid*. The societies are often compared, but the comparison is misleading, the

8. Phrase used by Barritt and Booth, 1972: Preface.

situation of Catholics in Northern Ireland being in no way comparable to that of Africans in South Africa.

The antagonisms between Catholics and Protestants in Northern Ireland were kept alive in the nineteenth century and the first decades of the twentieth century by the broader struggle in Ireland for Catholic emancipation, for land reform, for Home Rule, and finally for national independence. These antagonisms also found expression in the North, and particularly in Belfast, in periodic rioting. Elections, the threat of political change, provocative rituals of domination staged by Protestants, and rituals of protest celebrated by Catholics, provided occasion for the sectarian riots (in 1813, 1832, 1835, 1841, 1843, 1852, 1857, 1864, 1872, 1880, 1884, 1886, 1898, 1907, 1909).[9] Some of these were of short duration; others continued, with great ferocity, over relatively long periods of time. And, following partition in 1920, the establishment of Northern Ireland as a separate political unit within the United Kingdom was accompanied by protracted violence.

Partition in a society so divided along religious lines assured political domination by the Protestants, who constituted some two-thirds of the population (820,000 Protestants as against 430,000 Catholics), a ratio more or less maintained to the present time. In effect, Catholics were appreciably disenfranchised. Other inequalities were associated with political domination, or were superimposed in the consolidation of Protestant power. Catholics complained of the gerrymandering of local government electoral boundaries, and of discrimination in public employment and in the allocation of public housing. The complaints were well founded, though there is controversy over the extent of these abuses of Protestant power.[10] There were also legitimate Catholic complaints of bias in the administration of justice and in the maintenance of law and order. The Royal Ulster Constabulary, and the Ulster Special Constabulary (an exclusively Protestant force), became identified with the Protestant establishment.

The pluralism in the society is not confined to the public domain. The sectarian divisions permeate most sectors. There is a measure of segregation, and of discrimination, in private employment, with more regional underdevelopment, and higher rates of unemployment, in Catholic areas.[11] Neighbourhoods, and such communal facilities as recreation centres and public houses, are largely segregated. The churches are

9. Budge and O'Leary, 1973:Ch. 3.
10. See Darby, 1976:75–9.
11. ibid., 146–51.

essentially exclusive, and the schools are highly segregated, given the desire of the Catholic authorities to control the religious education of their members. Moreover, the segregation of activities extends far beyond these nuclear institutions. Boal demonstrates[12] the superimposition of physical segregation and segregation of activities in two areas of Belfast, the activity segregation affecting newspaper reading, route to bus stops, shopping for groceries, support of football teams, political affiliation and, most markedly, the close-knit networks with friends and relatives. The effect is to create an intense local community sentiment, coinciding with religious affiliation. The segregation of activities, the fierce political commitments, the infusion of routine activities with communal significance, the small scale of the society with its intensity of interpersonal relations, are highly reminiscent of Zanzibar in the years immediately preceding the revolution and the slaughter of Arabs.[13]

The segregation, and its associated communal and political expressions, are not exclusively phenomena of the working-class areas of Belfast, though manifested there in extreme form. Busteed demonstrates the correspondence of the map of voting behaviour in the 1969 elections with the map of religious distribution.[14] Darby, rejecting the view that Catholics and Protestants in Northern Ireland only live among people of their own religion, speaks instead of a series of religious enclaves, but adds that these enclaves, whether of large groups or of individuals, 'see themselves as ethnic units, distinct from the other ethnic units beside or around them'.[15] The large enclaves are of course a haven for terrorists, their natural habitat.

The structural pluralism is reflected also in ideological polarization. This was most marked in the earliest years, when Catholics denied the legitimacy of the new state, and a considerable minority boycotted its institutions. There seemed no possibility of reconciliation between a Catholic minority seeking a united Ireland, and a Protestant majority committed to union with Britain, or to loyalty to the constitution of the state and maintenance of Protestant domination. Yet there were indications in later years of an increasing accommodation. The Irish Republican Army failed to enlist popular support in its campaign for a united Ireland in 1956–62. And the launching of a Civil Rights movement in 1967/8 indicated a willingness on the part of many Catholics

12. Boal, 1969 : 30–50.
13. See Kuper, 1977 : 145–70.
14. Busteed, 1972 : 32–3.
15. Darby, op. cit., 32–3.

to work for reform of the existing system. But violent Protestant repression of the Civil Rights movement, and participation in the movement by the I.R.A., rapidly led to escalating violence and extreme polarization, which brought the country to the brink of civil war.

This was averted by the entry of British army units in 1969. Since then, reforms have responded to Catholic grievances, diminishing the level of discrimination against Catholics. The civil rights issues seem no longer so intractable, though the attempt to introduce power-sharing was defeated by Protestant workers. The Northern Ireland Parliament was prorogued in 1972, and abolished in 1973. Under British direct rule, there has been an appreciable dismantlement of Protestant hegemony. But attitude surveys still show considerable ideological dissent on constitutional issues; however, many in both camps view British direct rule 'as a second best or "least worst" alternative'.[16]

At the present time, the ideological extremes are represented by the Democratic Unionist Party under the leadership of Paisley, and by the Provisional I.R.A. Paisley has a large Protestant following – in 1979 he was elected to the European Parliament with an overwhelming first preference vote of 170,000 – and he enjoys paramilitary support. He is committed to traditional loyalism and Protestant domination, heavily laced with religious bigotry. The Provisional I.R.A. are a small body of men whose increasingly sophisticated command of terrorist technology renders them less dependent on popular support. Their policy is 'to get rid of the artificial statelet, the prop that sustains loyalism. Once you have got to get rid of that, once the people who have been fed and nurtured on the neo-fascist ideologies of demagogues and party leaders like Paisley are free of them, then you are in a situation where you can honestly develop within a 32-county democracy radical policies.'[17] The very existence of the state is in issue.

Given the continuity of violence in Northern Ireland during the nineteenth and early twentieth century, the discrimination against Catholics and the ideological polarization, there was an inevitability of violence in the new state; and the years of economic depression saw rioting in 1931, 1932 and 1935. Yet there followed a period of relative peace, marked by industrial development, the broadening of social welfare benefits, and the extension of educational opportunity. But the violence

16. See the report by Rose, McAllister and Mair (1978) on surveys from 1968 to 1978.

17. Gerry Adams, 'Provisional Sinn Fein Vice-President and leading Republican theoretician and strategist', 1979:7.

was only submerged, and it surfaced in the riots against the flying of a republican flag (the tricolour riots of 1964), and in the founding of a Protestant counterpart to the I.R.A. (with murders in 1966). And demands for reforms by the Civil Rights movement rapidly precipitated murder and destruction. In the process, there has been a redistribution of population, as Catholics and Protestants fled from vulnerable areas to the protection of segregated neighbourhoods, a 'demographic purification'. The intervention of Protestant paramilitary groups in 1972 demonstrated the ease with which both sides could resort to indiscriminate sectarian slaughter. When the Protestant paramilitaries withdrew, the Provisional I.R.A. continued to campaign by the sniper's bullet, the booby-trapped car, the land mines, the bombs in public places, and now the added refinement of explosives detonated by remote control.

Over the last decade, during what is referred to as 'The Troubles' (a phrase corresponding to *les événements* for the genocide in Burundi), almost 2,000 have been killed, over 70 per cent being civilians (excluding police).[18] And this statistic takes no account of the many thousands wounded, crippled for life, or deliberately maimed, nor does it take account of the anguish of bereavement and of homes destroyed and of living under terrorism, or the devastation of the country and its resources.

It is massive destruction. Yet there are curious features to the present violence, and indeed to the violence over the last 150 years. Thus the Commission investigating the disturbances in Londonderry on 1 November 1883 expressed its 'surprise that after two parties entertaining old feelings of political and religious rancour towards each other, had been brought into such dangerous contact under circumstances calculated to exasperate them, only two persons received gunshot wounds of a serious character'.[19] In an earlier riot in 1864, there had been a whole series of horrifyingly violent confrontations following the provocative desecration of funeral ceremonial in a lampooning of a great Catholic leader – battles between rioting mobs, battles between Protestant shipwrights and Catholic navvies, attacks on churches, on schools, on passers-by. Yet the reported deaths were only 12, and the injured only 100 during a period of 18 days' rioting, though to be sure, the total number of casualties must have exceeded the number reported.

By way of further example, in the current violence, certain episodes

18. The figures are from 1969 to August 1979, *Fortnight* (October–November 1979), 16.
19. British Parliamentary Papers, 1970:3.

have been singled out as specially horrifying. There was *Bloody Sunday*, and there was *Bloody Friday*. On *Bloody Sunday* (30 January 1972), British soldiers killed 13 young Catholic men during the course of a civil rights demonstration in Londonderry. On *Bloody Friday* (21 July 1972), twenty-two bombs planted by the Provisional I.R.A. in Belfast killed 9 people and injured some 130. There have been other massacres – 12 men and women burnt to death by a Provisional I.R.A. napalm-type bomb at La Mon House in February 1978, during the annual dinner of the Junior Motorcycle Club and a dinner party of the Irish Collie Club, with some 450 visitors altogether in different rooms of the restaurant; 18 soldiers slaughtered by remote control bombs at Warrenpoint (Provisional I.R.A., August 1979); and outside of Northern Ireland in 1974, 20 murdered in public houses in Birmingham (by a section of the I.R.A. living in England), and 28 in Dublin and Monaghan (car bombs laid by Protestant terrorists).

But however agonizing these tragedies, the number of casualties, comparatively speaking, is relatively small. This is true for both the nineteenth and twentieth centuries.[20] One has only to recall the Muslim riots in Algeria, in Sétif and neighbouring areas, on 8 May 1945, day of the celebration of victory in the Second World War, when Muslims killed 103, with some 100 wounded and mutilated, and the French reprisals were a death toll of 1,500 according to their estimates, and 50,000 according to the estimates of the National Liberation Front. If one totals all the reported deaths from sectarian conflict over the last 150 years, including the 544 killed in the turbulent period 1920–22, when Northern Ireland was constituted as a separate state, they fall far below the casualties of the recent sectarian battles in Lebanon, or the numbers massacred in short periods in the ethnic conflicts of Rwanda and Burundi. One can hardly imagine that the killing of 13 people in Rwanda or Burundi or Lebanon could be so horrifying as to earn the epithet 'Bloody Sunday'. Clearly, there are powerful restraints acting against genocidal conflict in Northern Ireland.

Yet one must also remember that the Provisional I.R.A. has shown itself quite capable of the genocidal murders of men, women and children, as in the bombings in public places, or the murders on a fishing cruise of the seventy-nine-year-old Lord Mountbatten, and members of his family, Lady Brabourne, eighty-two years old, his young grandson, and a young boatman, with other members of the family

20. See Table 3.1, Religious Riots in Belfast 1813–1912, in Budge and O'Leary, op. cit., 89.

escaping purely by chance. And in an earlier period, Protestant para-militaries engaged extensively in indiscriminate sectarian murder, including the killing of 17 at McGurk's Bar in 1971.

In South Africa, the pluralism has deep historical roots in the wars between black and white, in conquest and expropriation of land, in economic exploitation, and in racial domination and discrimination. There were signs in the late 1930s, and during and immediately after the Second World War, that racial barriers were becoming less rigid. But this trend was reversed in 1948, when Afrikaner nationalists took power, and introduced the systematic racism of *apartheid* to secure Afrikaner (and white) domination, and to recover ground lost to racial tolerance. *Apartheid* represented a qualitative change. Established about the same time as the United Nations, it is an almost clause-by-clause denial of the Universal Declaration of Human Rights.

The structure of *apartheid* is notoriously well known. The government's strategies were directed to the monopoly of political power; the removal of African affairs from politics to the safe containment of administration; the fragmentation of the overwhelming African majority into its tribal groups, with domesticated tribal authorities, and a renaissance of tribal culture and pride; and, most startling of all, the systematic control under penal sanctions of a great range of social relationships, so as to achieve the maximum possible separation between the races, and particularly the avoidance of contact on a basis of equality.

The pattern is clear in the earliest laws passed by the government. The Prohibition of Mixed Marriages Act of 1949 provided that a marriage could not be solemnized between a European (white) and a non-European (non-white). The Immorality Act of 1950 extended an earlier prohibition against 'illicit carnal intercourse' between Europeans and 'Natives' to all non-Europeans (that is, including 'Asiatics' and 'Coloureds'). The Group Areas Act, also of 1950, provided machinery, 'by compulsion, if necessary', for physical segregation in residence and trade. These three laws, passed in the first two years of taking office, thus control the intimacy of sex and neighbour relations by racial criteria. In the ensuing years, a vast superstructure of racial quarantine was erected, extending from the most intimate physical contacts to the intellectual and the spiritual.

Another of the key laws passed in the first two years was the Suppression of Communism Act of 1950. This introduced the crime of communism, defined not only as Marxian socialism, but also as any doctrine or scheme to bring about any political, industrial, social or economic change by illegal means. Since control of legal change would be ensured by a complete monopoly of constitutional power, the Suppression of Communism Act filled the gap in total control, by the provision of extreme criminal sanctions against change by illegal means. This act must be seen as part of a vast repressive apparatus of laws and police powers, continually extended and 'perfected' in the repression of political protest or challenge. It is a process of substituting 'rule by law' for 'the rule of law'.

The administrative basis for systematized racism is, of course, a clear system of definition and racial identification. The machinery for this was provided in another key act, also introduced in the first two years, the Population Registration Act of 1950. Pursuant to this act, the whole population was racially classified. To be sure, there was very appreciable physical identifiability of the racial groups. But the main problem arose in the identification of Coloureds, since there had been much intermingling between whites (particularly Afrikaners) and Africans. Hence, some form of identification outside of physical features was necessary, as in the case of Jews in Germany. Indeed, the problems of the *apartheid* government in relation to Coloureds are somewhat reminiscent of the problems experienced by the Germans in relation to the *mischlinge*.

I mention these laws because they recall some of the early steps taken by the Nazis against the Jews – the Law for the Protection of German Blood and Honour, prohibiting marriage and extramarital intercourse between Jews and citizens of German or related blood; the exclusion from citizenship; the definition and identification; the expropriation; the social separation; and the physical concentration and segregation. There are details, too, which are strongly reminiscent of the Nazi regime – the campaigns of vilification against the Indian population of South Africa, in which sections of the English-speaking people of Natal vigorously participated; and the problem of securing a share of the profits of expropriation for the State.[21] Even the ideology of *apartheid*, in its revised form of separate development to enable each race to realize its distinctive qualities, appears to have been taken verbatim from the explanations of Nazi race policies offered by German missions abroad in the 1930s.[22] And then there is the concern for legality and for bureau-

21. See Hilberg, 1961:86ff., and Kuper, Watts and Davies, 1958:166. In *Passive Resistance in South Africa* (1957:Ch. 2), I have analysed the early *apartheid* laws.
22. See Hilberg's account of this German diplomatic propaganda, op. cit., 45.

cratic nicety. Indeed, the South African government has carried the bureaucratic and legalistic organization of systematic racism far beyond anything developed by the Nazis. These similarities seem too close to be coincidental; and they are all the more disturbing since there were vigorous Nazi and pro-German movements among Afrikaner nationalists in the 1930s.

Given the ideological similarity in the hierarchical ordering of races with distinctive life chances, it was to be expected that the United Nations would assimilate *apartheid* to the same general category of crimes as nazism. And it was to be expected too that *apartheid* would be equated with genocide. Although in U.N. practice genocide is a protected crime, and the U.N. members who commit the crime are safeguarded as if they were an endangered species, in U.N. theory genocide is the most heinous of crimes.

The assimilation of *apartheid* to the same class of crimes as nazism is made explicitly or by implication in many U.N. documents.[23] Thus, a resolution of the General Assembly[24] reaffirms in a preamble 'that nazism, including its present-day manifestations, racism and similar totalitarian ideologies and practices, which are based on terror and racial intolerance, are incompatible with the purposes and principles of the Charter of the United Nations and constitute a gross violation of human rights and fundamental freedoms which may jeopardize world peace and the security of peoples'. In a subsequent clause, the resolution renewed '*its strong condemnation* of racism, nazism, *apartheid* and all other totalitarian ideologies and practices'. Apart from explicit condemnation, the assimilation is implicit in the application of categories of interpretation and judgment derived from the Charter for the International Military Tribunal at the Nuremberg Trials, as in the many U.N. declarations that *apartheid* constitutes a crime against humanity, or the analysis of the applicability of the Nuremberg principles to *apartheid*.[25]

I am not sure that I fully understand the declarations and decisions

23. See, for example, Resolutions of the General Assembly, 2438 (19 December 1968), 2713 (15 December 1970), 2839 (18 December 1971) and the International Convention on the Suppression and Punishment of the Crime of *Apartheid* (30 November 1973).

24. No. 2545, dated 11 December 1969.

25. The report E/CN. 4/1075, dated 15 February 1972, lists a number of resolutions declaring or reaffirming that *apartheid* is a crime against humanity (pp. 5–6), and makes a point by point application of the Nuremberg principles to *apartheid*.

of the U.N. on *apartheid* and genocide; they are most complex. Preambular paragraphs are often an arena of political struggle, and their final form presumably offers an interpretative framework for the substantive clauses. In the following preambular clause, the identification of *apartheid* with genocide seems quite clear:

> *Reaffirming* that racism, nazism and the ideology and policy of *apartheid* are incompatible with the objectives of the Charter of the United Nations and the Universal Declaration of Human Rights, the Convention on the Prevention and Punishment of the Crime of Genocide, the United Nations Declaration on the Elimination of All Forms of Racial Discrimination, the International Convention on the Elimination of All Forms of Racial Discrimination and other international instruments.[26]

But there is no need to turn to preambular paragraphs, which in some ways constitute a propaganda barrage. There is in fact a voluminous U.N. literature seeking to establish the identification of *apartheid* with genocide.

The prime mover in this enterprise was the Ad Hoc Working Group of Experts, established by the Commission on Human Rights in 1967 to investigate the torture and ill-treatment of persons in police custody in South Africa. In the process of gathering evidence from members of resistance groups, victims of *apartheid* repression, the Experts extended their task into a sort of preparatory examination of the South African government on charges of genocide under *apartheid*. And they concluded that 'the intention of the Government of South Africa to destroy a racial group, in whole or part, not being established in law, the evidence nevertheless reveals certain elements which correspond to the acts described in Article II (a), (b) and (c) of the United Nations Convention on the Prevention and Punishment of the Crime of Genocide and which may, as such, establish the existence of the crime of genocide'.[27] This line of investigation was approved by the Commission on Human Rights, and the Ad Hoc Group of Experts continued its prosecution of the South African government.

Two of its key reports deal respectively with the relationship between *apartheid* and genocide,[28] and with the question of *apartheid* from the point of view of international penal law.[29] In the former report, the

26. No. 2438, dated 19 December 1968.
27. E/CN. 4/950, para, 1137, dated 28 February 1967.
28. E/CN. 4/984/Add. 18, dated 28 February 1969.
29. E/CN. 4/1075, dated 15 February 1972.

Experts concluded that 'in the present state of South African legislation, the Group cannot say that the South African Government has expressed an intention to commit genocide. However, the members of political groups who have testified consider that certain elements of genocide exist in the practice of *apartheid*.' They therefore recommended 'that the Commission should request the General Assembly through the E.C.O.S.O.C. to take into account the development of the *Apartheid* policies and to revise the Genocide Convention with a view to making the *Apartheid* policies as they are practised by the South African authorities punishable under this Convention'.[30] In the second report, the Experts developed the case for the prosecution further by applying, point by point, the Nuremberg Principles (including crimes against peace, war crimes and crimes against humanity – massacres, exterminations, deportations etc.). The conclusions are quite predictable; and the report again recommended a revision of the Genocide Convention, in particular to make 'inhuman acts resulting from the policies of *apartheid*' punishable under that Convention.[31]

This recommendation does not seem very feasible, given the large number of member states who have signed and ratified the Convention. It is puzzling to know why the Experts should have made this recommendation at all. Perhaps they felt insecure in their conclusions and thought to dissolve doubt by the simple device of amending the Convention so as to incorporate a judgment that the policies and practices of *apartheid* constituted genocide within the terms of the Convention. In the result their recommendation was not accepted. Instead a separate Convention was drafted, the International Convention on the Suppression and Punishment of the Crime of *Apartheid*,[32] and this Convention is now in force. It establishes *apartheid* as a distinctive crime. The parties to the Convention declare that those organizations, institutions and individuals who commit the crime of *apartheid* are criminal, and the link with genocide is provided by the following preamble: '*Observing* that, in the Convention on the Prevention and Punishment of the Crime of Genocide, certain acts which may also be qualified as acts of *apartheid* constitute a crime under international law.' I think it is only in this limited manner that the recommendation of the Experts for the amendment of the Genocide Convention was taken up.

30. E/CN. 4/984/Add. 18, paras. 36 and 39.
31. E/CN. 4/1075, para. 161.
32. General Assembly Resolution 3068, dated 30 November 1973.

The present position seems to be that *apartheid* and genocide have been brought into the most intimate contact, but that the union has not been consummated. Only those acts committed in pursuance of *apartheid* policy, which constitute genocide under international law, would be punishable as such. The Convention is a warning to members of the South African government that they cannot rely on the immunities normally extended by the United Nations to its member states, and that they may have to answer to charges of genocide.

There are further puzzling features about the equating of *apartheid* and genocide. The witnesses testifying before the Ad Hoc Group of Experts were committed to the overthrow of the South African government. They hated *apartheid* and they were outraged by its injustice and its brutality. They had also suffered personally at the hands of the Security Branch, the courts, police and prison warders, for their political opposition to the government. It was to be expected that, under the encouragement and indeed coaxing of the Experts, they would be ready to denounce the regime as practising genocide. Yet there was division of opinion, with some witnesses resisting this conclusion. There must be ambiguity in the situation, which does not admit of an easy judgment.

There is some ambiguity in the pattern of massacres or slaughter. The 1950s were a period of protracted challenge to the government, starting with the May Day protests in 1950, and continuing, through the non-violent resistance campaign of 1952 and the Congress of the People in 1955, to the anti-pass law protest at Sharpeville in 1960. In the May Day protests, the police killed 18 Africans, and in four separate disturbances during the resistance campaign, they killed 34 Africans; there were 5 murders of whites by Africans. At Sharpeville, the police fired on a large crowd of African protesters, and murdered 69 (including 8 women and 10 children). Meanwhile there were protests and revolts in the rural areas, with 16 killed by police at Witzieshoek in 1950, and 11 at Ngqusa Hill in 1960. In South West Africa, in Windhoek in 1959, there were 11 African deaths in the suppression of a protest against removal from a location.[33] The most massive killings were in 1976, during and in the aftermath of a revolt, initiated by African schoolchildren, against the government's proposed language policy for African schools, and more generally against *apartheid*. One of the South African newspapers published a carefully documented list of 499 identified victims in 1976.[34] The official figure was 386 killed by police action. The United Nations

33. I have followed the figures given by Sachs, 1975:228.
34. Herbstein, 1979:225.

Ad Hoc Group of Experts quoted the International Defence and Aid Fund for Southern Africa as having established beyond doubt that 617 persons died between 16 June and December 1976, 'although the actual figure must certainly be over 1,000 (some of the victims were barely five or six years of age)'.[35] For 1977, the Experts quoted an official figure of 149 killed, including 11 children.[36]

This is not a complete record of police massacre, and one would also have to allow for many deaths resulting, not from police action against demonstrating crowds, but from action against individuals in the course of the daily routine. But even making such allowance, I would have expected far worse from the *apartheid* government. I share the view expressed by one of the witnesses before the Ad Hoc Group of Experts 'that the combination of racial attitudes in South Africa, and the power that the Government has, approaches the policies which led to genocide in Europe in recent decades. If by genocide one means the actual physical extermination of population – that is, the extreme form of genocide – I would say that stage has not yet been reached in South Africa, and one hopes that international exposure and pressure will be sufficiently strong to prevent it from ever being reached.'[37] The *apartheid* policies of the South African government have a strong genocidal potential in relation to Africans. The government segregates, and socially isolates, Africans, denying them membership in the wider community, and withholding the protection of a common humanity; it systematically deprives Africans of a wide range of basic human rights; it uproots vast numbers living in settled communities, so as to eliminate 'black spots', and it resettles them, in many cases with little or no regard for their survival; it tolerates health conditions which take a heavy toll of infant mortality, and generally of preventable deaths; it permits a wage structure which, apart from the extreme discrimination against Africans, denies hundreds of thousands an adequate level for sustenance; it canalizes African labour in a dehumanization to the level of a commodity; it condones, perhaps even authorizes, the torturing to death of political prisoners; and it subjects Africans to a daily routine of humiliation and deprivation. Yet the genocidal massacre of whole sections, including

35. A/32/226, 10 October 1977, para. 19.
36. E/CN. 4/1311, 26 January 1979, para. 51.
37. Albie Sachs, E/CN. 4/950, p. 229. Sachs continues that if one means by genocide humiliation on the grounds of race, deprivation of facilities and human rights, then this is part of official policy. But, of course, this is not genocide within the U.N. definition.

men, women and children, is not part of government practice, and the murders are on a smaller scale than one would expect from so tyrannical and brutal a regime. Here, too, there must be powerful restraints against genocide.

In looking at the restraints on genocidal massacre in Northern Ireland, the simple answer may be the one suggested to me by Pierre van den Berghe in comment on an earlier article – the presence of the British Army. According to this view, the withdrawal of the British Army at the present time would precipitate, as many people fear, genocidal conflict or at any rate civil war, with the Provisional I.R.A. seeking to establish control over Catholic areas, and Protestants driving out Catholics in an attempt to consolidate their power. The conflict would almost certainly draw in the Republic of Ireland, and have its repercussions also in such cities as Glasgow and Liverpool. These predictions are, of course, based on the assumption that there are no effective internal restraints against genocidal conflict.

This assumption is perhaps questionable. The violence seems to operate within limits. These limits are no doubt partly imposed by the ability of each of the contending parties to engage in effective reprisals, and in the case of the Provos, by the fact that they are recruited from a minority group. In any event, the violence does not exceed a certain limited scale of murder or massacre; and politicians are generally spared, as are clergymen. While unarmed men seem fair game, the killing of women and children arouses general revulsion. There was a murder of this type in October 1977, when the Provos killed, in her sleep, a young woman who was a part-time member of the Ulster Defence Regiment. Her three-year-old daughter in the next room screamed, and the gunmen fired through the partition, missing the child, but riddling with bullets the toy she was cuddling. The incident became an important item of news. The Catholic Primate of All Ireland described it as saddening and sickening. The Church of Ireland Primate condemned it as a savage act that had caused deep revulsion throughout the whole area. Father Faul denounced the murder as an absurd, savage and sickening action: to make an attack on women and children was to bring human actions to the lowest level of ignominy. There were condemnations by spokesmen for the political parties, and the presence at the funeral of most of the inhabitants of the predominantly Catholic village near the home of the murdered woman was expressive of similar sentiments.

I am not suggesting that the Provos recognize a moral obligation to spare women and children. The continuous practice of terrorism, and the strength of their ideological commitment, would make them reckless of the moral consequences of their actions. But I am suggesting that they feel obliged to respond to the values of the wider society. And so we find a spokesman for the Provos expressing regret for the murder of the young boatman who accompanied Lord Mountbatten on his last fishing cruise: 'it should have been a more mature man, an older man who would have been able to weigh up the political company he was keeping, and the repercussions of it'.[38] Presumably a more mature man would (or should) have understood that it was a capital offence to serve as boatman to Lord Mountbatten on his usual holiday visit to Ireland.

Further restraints flow from the interdependence of Protestants and Catholics in an appreciably industrialized society. However crippled by extreme crises, the society generally continues to function: and this involves a whole series of understandings between members of the different religious groups and their community leaders, and even with the paramilitary organizations.[39] These understandings make possible the daily routine of work, the provision of supplies, and some access to social services.

There is a broader level of interdependence affecting internal relations in Northern Ireland, through participation in the institutions of the United Kingdom, and common membership in such national organizations as trade unions. The equal availability to all sections of the social services of the United Kingdom exercises some restraint on extreme polarization.[40] And now there is the beginning of involvement in the institutions of the European Community, with access also to its human rights organizations. In January 1978, in response to a complaint by the Republic of Ireland against Britain, the European Court of Human Rights found that the interrogation techniques used by British Security Forces on some of the internees in Northern Ireland in 1971 were inhuman and degrading, though not amounting to torture. The European Commission and the European Court of Human Rights offer a forum for the hearing of complaints, and the services of the European Community will certainly continue to be available in the search for a

38. *Irish Times*, 1 September 1979, 5.
39. This is analysed in Darby and Williamson, 1978.
40. J. L. P. Thompson, 1979, sees in *dual incorporation* (i.e. equality between Catholics and Protestants in the United Kingdom, and inequality in Northern Ireland) a stimulus to conflict.

resolution of the present conflict. The involvement of Northern Ireland in the European Community may perhaps also contribute to restraint by extending the boundaries of the society, as it were, beyond its parochial divisions.

We might add to these restraining factors many others, such as the internal search for conciliation by middle-of-the-road political parties, and by peace and ecumenical movements. Yet we know enough of the highly explosive nature of plural societies of the type of Northern Ireland to realize how easily these restraining factors can be overwhelmed in polarizing conflict. And this is particularly true where either of the parties feels threatened by significant political change and resorts to terrorism. The situation may be so rapidly transformed, and relationships become so extremely polarized, that normal social processes and restraints are swept aside. And since the Provos are committed to the establishment of a united Ireland by force, and since Protestants are resistant to incorporation, terrorism is likely to be a continuing feature of the scene.

In the circumstances, the removal of the British presence and the withdrawal of the British Army before a political solution is achieved would seem to be an invitation to bloodshed. And even if some more or less acceptable political solution were found, there would be a need for continued vigilance, since the social foundations for conciliation are so fragile.

The fear in Northern Ireland is that under certain conditions of change and threat, sections of the Catholic and Protestant populations might engage in genocidal massacre. One hardly supposes that the British government or its army might be guilty of genocide. Indeed the British Army in Northern Ireland has been cast in a largely non-military and highly vulnerable role. In South Africa, on the other hand, the fear is that the South African government itself might engage in genocidal massacres. Many people already equate *apartheid* with genocide. I have taken a different view – that the policies and practices of *apartheid* have considerable genocidal potential, but that the level of violence and murder by the South African government and its agents, high as it is, falls below what one would predict, and that this suggests the pressure of powerful restraints on the government.

Internally, these restraints derive quite obviously from a combination of economic forces and demographic factors. The South African economy rests on the labour of Africans, Coloureds and Indians, particularly Africans who are the overwhelming majority of workers in primary and secondary industry. A recent Government Manpower Survey shows the estimated number of employed Africans in all categories, excluding domestic service and agriculture, as almost three million, compared with a little over one and a quarter million whites. The number of African workers and the corresponding dependence on Africans have greatly increased under *apartheid*. There is, then, what Sartre described as an infra-structural restraint on genocidal attacks on the subordinate group by reason of the dependence on its labour.

The demographic restraint arises from the great preponderance of Africans in the population. In the period 1946 to 1977, the African population has grown from about 7,832,000 (1946 census) to over 19,000,000 (estimate). For Coloureds, the comparable figures are from 930,000 to 2,400,000; for Asians, from 285,000 to 765,000; and for whites from about 2,373,000 to an estimated 4,365,000. Whites are a declining proportion of the population. And if one projects present rates of population growth to the year 2000, the disproportion is overwhelming. The government did seek to strengthen the white population by its immigration policies; and *apartheid* could certainly be expected to discourage growth in the African population. But there was really nothing the government could do by way of genocidal massacres to change significantly the proportion of Africans to whites. The disparity and numbers are far too great, quite apart from other restraints. The elements of genocide listed by the United Nations Ad Hoc Group of Experts – separation of families, population policies including deliberate malnutrition and birth control, the transfer of children, the imprisonment and ill-treatment of non-white political leaders and non-white prisoners in general, the killing of the non-white population through a system of slave or tied labour, especially in the so-called transit camps, and the banning of Indians, under Group Areas, to areas lacking the conditions for the exercise of their traditional occupations – hardly seem to address this demographic disproportion, though the crowding of Africans into Bantustans lacking in the means for an adequate livelihood is a more serious allegation.

Instead of a genocidal solution, the government has been obliged to fall back on two devices – the fragmentation of the African population and the denial of citizenship. These policies were pursued initially through Bantu authorities for the different ethnic African groups, and the cultivation of their distinctive cultures, languages and traditions, so as to develop a divisive, self-reproducing tribal sentiment and solidarity. The policies have now taken the form of the establishment of 'independent' satellite Bantustans, with African citizenship linked to the ethnic (tribal) homeland. If these plans are fully realized, then Africans within the highly industrialized core areas would have somewhat the status of foreign workers, comparable to the many foreign workers in European countries.

I have not mentioned restraint by moral values. It must certainly be present in government circles. But my assumption is that the moral restraints against large-scale massacre would be swept aside in a situation of crisis. A government which systematically engages in the practices of *apartheid* will hardly draw a line at massacre. And the handling of the schoolchildren's revolt in 1976 is some indication of the government's likely response to serious challenge. But nevertheless, there are moral restraints acting within the wider society.

Discussions of 'the failure of political liberalism in South Africa' have about the same quality of significance and discovery as discussions on the failure of political liberalism in Nazi Germany or in the U.S.S.R. under Stalin. The Act of Union sacrificed the liberalism of the Cape Colony. And though, even today, there are many harmonious relationships across racial barriers, the whole structure of *apartheid* is inimical to liberalism, and it has been a major target of attack by the government from the earliest years. The emphasis on human freedom, on the dignity and worth of the individual, on the equal enjoyment of human rights, on freedom from discrimination, on full participation in a common society, is the very antithesis of the practice of *apartheid*. The astonishing fact is that these values should have survived at all. They continue to be vigorously expressed in public criticism of *apartheid*, in the press, and by members of the opposition in parliament, notwithstanding the many restraints on freedom of expression. And they derive an added significance within South Africa by the reinforcement they receive from the outside world.

As for the external pressures on the South African government, these are indeed massive. *Apartheid* is universally reviled. It is special anathema to the élite of African nations, and the Organization of African Unity is committed to the overthrow of the *apartheid* regime. Moreover, South Africa's neighbours are increasingly independent African states, opposed to *apartheid*. Even South Africa's major trading partners, and such embarrassed allies as it has, cannot detach themselves from the universal condemnation. Disturbances in South Africa have an adverse effect on the country's economy, and its economic standing in the outside world. In many countries, there are popular movements seeking to isolate South Africa, and to exercise pressure for other punitive action. And in the United Nations, South Africa is under continuous attack, with U.N. concern going back to a complaint in the General Assembly in 1946 of discriminatory treatment against South African residents of Indo-Pakistani origin.

Because of a certain openness of the society to observation and criticism – quite out of keeping with the nature of the regime – events in South Africa are almost immediately known in the outside world. And atrocities have the appearance of being perpetrated in full view on the world stage, provoking immediate reaction. In consequence, there is wide international coverage and condemnation. Sharpeville was debated in the U.N. Security Council! The reports of the Experts on the schoolchildren's revolt were submitted to the U.N. Commission on Human Rights and the General Assembly. And the torture and murder of an outstanding leader of the Black Consciousness Movement, Steve Biko, became an international *cause célèbre*.

It is difficult to know the effect of international surveillance. The changing form of *apartheid*, from separation, to separate development, to 'independent' Bantustans, seems to be a response, in part at any rate, to international pressure. But the fundamental nature of *apartheid* as a totalitarian system of racial domination and exploitation has not changed, though there may be significant changes in the attitudes of the electorate.[41] However, the most extreme manifestations of conflict in massacre must surely be restrained by the certainty of immediate hostile international reaction.

In cases of very sharp and destructive conflict in plural societies, the condition for non-genocidal conflict would seem to be the presence of an effective peace-keeping force, as in Northern Ireland, and the continuous pressure of international public opinion, as in South Africa.

41. See the discussion by Schlemmer (1978:75–85).

Appendix 1

Text of the Genocide Convention

The Contracting Parties

Having considered the declaration made by the General Assembly of the United Nations in its resolution 96 (1) dated 11 December 1946 that genocide is a crime under international law, contrary to the spirit and aims of the United Nations and condemned by the civilized world;

Recognizing that at all periods of history genocide has inflicted great losses on humanity; and

Being convinced that, in order to liberate mankind from such an odious scourge, international cooperation is required;

Hereby agree as hereinafter provided

ARTICLE I

The Contracting Parties confirm that genocide whether committed in time of peace or in time of war, is a crime under international law which they undertake to prevent and to punish.

ARTICLE II

In the present Convention, genocide means any of the following acts committed with intent to destroy, in whole or in part, a national, ethnical, racial or religious group, as such:

(a) Killing members of the group;
(b) Causing serious bodily or mental harm to members of the group;
(c) Deliberately inflicting on the group conditions of life calculated to bring about its physical destruction in whole or in part;
(d) Imposing measures intended to prevent births within the group;
(e) Forcibly transferring children of the group to another group.

ARTICLE III

The following acts shall be punishable:

(a) Genocide;
(b) Conspiracy to commit genocide;
(c) Direct and public incitement to commit genocide;
(d) Attempt to commit genocide;
(e) Complicity in genocide.

ARTICLE IV

Persons committing genocide or any of the other acts enumerated in article III shall be punished, whether they are constitutionally responsible rulers, public officials or private individuals.

ARTICLE V

The Contracting Parties undertake to enact, in accordance with their respective Constitutions, the necessary legislation to give effect to the provisions of the present Convention and, in particular, to provide effective penalties for persons guilty of genocide or any of the other acts enumerated in article III.

ARTICLE VI

Persons charged with genocide or any of the other acts enumerated in article III shall be tried by a competent tribunal of the State in the territory of which the act was committed, or by such international penal tribunal as may have jurisdiction with respect to those Contracting Parties which shall have accepted its jurisdiction.

ARTICLE VII

Genocide and other acts enumerated in article III shall not be considered as political crimes for the purpose of extradition.

The Contracting Parties pledge themselves in such cases to grant extradition in accordance with their laws and treaties in force.

ARTICLE VIII

Any Contracting Party may call upon the competent organs of the United Nations to take such action under the Charter of the United Nations as they consider appropriate for the prevention and suppression of acts of genocide or any of the other acts enumerated in article III.

ARTICLE IX

Disputes between the Contracting Parties relating to the interpretation, application or fulfilment of the present Convention, including those relating to the responsibility of a State for genocide or any of the other acts enumerated in article III, shall be submitted to the International Court of Justice at the request of any of the parties to the dispute.

ARTICLE X

The present Convention, of which the Chinese, English, French, Russian and Spanish texts are equally authentic, shall bear the date of 9 December 1948.

ARTICLE XI

The present Convention shall be open until 31 December 1949 for signature on behalf of any Member of the United Nations and of any non-member State to which an invitation to sign has been addressed by the General Assembly.

The present Convention shall be ratified, and the instruments of ratification shall be deposited with the Secretary-General of the United Nations.

After January 1950, the present Convention may be acceded to on behalf of any Member of the United Nations and of any non-member State which has received an invitation as aforesaid.

Instruments of accession shall be deposited with the Secretary-General of the United Nations.

ARTICLE XII

Any Contracting Party may at any time by notification addressed to the Secretary-General of the United Nations, extend the application of the present Convention to all or any of the territory for the conduct of whose foreign relations that Contracting Party is responsible.

ARTICLE XIII

On the day when the first twenty instruments of ratification or accession have been deposited, the Secretary-General shall draw up a *procès-verbal* and transmit a copy of it to each Member of the United Nations and to each of the non-member States contemplated in article XI.

The present Convention shall come into force on the ninetieth day following the date of deposit of the twentieth instrument of ratification or accession.

Any ratification or accession effected subsequent to the latter date shall become effective on the ninetieth day following the deposit of the instrument of ratification or accession.

ARTICLE XIV

The present Convention shall remain in effect for a period of ten years as from the date of its coming into force.

It shall thereafter remain in force for successive periods of five years for such Contracting Parties as have not denounced it at least six months before the expiration of the current period.

Denunciation shall be effected by a written notification addressed to the Secretary-General of the United Nations.

ARTICLE XV

If, as a result of denunciations, the number of Parties to the present Convention should become less than sixteen, the Convention shall cease to be in force as from the date on which the last of these denunciations shall become effective.

ARTICLE XVI

A request for the revision of the present Convention may be made at any time by any Contracting Party by means of a notification in writing addressed to the Secretary-General.

The General Assembly shall decide upon the steps, if any, to be taken in respect of such request.

ARTICLE XVII

The Secretary-General of the United Nations shall notify all Members of the United Nations and the non-member States contemplated in article XI of the following:

(a) Signatures, ratifications and accessions received in accordance with article XI;

(b) Notifications received in accordance with article XII;

(c) The date upon which the present Convention comes into force in accordance with article XIII;

(d) Denunciations received in accordance with article XIV;

(e) The abrogation of the Convention in accordance with article XV;

(f) Notifications received in accordance with article XVI.

ARTICLE XVIII

The original of the present Convention shall be deposited in the archives of the United Nations.

A certified copy of the Convention shall be transmitted to all Members of the United Nations and to the non-member States contemplated in article XI.

ARTICLE XIX

The present Convention shall be registered by the Secretary-General of the United Nations on the date of its coming into force.

Violation of Human Rights

V. QUESTION OF THE VIOLATION OF HUMAN RIGHTS AND FUNDA-
MENTAL FREEDOMS, INCLUDING POLICIES OF RACIAL DISCRIMINA-
TION AND SEGREGATION AND OF APARTHEID, IN ALL COUNTRIES,
WITH PARTICULAR REFERENCE TO COLONIAL AND OTHER DEPENDENT
COUNTRIES AND TERRITORIES: REPORT OF THE SUB-COMMISSION
UNDER COMMISSION ON HUMAN RIGHTS RESOLUTION 8 (XXIII).

91. By resolution 8 (XXIII) of 16 March 1967, the Commission on Human
Rights requested the Sub-Commission to prepare for the use of the Commission a report containing information on violations of human rights and
fundamental freedoms from all available sources.

92. The Sub-Commission considered this item at its 645th, 646th, 649th, 650th
and 660th meetings.

93. Some members emphasized that the Sub-Commission should concentrate
on serious violations of human rights such as *apartheid* and racial discrimination. Other members drew attention to the fact that the agenda item related
to violations of human rights and fundamental freedoms in all countries.

94. At the 646th meeting on 22 August 1972, Mr James submitted the text
of a telegram which he proposed that the Chairman of the Sub-Commission
should send to the President of Uganda. The proposed telegram (E/CN. 4/
Sub. 2/XXV/CRP. 3) was worded as follows:

Your Excellency,
    The United Nations Sub-Commission on Prevention of Discrimination
and Protection of Minorities, now meeting in New York, has noted with
concern the decision of the Ugandan Government to require all Asians –
including those holding Ugandan citizenship – to leave your country.
    The internal affairs of your distinguished country are not a matter for
the Sub-Commission, but it does have a particular responsibility in the
field of human rights entrusted to it by the United Nations Commission on
Human Rights. The Sub-Commission has asked that I communicate to you
its serious concrn over this situation, and to ask you to give particular
attention to the humanitarian aspects of the situation arising out of the
decision affecting those Asians living in Uganda who do not have Ugandan

citizenship. The Sub-Commission has also expressed its concern over the decision to require Asians holding Ugandan citizenship to leave your country as well.

The Sub-Commission, fully aware of the magnificent record of your great country in the field of human rights, is convinced that you will give these matters your most careful personal attention.

95. Several members stated that the Sub-Commission had no mandate to send telegrams to heads of State. Its terms of reference were confined to conducting studies and carrying out tasks specifically entrusted to it by its parent bodies.

96. At the 649th meeting on 23 August 1972, the Sub-Commission by 13 votes to 9 with 1 abstention decided to give precedence to a motion proposed by Mr Sekyiamah not to send the telegram, over a proposal by Mr Morga that the Sub-Commission first hear the Observer from Uganda, who had requested a hearing. Mr Sekyiamah's proposal that the Sub-Commission not send the telegram was adopted by 14 votes to 1 with 6 abstentions.

97. The Observer from Uganda stated, *inter alia*, that all genuine Ugandan citizens, regardless of race, would be allowed to stay in the country. Moreover, the expulsion of undesirable aliens was not unprecendented. This was particularly true of persons who had forged their citizenship papers and those of double and triple citizenship who had transferred large amounts of foreign exchange to other countries.

98. At the 646th meeting on 24 August 1972, Mr James submitted a draft resolution (E/CN. 4/Sub. 2/L. 572) as follows:

The Sub-Commission on Prevention of Discrimination and Protection of Minorities,

Recalling the statements in the preamble and text of the Universal Declaration of Human Rights to the effect that all human beings are born free and equal in dignity and rights,

Noting with regret that situations continue to arise in which the human rights of individuals who are not citizens of the nations in which they live are violated,

Recognizing that this matter involves complex questions of international law,

Recommends the Commission on Human Rights to reaffirm the principle that human rights apply to all human beings, and to consider how effective international legal protection for individuals who are not citizens of the country in which they live can be established.

99. Certain members of the Sub-Commission stated that Mr James' draft

resolution did not directly raise human rights questions but rather problems
of international law, and that the matter was one not for the Commission on
Human Rights but for the International Law Commission. Other members
considered that the second preambular paragraph contained an implication
concerning certain States.

100. In the light of the discussion, at the 660th meeting on 30 August 1972,
Messrs Gros Espiell, Inglés, James and Nettel submitted a draft resolution
(E/CN. 4/Sub. 2/L. 577), replacing the draft resolution earlier submitted by
Mr James. The new draft resolution read as follows:

*The Sub-Commission on Prevention of Discrimination and Protection of
Minorities,*

Recalling and reaffirming the statements in the preamble and text of the
Universal Declaration of Human Rights to the effect that all human beings
are born free and equal in dignity and rights,

Noting with regret that situations continue to arise in which the human
rights of individuals and groups of individuals who are not citizens of the
nations in which they live can be jeopardized,

Recognizing that this matter involves complex questions,

1. *Recommends* that the Commission on Human Rights should review
the present provisions for the international protection of the human rights
of individuals who are not citizens of the country in which they live, and
to consider what action, in the field of human rights, would be desirable;

2. *Decides* to place the matter of the human rights of individuals who are
not citizens of the country in which they live on its agenda for the twenty-
sixth session of the Sub-Commission.

101. In the light of the debate, the co-sponsors withdrew the second preambular paragraph and reworded the third preambular paragraph to read as
follows:

'*Recognizing* that the question of the enjoyment of human rights by individuals who are not citizens of the country in which they live gives rise to
complex legal and political problems,'.

102. A proposal by Mr Sanchez to delete operative paragraph 2 was approved
by 8 votes to 6, with 10 abstentions.

103. Some members said that they had voted under a misapprehension, and
asked for the vote to be taken again. After discussion, the Chairman ruled
that another vote on operative paragraph 2 be taken.

104. A proposal by Mr Al-Qaysi to delete operative paragraph 2 was rejected by 9 votes to 7 and 4 abstentions.

105. The sponsors orally revised the first operative paragraph to read as follows:

> '*Recommends* that the Commission on Human Rights should consider the problem of the applicability of the present provisions for the international legal protection of the human rights of individuals who are not citizens of the country in which they live and to consider what measures in the field of human rights would be desirable;'.

106. After the withdrawal of operative paragraph 2 by the sponsors, the draft resolution as a whole, as orally amended, was adopted by 12 votes to 1 with 10 abstentions. The text of the resolution appears in Chapter XIV as resolution 8 (XXIV).

The Turkish Genocide Against the Armenians and the United Nations Memory Hole

The process of pushing the Turkish Genocide down the United Nations memory hole can be traced through the proceedings of the Sub-Commission on Prevention of Discrimination and Protection of Minorities. There was a discussion in 1972 of a preliminary report on genocide (E/CN. 4/1101–E/CN. 4/Sub. 2/332). In 1973, at the 26th Session, the Special Rapporteur submitted a further report on the Study of the Question of the Prevention and Punishment of the Crime of Genocide. Paragraph 30 contained the following reference in the historical section of the study.

> Passing to the modern era, one may note the existence of relatively full documentation dealing with the massacres of Armenians, which have been described as 'the first case of genocide in the twentieth century'. (E/CN. 4/Sub. 2/L.583 dd. 25 June 1973)

The reader will appreciate the extreme tact of the reference. No mention is made of the role of the Ottoman Empire in this genocide. It is as if the genocide happened of itself.

The meeting of the Sub-Commission in the following year reports discussion of the draft study in the Commission on Human Rights.

> ... many speakers considered that the Special Rapporteur of the Sub-Commission, in preparing the final version of the study on the subject-matter, should avoid references to specific incidents that had taken place in the past, before the contemporary notion of genocide had been elaborated. It was pointed out that there was the dangerous pitfall of confusing the crime of genocide with the eventual consequences which might occur as a result of a given war and of making such parallels without taking into account the historical and socio-economic background of the past events. In that connection all speakers urged the Special Rapporteur to delete, in the final version of his report, paragraph 30 of his progress report, submitted to the Sub-Commission at its twenty-sixth session (E/CN. 4/Sub. 2/L. 583). Some speakers expressed the view that, although many studies prepared by the Sub-Commission contained historical introductions that helped in the understanding of contemporary situations, reference to events

that had given rise to controversial explanations and evaluations in different publications should be avoided.

At the meetings in 1975, the matter was discussed further, one of the members contributing the observation that the 1915 incidents between Turks and Armenians constituted a historical fact, but in a civilized international community, consideration should also be given to the desire of a state not to be defamed on account of its past acts, which had been perpetrated by a previous generation and were probably regretted by the present generation (E/CN. 4/Sub. 2/SR. 736).

In 1978, the Special Rapporteur presented the final report. The historical section 'had been collapsed down to the Nazi genocide. The Turkish genocide had disappeared down the memory hole. Representatives of non-governmental organizations and members of the Sub-Commission protested. However, the final responsibility for the study rests with the Rapporteur, and he replied as follows:

> Concern had been expressed that the study on genocide might be diverted from its intended course and lose its essential purpose. Consequently, it had been decided to retain the massacre of the Jews under Nazism, because that case was known to all and no objections had been raised; but other cases had been omitted, because it was impossible to compile an exhaustive list, because it was important to maintain unity within the international community in regard to genocide, and because in many cases to delve into the past might reopen old wounds which were now healing. That procedure seemed to him to be only logical. He had not abandoned his responsibilities and, if the Sub-Commission considered that the historical chapter of the study should include all cases, he suggested that it should take a formal decision to review the chapter and to include, for example, the Armenian case. He would, however, need to have the necessary evidence. (E/CN. 4/Sub. 2/SR. 822)

No such decision was taken. But at the meeting of the Human Rights Commission in the following year, there was an active campaign to re-insert reference to the genocide against Armenians: and the Rapporteur was asked to take account of the statements made to the Commission, and other communications on the subject. So it seems that the Turkish genocide against the Armenians may be restored to the memory of the United Nations.

A curious footnote to this episode is provided by a former representative of the U.S.A. on the Commission. When the Turks had lobbied for the deletion of reference to their genocide, the instructions to the U.S. representative were to take a neutral stand, since the U.S.A. was trying to get the Turks to eliminate their poppy crop, used in the export of heroin to the United States (Hoffman, 1978: 18).

Bibliography

ADAMS, GERRY 'Provisional Sinn Fein Vice-President and leading Republican theoretician and strategist', interview, *Hibernia*, 25 October 1979, pp. 1, 6, 7.

AIKMAN, D. 'Cambodia: An Experiment in Genocide', *Time*, 31 July 1978, pp. 39–40.

AINSZTEIN, REUBEN 'Myth of the Yalta "Victims"', *Sunday Times*, 12 March 1978, p. 16.

ALBINO, OLIVER *The Sudan: A Southern Viewpoint*. London: Oxford University Press, 1970.

ALIER, ABEL 'The Southern Sudan Question', in Wai, *The Southern Sudan*, 1973.

AMNESTY INTERNATIONAL *The Human Rights Situation in Uganda*. London, 1977. *Indonesia: An Amnesty International Report*. London, 1977. Letter to the Editor ('What Happened in Indonesia? An Exchange'), *New York Review of Books*, 9 February 1978, p. 44.

ANDEMICAEL, BERHANYKUN *The OAU and the UN: Relations between the Organization of African Unity and the United Nations*. New York: Africana Publishing Co., 1976.

ANDERSON, BENEDICT R., and MCVEY, RUTH T. *A Preliminary Analysis of the October 1, 1965 Coup in Indonesia*. Ithaca: Southeast Asia Program, Cornell University, 1971.

ARENDT, HANNAH *Eichmann in Jerusalem*. New York: Viking Press, 1969. 'Lying in Politics: Reflections on the Pentagon Papers', *New York Review of Books*, 18 November 1971, pp. 30–39.

ARENS, RICHARD *Genocide in Paraguay*. Philadelphia: Temple University Press, 1976.

ARLEN, MICHAEL J. *Passage to Ararat*. New York: Farrar, Straus and Giroux, 1975.

ARNETT, E. J. *The Rise of the Sokoto Fulani, Being a Paraphrase and in Some Parts a Translation of the Infaku'l Maisuri of Sultan Mohammed Bello*. Kano: n.p., 1922.

BANGLA DESH DOCUMENTS
See Indian Ministry of External Affairs.

BARAKAT, HALIM *Lebanon in Strife*. London: University of Texas Press, 1977.

Genocide

BARRITT, D. P. and BOOTH, A. *Orange and Green.* Northern Friends Peace Board, 1972.

BARRON, JOHN, and PAUL, ANTHONY *Peace with Horror.* London: Hodder & Stoughton, 1977.

BEARDSLEY, MONROE C. 'Reflections on Genocide and Ethnocide', in Arens, *Genocide in Paraguay,* 1976, pp. 85–101.

BEDAU, HUGO ADAM 'Genocide in Vietnam?', in Held, Morgenbesser and Nagel, *Philosophy, Morality and International Affairs,* 1974, pp. 5–46.

BELL, WENDELL, and FREEMAN, WALTER E. (eds.) *Ethnicity and Nation Building.* London: Sage Publications, 1974.

BENOIT, Y. 'Indonesia: 500,000 morts', *Guerres et Paix* (Paris), 2 (1966), 69–73.

BERLIN, ISAIAH 'The Rationality of Value Judgements', in Friedrich, *Rationality in Decision,* 1964.

BERNARD, V., OTTENBERG, P., and REDL, F. 'Dehumanization: A Composite Psychological Defense in Relation to Modern War', in Schwebel, *Behavioral Science and Human Survival,* 1965.

BESHIR, MOHAMMED OMER *The Southern Sudan: Background to Conflict.* Khartoum: Khartoum University Press, 1970.

BOAL, F. W. 'Territoriality on the Shankill–Falls Divide, Belfast', *Irish Geography* (1969), 30–50.

BODLEY, JOHN H. *Victims of Progress.* London: Cummings Publishing Co., 1975.

BOWEN, M., FREEMAN, G., and MILLER, KAY *Passing By: The United States and Genocide in Burundi.* New York: Carnegie Endowment for International Peace, 1973.

BOYAJIAN, DICKRAN H. *Armenia: The Case for a Forgotten Genocide.* New Jersey: Educational Book Crafters, 1972.

BRITISH PARLIAMENTARY PAPERS *Civil Disorder, 8, Northern Ireland, Sessions 1884–1887.* Dublin: Irish University Presses, 1970.

BRYCE, VISCOUNT J. *The Treatment of Armenians in the Ottoman Empire, 1915–1916.* London: His Majesty's Stationery Office, 1916. (See Toynbee, 1916.)

BUCHHEIT, LEE C. *Secession: The Legitimacy of Self-Determination.* New Haven: Yale University Press, 1978.

BUDGE, IAN, and O'LEARY, CORNELIUS *Belfast: Approach to Crisis.* London: Macmillan, 1973.

BUDIARDJO, CARMEL 'The Abuse of Human Rights in Indonesia', in Foundation for the Study of Plural Societies, *Case Studies on Human Rights and Fundamental Freedoms: A World Survey,* III, 1975–6, 209–41.

BULLOCH, JOHN *Death of a Country: The Civil War in Lebanon.* London: Weidenfeld & Nicolson, 1977.

BUSTEED, M. A. *Northern Ireland: Geographical Aspects of a Crisis.* School of Geography, Research Paper No. 3, University of Oxford: 1972.

CALDWELL, MALCOLM, and TAN, LEK *Cambodia in the Southeast Asian War.* New York: Monthly Review Press, 1973.

CAMPBELL-JOHNSON, ALAN *Mission with Mountbatten.* London: Hale, 1951.

CAPUTO, PHILIP *A Rumor of War.* New York: Holt, Rinehart & Winston, 1977.

CARNEY, TIMOTHY MICHAEL *Communist Party Power in Kampuchea (Cambodia): Documents and Discussion.* Ithaca: Southeast Asia Program, Cornell University Press, 1977.

CARZOU, JEAN-MARIE *Un Génocide exemplaire: Arménie 1915.* Paris: Flammarion, 1975.

CASSESE, ANTONIO *Current Problems in International Law.* Milan: Guiffre, 1975.

CHAUDHURI, KALYAN *Genocide in Bangladesh.* Bombay: Orient Longman, 1972.

CHOMSKY, NOAM 'The Western Press and Cambodia', *Journal of Contemporary Asia,* 7, 4 (1977), 548–54.

CHOMSKY, NOAM, and HERMAN, EDWARD S. 'Distortions at Fourth Hand', *The Nation,* 25 June 1977, pp. 789–94. *After the Cataclysm: Postwar Indochina and the Reconstruction of Imperial Ideology.* Nottingham: Spokesman, 1979.

CLASTRES, PIERRE 'De l'ethnocide', *L'Homme,* 14 (July–December 1974), 101–10.

CLIFFORD-VAUGHAN, F. M. (ed.) *International Pressures and Political Change in South Africa.* Cape Town: Oxford University Press, 1978.

COHEN, STEPHEN F. 'Old and New Approaches: Bolshevism and Stalinism', in Tucker (ed.), *Stalinism: Essays in Historical Interpretation,* 1977, 3–29.

COHN, NORMAN *Warrant for Genocide.* New York: Harper & Row, 1967.

COLLINS, LARRY, and LAPIERRE, DOMINIQUE *Freedom at Midnight.* New York: Simon & Schuster, 1975.

COMITÉ DES DÉLÉGATIONS JUIVES *Les pogromes en Ukraine sous les gouvernements ukrainiens 1917–1920.* Paris: 1927.

CONQUEST, ROBERT *The Great Terror: Stalin's Purge of the Thirties.* New York: Macmillan, 1968. *The Nation Killers: The Soviet Deportation of Nationalities.* New York: Macmillan, 1970.

COSER, LEWIS A. 'The Visibility of Evil', *Journal of Social Issues,* 25, 1 (1969), 101–9.

COURRIÈRE, YVES *Le Temps des léopards.* Paris: Fayard, 1969.

DADRIAN, VAHAKN N. 'Factors of Anger and Aggression in Genocide', *Journal of Human Relations,* 19, 3 (1947), 394–416. 'A Typology of Genocide', *International Review of Sociology,* 2 (1975). 'The Structural-Functional Components of Genocide', in Drapkin and Viano, *Victimology,* Vol. IV, 1974–5. 'The Common Features of the Armenian and Jewish

Cases of Genocides: A Comparative Victimological Perspective', in Drapkin and Viano, *Victimology*, Vol. IV, 1974–5.

DALLIN, ALEXANDER, and BRESLAUER, GEORGE W. *Political Terror in Communist Systems*. Stanford: Stanford University Press, 1970.

DARBY, JOHN *Conflict in Northern Ireland*. New York: Barnes & Noble, 1976.

DARBY, JOHN, and WILLIAMSON, ARTHUR *Violence and the Social Services in Northern Ireland*. London: Heinemann, 1978.

DAVIDSON, EUGENE *The Nuremberg Fallacy*. New York: Macmillan, 1973.

DEBRÉ, FRANÇOIS *Cambodge: La révolution de la forêt*. Paris: Flammarion, 1976.

DEMARIS, OVID *Brothers in Blood*. New York: Charles Scribner's Sons, 1977.

DESJARDINS, THIERRY *Le Martyre du Liban*. Paris: Plon, 1976.

DES PRES, TERRENCE *The Survivor: An Anatomy of Life in the Death Camps*. New York: Oxford University Press, 1976.

DICKS, HENRY VICTOR *Licensed Mass Murder: A Socio-Psychological Study of Some S.S. Killers*. London: Sussex University Press, 1972.

DJABAGUI, VASSAN-GHIRAY 'Soviet Nationality Policy and Genocide', *Armenian Review*, 20 (Winter 1967), 45–56.

DOMINGUEZ, JORGE I., RODLEY, NIGEL S., WOOD, BRYCE, and FALK, RICHARD *Enhancing Global Human Rights*. New York: McGraw-Hill, 1979.

DONAT, ALEXANDER *The Holocaust Kingdom*. New York: Holt, Rinehart & Winston, 1965.

DONNEDIEU DE VABRES *Le Procès de Nuremberg*. Paris: Editions Domat Montchrestien, 1947.

DRAPKIN, ISRAEL, and VIANO, EMILIO (eds.) *Victimology*. Lexington: Lexington-Books D. C. Heath, Vol. IV, 1974–5.

DROST, PIETER *Genocide* (Vol. I) and *The Crime of State* (Vol. II). Leyden: A. W. Sythoff, 1959.

DU BOIS, VICTOR D. *To Die in Burundi*. American University Field Staff Reports, Central and Southern African Series, Vol. XVI, no. 4. New York, September 1972.

DUTT, R. PALME 'India, Pakistan, Bangladesh', *Labour Monthly*, 54 (January 1972), 4–12.

EADS, BRIAN 'The Prison Camp State', *Observer*, 30 October 1977.

ECKHARDT, ALICE 'The Holocaust: Christian and Jewish Responses', *Journal of the American Academy of Religion*, 42, 3 (September 1974), 453–69.

EIDELBERG, SHLOMO (ed.) *The Jews and the Crusaders*. Madison: University of Wisconsin Press, 1977.

EMERSON, RUPERT 'Self-Determination Revisited in the Era of Decolonization', Occasional Paper, no. 9, Center for International Affairs, Harvard

University (December 1964). 'The Fate of Human Rights in the Third World', *World Politics*, 27 (January 1975), 201–26.

EPRILE, CECIL *War and Peace in the Sudan 1955–1972*. Newton Abbot: David & Charles, 1974.

ESMAN, MILTON J. (ed.) *Ethnic Conflict in the Western World*. Ithaca: Cornell University Press, 1977.

FACKENHEIM, EMIL L. *The Jewish Return into History*. New York: Schocken, 1978.

Fact Finder, The Volume 31, no. 15 (16 June 1973).

FALK, RICHARD A. 'The Beirut Raid and the International Law of Retaliation', *American Journal of International Law*, 63 (July 1969), 415–43. 'Ecocide, Genocide and the Nuremberg Tradition', in Held, Morgenbesser and Nagel, *Philosophy, Morality and International Affairs*, 1974, pp. 123–37. *The Vietnam War and International Law*. Princeton University Press, 1976, Vol. 4.

FALK, RICHARD A. (ed.) *The International Law of Civil War*. Baltimore: John Hopkins Press, 1971.

FEIN, HELEN *Accounting for Genocide*. New York: The Free Press, 1979.

FOUNDATION FOR THE STUDY OF PLURAL SOCIETIES *Case Studies on Human Rights and Fundamental Freedoms: A World Survey*. 5 Vols. The Hague: Nijhoff, 1975–6.

FRANKEL, BORIS 'The "Gulag Archipelago" and the Left', *Theory and Society*, 1:4 (1974).

FRIEDLANDER, ALBERT H. *Out of the Whirlwind*. New York: Schocken, 1976.

FRIEDLÄNDER, SAUL 'Some Aspects of the Historical Significance of the Holocaust', *The Jerusalem Quarterly*, 1 (Fall 1976), 36–59.

FRIEDMAN, PHILIP 'The Extermination of the Gypsies: A Nazi Genocide Operation against an Aryan People', *Jewish Frontier*, January 1951, 7–11.

FRIEDRICH, CARL (ed.) *Rationality in Decision*. Nomos, Vol. III. New York, 1964.

FROMM, ERICH *The Anatomy of Human Destructiveness*. Greenwich: Fawcett Publications, 1975.

GALBRAITH, FRANCIS J. Letter to the Editor ('What Happened in Indonesia? An Exchange'), *New York Review of Books*, 9 February 1978, p. 44.

GOLDBERG, ARTHUR J., and GARDNER, RICHARD N. 'Time to Act on the Genocide Convention', *American Bar Association Journal*, 58 (February 1972), 141–5.

GOLDENBERG, SYDNEY L. 'Crimes Against Humanity: 1945–1970', *Western Ontario Law Review*, X (1971), 1–55.

GORDENKER, LEO 'Symbols and Substance in the United Nations', *New Society* 35, 697 (12 February 1976), 324–6.

GOULD, STEPHEN JAY 'Koestler's Solution', *New York Review of Books*, 20 April 1978, pp. 35–7.

GOULDNER, ALVIN W. 'Stalinism: A Study of Internal Colonialism', *Telos*, 34 (Winter 1977–8), 5–48.

GRAETZ, H. *History of the Jews*. Philadelphia: The Jewish Publication Society of America, 6 Vols., 1894.

Grass Curtain, 1, 2 (August 1970), 3 (December 1970).

GREENLAND, JEREMY 'Ethnic Discrimination in Rwanda and Burundi', in Foundation for the Study of Plural Societies, *Case Studies On Human Rights and Fundamental Freedoms*, IV, 1975, 97–133.

GREGOR, A. JAMES *Fascism: The Contemporary Interpretations*. Morristown: General Learning Press, University Programs Modular Studies, 1973.

HALE, SONDRA 'Sudan Civil War: Religion, Colonialism and the World-System', in Suad and Pillsbury, *Muslim-Christian Conflicts: Economic, Political and Social Origins*, 1978, pp. 157–82.

HECHTER, MICHAEL *Internal Colonialism: The Celtic Fringe in British National Development, 1536–1966*. Berkeley: University of California Press, 1975.

HEDER, STEPHEN R. 'Origins of the Conflict', *Southeast Asia Chronicle*, 64 (September–October 1978), 3–18.

HELD, VIRGINIA, MORGENBESSER, SIDNEY, and NAGEL, THOMAS *Philosophy, Morality and International Affairs*. New York: Oxford University Press, 1974.

HELLER, CELIA S. *On the Edge of Destruction*. New York: Columbia University Press, 1977.

HEMMING, JOHN *The Conquest of the Incas*. New York: Harcourt, Brace Jovanovich, 1973.

HERBSTEIN, DENIS *White Man, We Want to Talk to You*. New York: Africana Publishing Co., 1979.

HILBERG, RAUL *The Destruction of the European Jews*. Chicago: Quadrangle Books, 1961.

HILDEBRAND, GEORGE, and PORTER, GARETH *Cambodia – Starvation and Revolution*. New York: Monthly Review Press, 1976.

HOCHHUTH, ROLF *The Deputy*. New York: Grove Press, 1964.

HODSON, H. V. *The Great Divide – Britain-India-Pakistan*. London: Hutchinson, 1969.

HOFFMAN, PHILIP E. Comments in *Thirty Years of Human Rights at the United Nations*. Columbia University Center for the Study of Human Rights, 1978, p. 18.

HOHENBERG, JOHN 'The Crusade that Changed the U.N.', *Saturday Review*, 9 November 1968.

HOROWITZ, IRVING LOUIS *Genocide: State Power and Mass Murder*. New Brunswick: Transaction Books, 1976.

HOUSEPIAN, MARJORIE 'The Unremembered Genocide', *Commentary* 42, 3 (September 1966).

HOVANNISIAN, RICHARD G. *Armenia on the Road to Independence.* Berkeley: University of California Press, 1967. *The Republic of Armenia.* Berkeley: University of California Press, 1971. 'The Armenian Question in the Ottoman Empire', *East European Quarterly*, 5 (March 1972), 1–26. 'The Ebb and Flow of the Armenian Minority in the Arab Middle East', *Middle East Journal*, 28 (1974), 39–52. 'The Critics' View: Beyond Revisionism', *International Journal of Middle East Studies*, 9 (August 1978), 379–88. *The Armenian Holocaust: A Bibliography relating to the Deportations, Massacres and Dispersion of the Armenian People, 1915–1923.* Cambridge, Massachusetts: Armenian Heritage Press, 1978.

HUGHES, JOHN *The End of Sukarno.* London: Angus & Robertson, 1968.

INDIAN MINISTRY OF EXTERNAL AFFAIRS *Bangla Desh Documents.* Madras: B. N. K. Press, 1971.

INSTITUTE FOR THE STUDY OF THE U.S.S.R. *Genocide in the U.S.S.R.: Studies in Group Destruction.* New York: The Scarecrow Press, 1958.

INTERNATIONAL COMMISSION OF JURISTS *The Events in East Pakistan 1971: A Legal Study.* Geneva: 1972. *Violations of Human Rights and the Rule of Law in Uganda.* Geneva: 1974. *Uganda and Human Rights, Reports to the United Nations.* Geneva: 1977.

INTERNATIONAL WAR CRIMES TRIBUNAL *Le Jugement de Stockholm.* Paris: Gallimard, 1967. *Russell II: Le Jugement final.* Paris: Gallimard, 1968.

JAULIN, ROBERT *L'Ethnocide à travers Les Amériques.* Paris: Fayard, 1972. *La décivilisation, politique et pratique de l'ethnocide.* Brussels: Presses Universitaires de France, 1974.

JONAS, GERALD 'Seeing the Universe Whole', *New York Times Book Review*, 2 April 1978, pp. 9, 16.

KAMM, HENRY 'The Agony of Cambodia', *New York Times Magazine*, 10 November 1977, pp. 40–43, 142–52.

KASFIR, NELSON *Still Keeping the Peace.* American University Field Staff Reports, Northeast Africa Series, Vol. XXI, no. 4 (April 1976).

KELMAN, HERBERT C. 'Violence without Moral Restraint: Reflections on the Dehumanization of Victims and Victimizers', *Journal of Social Issues*, 29, 4 (1973), 25–61.

KERNER, ROBERT J. (ed.) *Yugoslavia.* Berkeley: University of California Press, 1949.

KIRK-GREENE, A. H. M. 'The Cultural Background to the Nigerian Crisis', *African Affairs*, 262 (January 1967), 3–11. *Crisis and Conflict in Nigeria.* London: Oxford University Press, 1971.

KNOLL, ERWIN, and MCFADDEN, JUDITH NIES (eds.) *War Crimes and the American Conscience.* New York: Holt, Rinehart & Winston, 1970.

KOESTLER, ARTHUR *Janus: A Summing Up.* London: Hutchinson, 1978.

KOGON, EUGEN *The Theory and Practice of Hell.* New York: Octagon Books, 1973.

KOLAKOWSKI, LESZEK 'Intellectuals, Hope and Heresy', *Encounter*, XXXVII, 4 (October 1971), 42–8. 'Revolution and Reform', *Partisan Review* (Winter 1973), 52–64. 'Marxist Roots of Stalinism', in Tucker (ed.), *Stalinism: Essays in Historical Interpretation*, 1977, pp. 283–98.

KOVALY, PAVEL *Rehumanization or Dehumanization*. Boston: Branden Press, 1974.

KUPER, LEO *Passive Resistance in South Africa*. New Haven: Yale University Press, 1957. *Race, Class and Power*. London: Duckworth, 1974. *The Pity of It All*. Minneapolis: University of Minnesota Press, 1977. *The Theory of the Plural Society, Race and Conquest*. (In process of publication – UNESCO.

KUPER, LEO, and SMITH, M. G. (eds.) *Pluralism in Africa*. Berkeley: University of California Press, 1969.

KUPER, LEO, WATTS, HILSTAN, and DAVIES, RONALD L. *Durban: A Study in Racial Ecology*. New York: Columbia University Press, 1958.

KYEMBA, HENRY *State of Blood*. With a preface by Godfrey Lule. London: Transworld Publishers, 1977.

LACOUTURE, JEAN 'The Bloodiest Revolution', *New York Review of Books*, 31 March 1977, 9–10. 'Cambodia: Corrections', *New York Review of Books*, 26 May 1977, 46.

LAMB, HAROLD *Genghis Khan*. New York: Pinnacle Books, 1927.

LAVERGNE, BERNARD, and LAURIÈRE, HERVÉ 'Genocide in the Puppet State of Croatia', *Contemporary Review*, 224, 1301 (June 1974), 291–8.

Law Reports of Trials of War Criminals London: United Nations War Crimes Commission, H.M.S.O., 1948, Vols. VI, VII, XIX.

LEGUM, COLIN 'The Massacre of the Proud Ibos', *Observer*, 16 October 1966, p. 12.

LEMARCHAND, RENÉ *Rwanda and Burundi*. New York: Praeger Press, 1970. 'Revolutionary Phenomena in Stratified Societies: Rwanda and Zanzibar', *Civilisations*, 18 (1968), 16–51. 'Ethnic Genocide', *Issue*, Summer 1975, pp. 9–16.

LEMARCHAND, RENÉ, and GREENLAND, JEREMY *Problèmes du Burundi*. Brussels: Colloque International, 27–8 December 1974.

LEMARCHAND, RENÉ, and MARTIN, DAVID *Selective Genocide in Burundi*. London: Minority Rights Group, Report No. 20, 1974.

LEMKIN, RAPHAEL *Axis Rule in Occupied Europe*. Washington: Carnegie Endowment for International Peace, 1944. 'Genocide – A Modern Crime', *Free World*, 9 (April 1945), 39–43. 'Genocide', *The American Scholar*, 15, 2 (Spring 1946), 227–30. 'Genocide as a Crime under International Law', *American Journal of International Law*, XLI (1947), 145–71. 'Genocide as a Crime under International Law', *United Nations Bulletin*, IV (1948), 70–71.

LEPSIUS, JOHANNES *Armenia and Europe*. London: Hodder & Stoughton, 1897. *Le rapport secret de Johannes Lepsius ... sur les massacres d'Arménie.* Paris: Payot, 1918. *Deutschland und Armenien, 1914–1918, Sammlung Diplomatischer Aktenstücke.* Potsdam, 1919.

LEV, DANIEL S. 'Indonesia 1965: The Year of the Coup', *Asian Survey*, VI, 2 (February 1966), 103–10.

LEVAK, ALBERT E. 'Provincial Conflict and Nation-Building in Pakistan', in Bell and Freeman, *Ethnicity and Nation Building*, 1974, pp. 203–22. 'Discrimination in Pakistan: National, Provincial, Tribal', in Foundation for the Study of Plural Societies, *Case Studies on Human Rights and Fundamental Freedoms*, Vol. 1, 1975, 281–308.

LÉVY, BERNARD-HENRI *La Barbarie à visage humain.* Paris: Grasset, 1977.

LEVY, REUBIN *The Social Structure of Islam.* Cambridge: Cambridge University Press, 1957.

LEWIS, NORMAN *Genocide: A Documentary Report on the Conditions of Indian Peoples in Brazil.* Berkeley: Indigena and American Friends of Brazil, 1974. 'The Camp at Cecilio Baez', in Arens, *Genocide in Paraguay*, 1976, pp. 58–68.

LISKOFSKY, SIDNEY 'Coping with the "Question of the Violation of Human Rights and Freedoms" ', *Revue des Droits de L'Homme*, VIII, 4 (1975).

LLOYD, P. C. 'The Ethnic Background to the Nigerian Crisis', in Panter-Brick, *Nigerian Politics and Military Rule: Prelude to the Civil War*, 1970.

LOEWENBERG, PETER 'The Psychohistorical Origins of the Nazi Youth Cohort', *The American Historical Review*, 76, 5 (December 1971), 1457–1502. 'Psychohistorical Perspectives on Modern German History', *Journal of Modern History*, 47, 2 (June 1975), 229–79.

LORENZ, KONRAD 'On Killing Members of One's Own Species', *Bulletin of the Atomic Scientists*, October 1970, pp. 3–5, 51–6. *On Aggression.* New York: Harcourt Brace & World, 1977.

LUKE, SIR HARRY *The Making of Modern Turkey.* London: Macmillan, 1936.

MACBRIDE, SEAN *The 1979 Sean MacBride Human Rights Lecture.* London: Amnesty International, 1979.

MANVELL, ROGER, and FRAENKEL, HEINRICH *Incomparable Crime; Mass Extermination in the 20th Century: The Legacy of Guilt.* London: Heinemann, 1967.

MARCUS, JACOB R. *The Rise and Destiny of the German Jew.* Cincinnati: Union of American Hebrew Congregations, 1934.

MARKOVIĆ, MIHAILO 'Stalinism and Marxism', in Tucker (ed.), *Stalinism: Essays in Historical Interpretation*, 1977, pp. 299–319.

MARTIN, DAVID *Selective Genocide in Burundi – Part II.* London: Minority Rights Group, Report No. 20, 1974.

MASCARENHAS, ANTHONY *The Rape of Bangladesh.* Delhi: Vikas Publications, 1971.

MEDVEDEV, ROY A. *Let History Speak.* New York: Alfred A. Knopf,

1971. 'New Pages from the Political Biography of Stalin', in Tucker (ed.), *Stalinism: Essays in Historical Interpretation*, 1977, pp. 199–235.

MELADY, THOMAS PATRICK *Burundi: The Tragic Years.* Maryknoll: Orbis Books, 1974.

MELSON, R., and WOLPE, H. (eds.) *Nigeria: Modernization and the Politics of Communalism.* East Lansing: Michigan State University Press, 1971.

MILLER, S. 'Our Mylai of 1900', *Transaction*, September 1970, p. 19.

MOON, PENDEREL *Divide and Quit.* Berkeley: University of California Press, 1962.

MORGENTHAU, HENRY *Ambassador Morgenthau's Story.* New York: Doubleday, 1918.

MORRIS, ROGER 'The United States and Burundi: Genocide, Nickel and Normalization', *The Progressive*, April 1974, pp. 27–9.

MORRIS-JONES, W. H. 'Pakistan Post-mortem and the Roots of Bangladesh', *Political Quarterly*, 43 (April 1972), 187–200.

NAFZIGER, E. W., and RICHTER, W. L. 'Biafra and Bangladesh: The Political Economy of Secessionist Conflict', *Journal of Peace Research*, 13, 2 (1976), 91–109.

NALBANDIAN, LOUISE *The Armenian Revolutionary Movement. The development of Armenian political parties through the nineteenth century.* Berkeley: University of California Press, 1963.

NANSEN, FRIDTJOF *Armenia and the Near East.* London: Allen & Unwin, 1928.

NEKRICH, ALEKSANDR M. *The Punished Peoples: The Deportation and Fate of Soviet Minorities at the End of the Second World War.* New York: Norton, 1978.

NEWMAN, FRANK C. 'The international bill of human rights: does it exist?', in Cassese, *Current Problems in International Law*, 1975, pp. 107–16.

NIXON, CHARLES R. 'Self Determination: The Nigeria/Biafra Case', *World Politics*, 24 (July 1972), 473–97.

NORDLINGER, ERIC A. 'Military Governments in Communally Divided Societies: Their Impact upon National Integration', in Foundation for the Study of Plural Societies, *Case Studies on Human Rights and Fundamental Freedoms*, III, 1975–6, 535–64.

NYISZLI, MIKLOS *Auschwitz.* New York: Frederick Fell, 1960.

O'BALLANCE, EDGAR *The Secret War in the Sudan 1955–1972.* Hamden, Connecticut: Anchor Books, 1977.

O'BRIEN, CONOR CRUISE 'Biafra: Genocide and Discretion', *Listener*, 30 January 1969, pp. 129–31. *Herod: Reflections on Political Violence.* London: Hutchinson, 1978.

ODUHO, JOSEPH, and DENG, WILLIAM *The Problem of the Southern Sudan.* London: Oxford University Press, 1963.

OFUATEY-KODJOE, W. *The Principle of Self-Determination in International Law.* New York: Nellen Publishing Co., 1977.

OWEN, J. E. 'East Pakistan, 1947–1971', *Contemporary Review,* 221 (July 1972), 23–8.

OWEN, RICHARD 'Background to the Southern Sudan', *Grass Curtain,* 1, 2 (August 1970), 7–9.

OWEN, ROGER (ed.) *Essays on the Crisis in Lebanon.* London: Ithaca Press, 1976.

PALMIER, LESLIE *Communism in Indonesia.* New York: Doubleday, 1973.

PANTER-BRICK, S. K. (ed.) *Nigerian Politics and Military Rule: Prelude to the Civil War.* Institute of Commonwealth Studies, The Athlone Press: London, 1970.

PARIS, EDMOND *Genocide in Satellite Croatia, 1941–1945.* Chicago: American Institute for Balkan Affairs, 1961.

PARSONS, TALCOTT *Essays in Sociological Theory: Pure and Applied.* Glencoe, Illinois: The Free Press, 1949.

PATEL, H. 'General Amin and the Indian Exodus from Uganda', *Issue,* 2, 4 (Winter 1972), 12–22.

PAWELCZYŃSKA, ANNA *Values and Violence in Auschwitz.* Berkeley; University of California Press, 1979.

PAYNE, ROBERT *Massacre.* New York: Macmillan, 1973.

PERHAM, M. 'Reflections on the Nigerian Civil War', *International Affairs,* 46 (April 1970), 231–46.

POLIAKOV, LÉON *Harvest of Hate.* Westport: Greenwood Press, 1971. 'La "solution finale". Les aveux du langage', *Études Internationales de Psycho-sociologie Criminelle,* 14–15 (1968), 53–5.

POL POT Interview. *Journal of Contemporary Asia,* 7, 3 (1977), 418–22.

PONCHAUD, FRANÇOIS *Cambodia Year Zero.* Harmondsworth: Penguin, 1978.

QUINN, K. M. 'Cambodia 1976: Internal Consolidation and External Expansion', *Asian Survey,* 17 (January 1977), 43–54.

RAJAN, M. S., and ISRAEL, T. 'The United Nations and the Conflict in Vietnam', in Falk, *The Vietnam War and International Law,* IV, 114–143.

REITLINGER, GERALD *The Final Solution.* London: Valentine, Mitchell, 1961.

REY, LUCIEN 'Holocaust in Indonesia', *New Left Review,* 36 (March–April), 1966.

ROBINSON, N. *The Genocide Convention.* New York: Institute of Jewish Affairs, 1960.

ROSE, RICHARD, MCALLISTER, IAN, and MAIR, PETER *Is There a Concurring Majority about Northern Ireland?* Studies in Public Policy No. 22. Glasgow: University of Strathclyde, 1978.

231

ROUSSET, PIERRE 'Cambodia: Background to the Revolution', *Journal of Contemporary Asia*, 7, 4 (1977), 513–28.

RUBENSTEIN, RICHARD L. *The Cunning of History*. New York: Harper & Row, 1975.

RUSSELL OF LIVERPOOL, LORD *The Record: The Trial of Adolf Eichmann for His Crimes against the Jewish People and against Humanity*. New York: Knopf, 1963.

SACHAR, ABRAM LEON *A History of the Jews*. New York: Knopf, 1967.

SACHS, ALBIE 'The Instruments of Domination in South Africa', in Thompson and Butler, *Change in Contemporary South Africa*, 1975, pp. 223–49.

ST JORRE, JOHN DE 'The Red Cross Fights to Survive', *Observer*, 7 September 1969. *The Brothers' War: Biafra and Nigeria*. Boston: Houghton Mifflin Co., 1972.

SALIBI, KAMAL S. *Cross Roads to Civil War*. New York: Caravan, 1976.

SAMIZDAT *Voices of the Soviet Opposition*. New York: Monad Press, 1974.

SANFORD, N., COMSTOCK, C., and ASSOCIATES (eds.) *Sanctions for Evil: Sources of Social Destructiveness*. San Francisco: Jossey-Bass, 1971.

SARTRE, JEAN-PAUL 'On Genocide', *Ramparts* (February 1968), 37–42.

SAUNDERS, GEORGE (ed.) *Samizdat: Voices of the Soviet Opposition*. New York: Monad Press, 1974.

SCHERMERHORN, R. A. *Comparative Ethnic Relations: A Framework for Theory and Research*. New York: Random House, 1970.

SCHLEMMER, L. 'External Pressures and Local Attitudes and Interests', in Clifford-Vaughan, *International Pressures and Political Change in South Africa*, 1978, pp. 75–85.

SCHWEBEL, MILTON (ed.) *Behavioral Science and Human Survival*. Palo Alto: Science and Behavior Books, 1965.

SCHWELB, EGON 'Crimes Against Humanity', *The British Yearbook of International Law*, 23 (1946), 178–226.

SETON-WATSON, HUGH 'Yugoslavia', in Toynbee and Toynbee, *Survey of International Affairs, 1939–1946: The Realignment of Europe*, 1955, pp. 352–71.

SHAW, STANFORD J., and SHAW, EZEL KURAL *History of the Ottoman Empire and Modern Turkey*. Cambridge: Cambridge University Press, Vol. I, 1976, Vol II, 1977. 'The Authors Respond', *International Journal of Middle East Studies*, 9 (August 1978), 388–400.

SHAWCROSS, WILLIAM 'Cambodia', *Far Eastern Economic Review*, 95 (7 January 1977), 18–24; (14 January 1977), 30–35. 'Cambodia: Nightmare without End', *Far Eastern Economic Review*, 100 (14 April 1978), 32–4. 'The Third Indochina War', *New York Review of Books*, 6 April 1978, pp. 15–22, and correspondence with Gareth Porter, *New York Review of Books*, 20 July 1978, pp. 48–9. *Sideshow: Kissinger, Nixon and the Destruction of Cambodia*. New York: Simon & Schuster, 1979.

SHAWCROSS, WILLIAM, TERRY, ANTONY, and PRINGLE, PETER 'A Conspiracy to Oppress', *Sunday Times*, 14 March 1976.

SINGH, KHUSHWANT *Mano Majna*. New York: Grove Press, 1956.

SMITH, BRADLEY F. *Reaching Judgement at Nuremberg*. London: Deutsch, 1977.

SMITH, M. G. 'Pluralism in Pre-Colonial African Societies', in Kuper and Smith, *Pluralism in Africa*, 1969, Ch. 4. 'Race and Stratification in the Caribbean', in *Corporations and Society*. London: Duckworth, 1974, Ch. 9.

SOHN, L. B. 'The Improvement of the UN Machinery on Human Rights', *International Studies Quarterly*, 23, 2 (1979), 186–215.

SOHN, L. B. and BUERGENTHAL, T. *International Protection of Human Rights*. Indianapolis: Bobbs-Merrill, 1973.

SOLZHENITSYN, ALEKSANDR I. *The Gulap Archipelago*. Vols. I–III. New York: Harper & Row, 1974–8. *A World Split Apart*. New York: Harper & Row, 1979.

SONTAG, SUSAN 'Disease as Political Metaphor', *New York Review of Books*, 23 February 1978, pp. 29–33.

SOUVARINE, BORIS *Staline*. Paris: Editions Champ Libre, 1977.

STEINER, GEORGE *In Bluebeard's Castle*. New Haven: Yale University Press, 1971.

STORR, ANTHONY *Human Destructiveness*. New York: Basic Books, 1972.

SUAD, JOSEPH, and PILLSBURY, BARBARA (eds.) *Muslim–Christian Conflicts: Economic, Political, and Social Origins*. Boulder, Colorado: Westview Press, 1978.

SUDAN GOVERNMENT *Report of the Commission of Inquiry into the Disturbances in the Southern Sudan during August, 1955*. Khartoum: Sudan Government, 1956.

SUHL, YURI (ed.) *They Fought Back*. New York: Crown Publishing Co., 1967.

TAMUNO, TEKENA N. 'Separatist Agitations in Nigeria', *The Journal of Modern African Studies*, 8, 4 (December 1970), 563–84.

TAN, LEK HOR 'Cambodia's Total Revolution', *Index on Censorship* (January–February 1978), 3–10.

TAYLOR, TELFORD 'The Nuremberg War Crimes Trials', *International Conciliation*, 450 (April 1949), 243–371.

THOMPSON, J. L. P. *Dual Incorporation in Northern Ireland: A Theory of Social and Political Structure*. Dissertation, University of California, Los Angeles, 1979.

THOMPSON, LEONARD, and BUTLER, JEFFREY (eds.) *Change in Contemporary South Africa*. Berkeley: University of California Press, 1975.

TOLSTOY, NIKOLAI *Victims of Yalta*. London: Hodder & Stoughton, 1977.

TOPPING, SEYMOUR 'Slaughter of Reds gives Indonesia a Grim Legacy', *New York Times*, 24 August 1966, pp. 1, 16.

TORIGUIAN, SHAVARGH *The Armenian Question and International Law.* Beirut: Hamaskaine Press, 1973.

TORRÈS, HENRY *Le Procès des Pogromes.* Paris: Editions de France, 1928.

TOYNBEE, ARNOLD J. *Armenian Atrocities: The Murder of a Nation.* London: Hodder & Stoughton, 1915. *The Treatment of Armenians in the Ottoman Empire, 1915–1916.* London: His Majesty's Stationery Office, 1916. (See Bryce, Viscount J.) *A Study of History.* London: Oxford University Press, 1947. *Experiences.* London: Oxford University Press, 1969.

TOYNBEE, ARNOLD, and TOYNBEE, VERONICA M. (eds.) *Survey of International Affairs, 1939–1946: The Realignment of Europe.* London: Oxford University Press, 1955.

TRUMPENER, ULRICH *Germany and the Ottoman Empire 1914–1918.* Princeton: Princeton University Press, 1968.

TUCKER, FRANCIS IVAN SIMMS *While Memory Serves.* London: Cassell, 1950.

TUCKER, ROBERT C. (ed.) *Stalinism: Essays in Historical Interpretation.* New York: Norton & Company, 1977.

ULLMAN, RICHARD H. 'Human Rights and Economic Power: The United States versus Idi Amin', *Foreign Affairs*, no. 56, April 1978, 529–43.

UNITED NATIONS

(1) Reports of the proceedings and resolutions of the General Assembly, the Fourth Committee of the General Assembly, the Legal Committee, the Economic and Social Council, the Ad Hoc Committee on Genocide, the Commission on Human Rights, and the Sub-Commission on Prevention of Discrimination and Protection of Minorities.

(2) *Special Reports. Ad Hoc Working Group of Experts on Southern Africa.* E/CN. 4/950 dd. 27 October 1967. E/CN. 4/984/Add. 18 dd. 28 February 1969. E/CN. 4/1075, dd. 15 February 1972 (*Study concerning the question of apartheid from the point of view of international penal law*). A/32/226, dd. 10 October 1977 (*Deaths of detainees and police brutality in South Africa since the Soweto massacres in June 1976*). E/CN. 4/1311, dd. 26 January 1979 (*Violations of Human Rights in Southern Africa*).

(3) *Sub-Commission on the Prevention of Discrimination and Protection of Minorities.* E/CN. 4/Sub. 2/416, dd. 4 July 1978 (*Study of the Question of the Prevention and Punishment of the Crime of Genocide*).

(4) *United Nations Action in the Field of Human Rights.* New York: 1974.

UNITED STATES

CONGRESS

International Protection of Human Rights. Hearing before the Subcommittee on International Organizations and Movements of the Committee on Foreign Affairs – House of Representatives, Ninety-Third Congress, First Session. August to December 1973. Washington: U.S. Government Printing Office, 1974.

DEPARTMENT OF STATE *Report on Human Rights Practices in Countries Receiving U.S. Aid.* Washington: U.S. Government Printing Office, 1979. 'President Nixon Urges Senate Advice and Consent to Ratification of the Treaty on Genocide', *Bulletin*, 62 (16 March 1970), 350–53.

SENATE COMMITTEE ON FOREIGN RELATIONS *Hearings of May 24, 26, 1977 on the International Convention on the Prevention and Punishment of the Crime of Genocide,* Washington: U.S. Government Printing Office, 1977 (95th Congress, 1st Session).

Genocide Convention. Hearings Before a Sub-Committee of The Committee on Foreign Relations. U.S. Senate, 81st Congress, 1st Session, April–May 1970. Washington: U.S. Government Printing Office, 1970.

C.I.A. REPORT (DECEMBER 1968) 'Indonesia 1965, the Coup that Backfired'. *Hearings before the Sub-Committee on Future Foreign Policy Research and Development of the Committee on International Relations.* House of Representatives, Ninety-fourth Congress, 1976: pp. 226–36.

USVATOV, ALEXANDER, and SHMELYOV, GEORGI 'The Kampuchean Tragedy: From the World Press', *New Times*, 37 (September 1978), 18–20.

UWECHUE, RAPH 'Biafra: A Middle Way to Peace', *Observer*, 14 September 1969, p. 10.

VAN DEN BERGHE, PIERRE L. *South Africa: A Study in Conflict,* Berkeley: University of California Press, 1967. 'Pluralism and the Polity: A Theoretical Exploration', in Kuper and Smith, *Pluralism in Africa*, 1969, pp. 67–81.

VAN GARRSE, YVAN *A Bibliography of Genocide, Crimes against Humanity and War Crimes.* Sint Niklaas Waas: Studiecentrum voor Kriminologie en Gerechtelyke Geneeskunde, 1970.

VEENHOVEN, WILLEM A. (ed.) *Case Studies on Human Rights and Fundamental Freedoms.* The Hague: Nijhoff, 1975.

VUCINICH, WAYNE S. 'Yugoslavs of the Moslem Faith' and 'The Second World War and Beyond', in Kerner, *Yugoslavia*, 1949, pp. 261–75 and 353–86.

WAI, DUNSTAN M. (ed.) *The Southern Sudan: The Problem of National Integration.* London: Frank Cass, 1973.

WALKER, T. A. *A History of the Law of Nations.* Cambridge: Cambridge University Press, 1899.

WASHBURN, WILCOMB E. *The Indian in America.* New York: Harper & Row, 1975.

235

WEDGWOOD, C. V. *The Thirty Years War*. New Haven: Yale University Press, 1939.

WEINSTEIN, WARREN 'Burundi: Alternatives to Violence', *Issue*, 5, 2 (Summer 1975), 17–22.

WEINSTEIN, WARREN, and SCHRIRE, ROBERT *Political Conflict and Ethnic Strategies*. Syracuse: Syracuse University Press, 1976.·

WERFEL, FRANZ *The Forty Days of Musa Dagh*. New York: The Viking Press, 1934.

WERTHEIM, W. F. 'Indonesia before and after the Untung Coup', *Pacific Affairs*, 39, 1 and 2 (Spring–Summer 1966), 115–27.

WIESEL, ELIE *Legends of Our Time*. New York: Holt, Rinehart & Winston, 1968. *Night, Dawn, The Accident*. New York: Hill & Wang, 1972.

WOLF, ERIC R. 'Killing the Achés', in Arens, *Genocide in Paraguay*, 1976, pp. 47–57.

WOLFE, BERTRAM D. *Krushchev and Stalin's Ghost*. New York: Praeger, 1957.

WOLPERT, STANLEY *A New History of India*. New York: Oxford University Press, 1977.

Yellow Spot, The. New York: Knight Publications, 1936.

YOUNG, CRAWFORD *The Politics of Cultural Pluralism*. Madison: University of Wisconsin Press, 1976.

Index

Abdul-Hamid II, Sultan, 106, 115, 117
Aborigines:
    Australian, 59
    genocide against Tasmanians, 40
Aché Indians, genocide against, in Paraguay, 33–4, 40, 54, 162
Acholi, massacre of, in Uganda, 166
Adams, Gerry, 194n.
Adana massacres, 106
African Bourgeoisie, An (Kuper), 186
African Charter of Human Rights, 184
African Commission on Human Rights, 184
Afrikaners, 88, 197, 198
After the Cataclysm: Postwar Indochina and the Reconstruction of Imperial Ideology (Chomsky and Herman), 155n.
Aggression/frustration theories of genocide, 49, 51–2
Aggression, problems in definition of, 39
Ainsztein, Reuben, 142n.
Albigensians, Reuben, 142n.
Albigensians, suppression of, 13
Albino, Oliver, 71n., 72 and n., 73n.
Aleppo, 109, 111, 112, 117
Algeria:
    decolonization of, 60–61, 174
    French conquest and colonization of, 16, 45, 59, 60
    genocidal massacres in, 32, 60–61, 93, 139, 196
    numbers of victims in 60–61, 196
Algerians, dehumanization of, 88
Allied Control Council, 28
Alstötter, Joseph, 19n.
Ambassador Morgenthau's Story (Morgenthau), 161
America, colonization of North and South, 15, 59
American Committee for Armenian and

Syrian Relief, 113
Amin, 36, 165, 167, 168, 169
Amnesty International, 152 and n., 153n., 155, 167 and n., 186n.
Amritsar, genocidal massacre at, 65–6
Anderson, B. R., 151n.
Anglo-Egyptian Condominium, in Sudan, 70–71
Animal metaphors, 40, 54, 88
Animist religion:
    in Nigeria, 73
    in Sudan, 70
Anti-semitism, 85, 86, 136
    forms of, 42, 88, 120
    functional theory of, 50
    function of, in Third Reich, 94–5
    in Poland, 131
Anti-Slavery Society of Great Britain, 162
Apartheid, 191, 197–204, 206–9
    and genocide, 199–202, 203 and n., 206, 207, 208
    and United Nations, 199–202
    demography, economy and, 206–7
    ideology of, 198
    structure of, 197
Arabs:
    African genocide against, in Zanzibar, 17, 139, 174, 193
    in decolonization of Algeria, 60–61
    Sudanese, 70
Arendt, Hannah, 11 and n., 49, 122 and n.
Arens, Richard, 162 and n., 180
Argentina, human rights in, 186
Arlen, M. J., 113n., 115 and n., 117n.
Armenia and Europe (Lepsius), 116
Armenian Patriarchate, 106
Armenian Plateau, 106
Armenians:
    in Turkish army, 114
    nineteenth-century massacres of, 106

Index

Bureaucracy – *cont.*
120–22, 125–7, 131, 135, 137
in Soviet deportations, 147–8
in Turkish genocide against Armenians, 115, 116, 118–19, 135
Burundi:
constitution of, 187
disposal of bodies in, 101
Hutu massacres of Tutsi in, 63, 115, 139, 163
number of victims in, 63, 115, 164, 196
O.A.U. and genocide in, 164–5
social structure of, 62–3, 69, 93
Tutsi genocide against Hutu in, 17, 29, 33, 48, 50, 55, 57, 63, 90, 93, 103, 115, 139, 162–5, 176, 186, 187, 195
United Nations and genocide in, 164, 165
world reaction to genocide in, 163
Burundi: Alternatives to Violence (Weinstein), 163n.
Burundi: The Tragic Years (Melady), 163n.
Bushmen, genocide against, 40
Busteed, M. A., 193 and n.

Calcutta:
genocidal massacres in, 64
structure of city, 67–8
Cambodge: La révolution de la forêt (Debré), 154n.
Cambodia:
charges of U.S. genocide in, 34, 158–9
civil war in, 159
massacres of Vietnamese in, 159
penal system of, 160
(*see also* Kampuchea)
'Cambodia: Background to the Revolution' (Rousset), 155n.
'Cambodia: Nightmare without End' (Shawcross), 154n.
'Cambodia 1976: Internal Consolidation and External Expansion' (Quinn), 155n.
Cambodia Year Zero (Ponchaud), 138, 154n., 161
Campbell-Johnson, Alan, 66 and n., 67 and n., 68n., 103n.
Canada, colonization of, 59
Capitalism, and Sartre's theory of genocide, 44, 47, 50
Caputo, Philip, 17n.
Carzou, Jean-Marie, 113 and n.
Catholic church, and genocide in Burundi, 163

Catholics:
and German genocide against Jews, 130
and Wars of Religion, 14
in Northern Ireland, 48, 69, 90, 189, 191–7, 204, 205
in Serbo-Croat conflict, 89
in Sudan, 70
Caucasus, Soviet deportations from, 143
Central African Empire, genocide in, 186
Central Intelligence Agency (C.I.A.), 151 and n.
Cham, Kampuchean plans to eliminate, 172
Chamounists, in Lebanon, 81
Châteaubriant, martyrs of, 21, 32
Chattel slavery, 88
(*see also* Slavery)
Chaudhuri, Kalyan, 79 and n.
Chechens, Soviet deportation of, 140, 142, 143–4, 145, 190–91
Chile, human rights in, 186
and United Nations, 170, 179
China:
and genocide in Burundi, 163
and genocide in East Pakistan, 174
application of Marxism in, 99
Gang of Four, 91
Chinese:
as traders in Java, 42
massacres of, in Sumatra, 153
Vietnamese deportation of, 175
Chomsky, Noam, 155n., 175
Christians:
in Serbo-Croat conflict, 89
in Lebanon, 80–82, 83n., 103, 104
Maronite, 80, 81
medieval conflicts with Muslims, 12, 13, 14
medieval massacres of Jews, 12–14, 93
Nigerian, 73
Sudanese, 70
Turkish persecution of, 20
(*see also* Churches, Christian)
Churches, Christian:
and German genocide against Jews, 129–30, 136
and Soviet deportations, 148n.
(*see also* Christians)
Churchill, W. S., 21
Circassians, 106, 116
Civil Rights movement, Northern Ireland, 193–4, 195
Class struggle, 47

239

Genocide – *cont.*

and identifiability of target group, 53
and ideology, 54–5, 84–100
and metaphor, 40, 54, 85, 88, 90–91
and nuclear war, 46
and plural societies, 14, 17, 54, 56, 57
and racial difference, *see* Racial difference
and religious difference, *see* Religious difference
and social structure, 57–83 (*see also particular countries*)
and sovereign territorial state, 14, 17, 18, 37–8, 161–85
and technology, 14, 17, 35, 46, 51, 54, 55, 92, 101–2, 115
and terroristic government, 47
and theories of human destructiveness, 51
and totalitarian centralized government, 47, 49
and totalitarian ideologies, 17
as 'crime of governments', 37–8, 55, 56, 113
'biological', 30
cultural, 15, 30–31, 44
Dadrian's typology of, 105
deportation as cloak for, 112, 114–15, 135
domestic, 9, 46
etymology of, 22, 25, 27–8
euphemisms for, 104–5, 124, 137, 144, 152
first use of word, 22
Fromm's theory of, 52, 53
functional theories of, 50–51
in antiquity, 11
infra-structural restraint on, 207
in Middle Ages, 12–14
Koestler's theory of, 51–2
Lemkin's categories of, 30
Lemkin's definition of, 22
Lorenz's theory of, 51, 53
material advantages from, 43, 95, 124, 136
'physical', 30
problem of intent, 86–7, (*see also* Genocide Convention)
process of, *see* Process, genocidal
rationalization of, 85
recognition of, as crime in international law, 20–22, 24
restraints on, 46, 56, 85, 87, 187–91, 196, 204–9
Sartre's theory of, 14–15, 44–6, 47, 50

scapegoat type of, 18, 43, 54, 55, 93
sexual mutilations in, 66, 104, 152
Soviet conception of, 25, 46–7, 138–9
spontaneity and organization in, 102, 116, 119, 122
structural conditions excluding domestic, 187–9
U.N. definition of, 19
U.N. resolution (96–I) on, 23
(*see also* Genocide Convention, Ideology, Process)

Genocide Convention (United Nations Convention on the Prevention and Punishment of the Crime of Genocide), 10, 11, 19, 23n., 24–39, 55, 165, 175, 200
adoption of, 24, 29, 38
ambiguity in, 33
and *apartheid*, 201
and cultural genocide, 24, 30–31
and economic groups, 28
and political groups, 24–5, 26–30, 33, 38, 39, 56, 93–4, 138–9, 150, 176
and problem of intent, 24, 32–6, 86
and religious groups, 25–6, 27
and sovereign territorial state, 162
declared purpose of, 36
definition of genocide in, 19, 30–36, 39, 93–4, 186
enforcement of, 24, 36–9, 176, 177
ratification of, 187, 188
report of Ad Hoc Committee, 27
scope of genocide in, 30–36
text of, 210–14
universal enforcement, validity and repression in, 36
Génocide exemplaire: Arménie 1915, Un (Carzou), 113
Genocide in the U.S.S.R. (Institute for the Study of the U.S.S.R.), 146
Germans, Volga, Soviet deportation of, 145
Germany, German
condition of Jews in, 135–6
extermination of communists and social democrats, 24, 28
genocide against Gypsies, 22, 48, 94, 124
genocide against Herero, 16
genocide against Jews, *see* Jews
genocide against mental defectives, 94
genocide against Poles, 22–3, 48, 94, 124
genocide against Russians, 124
genocide, and demography, 48
genocide, and world domination, 46

243

United Nations – *cont.*
Special Committee on aggression, 39
Special Rapporteur, 177
Study of the Question of the Prevention and Punishment of the Crime of Genocide, 23n., 38n., 48n., 176–7, 187n., 219
Sub-Commission on Prevention of Discrimination and Protection of Minorities, *see under* Sub-Commission
United States of America (U.S.A.):
and Declaration of Moscow, 21
and East Pakistan genocide, 174
and East Timor genocide, 175
and Four-Power Agreement, 21
and U.N. Convention on Genocide, 29–30
and U.N. 'memory hole', 220
atomic bombing by, as genocide, 46, 102
Central Intelligence Agency (C.I.A.), 151 and n.
colonization of, 59, 69
Commission on Foreign Affairs, 163n.
Congress, 154, 174 and n.
declaration on Russian persecution of Jews, 20
genocide against Indians in, 40
'internal colonialism' in, 47
intervention in Romanian persecution of Jews, 20
intervention in Turkish persecution of Jews, 19
intervention in Vietnam, 17
involvement in Vietnam, Laos and Cambodia, as genocide, 14, 34–5, 45, 50, 55, 91–2, 139, 158–9, 174
Kampuchean indictment of, 158
Senate Foreign Relations Committee, 29, 163
United States and Burundi: Genocide, Nickel and Normalization' (Morris), 163n.
Urdu, 76
Uzbekistan, 145

Van den Berghe, Pierre, 161, 189n., 204
Vatican:
and genocide in Burundi, 163
and German genocide against Jews, 130
Venezuela, genocide in, 40
Vietcong, 158, 159
Vietnam:
deportation of Chinese, 175

invasion of Kampuchea, 154, 158, 172
United Nations and war in, 174
U.S. involvement in, as genocide, 14, 17, 34–5, 45, 50, 55, 91–2, 139, 174
war, 154
Vietnamese, Cambodian massacres of, 157, 159
Violations of Human Rights and the Rule of Law in Uganda (International Commission of Jurists), 167
Violence, theories of, 49
Vorkuta, 150 and n.
Vucinich, W. S., 89n.

Walker, T. A., 11n., 12
War crimes:
and international law, 21–2
and U.N. resolution (96–I) on genocide, 23
Warfare:
advanced technology in, 14, 17, 35, 46, 51, 54, 55, 92, 187
and genocidal conflict, 46, 51, 55
in hunting and gathering groups, 53
nuclear, 17, 46, 54
Warrant for Genocide (Cohn), 42
Wars of Religion, 12–14, 89 (*see also* Religious difference)
Watergate, 91
Watts, Hilstan, 198n.
Wedgwood, C. V., 14n.
Weimar Republic, 38
Weinstein, Warren, 163n.
Wertheim, W. F., 151n., 152 and n.
'Western Press and Cambodia, The' (Chomsky), 155n.
West Indies, colonization of, 15
Williamson, Arthur, 205n.
Wolf, Eric, 40–41 and n.
Wolfe, B. D., 96n., 140n.
Wolpert, Stanley, 16n.
World Conference on Religion and Peace, 185

Yellow Spot, The, 127n.
Yoruba, 73, 74
Young, Crawford, 79n.
Yugoslavia:
and Kampuchean genocide, 171
Croatian genocide against Serbs in, 89
genocidal bands in, 38

Zaire, 63, 166
Zambia, 166
Zanzibar, African genocide against Arabs in, 17, 139, 174, 193

Leo Kuper was born in South Africa and practised law there until the Second World War. Following military service, he taught sociology at the University of Birmingham, and worked on urban neighbourhood planning for the City of Coventry (published in *Living in Towns*). He taught at the University of Natal, South Africa, during the turbulent 1950s. His main books on South Africa, *Passive Resistance in South Africa* and *An African Bourgeoisie*, were both banned in that country. From Natal he moved to the University of California in Los Angeles. Now Professor Emeritus, he also served for some years as Director of the African Studies Centre. His writings include *Durban: A Study in Racial Ecology* (with Watts and Davies), *The College Brew* (a satirical novel set in an *apartheid* tribal university), *Race, Class and Power*, *The Pity of It All*, and *Pluralism in Africa* (edited with M. G. Smith). He received the Herskovits award for *An African Bourgeoisie*, and the Spivak Fellowship from the American Sociological Association for contributions to the study of group relations. He is married to Hilda Kuper, who has written extensively on Swaziland, and they have two daughters, both living in London.